C++ DEMYSTIFIED

JEFF KENT

McGraw-Hill/Osborne

New York   Chicago   San Francisco   Lisbon   London
Madrid   Mexico City   Milan   New Delhi   San Juan
Seoul   Singapore   Sydney   Toronto

The McGraw·Hill Companies

McGraw-Hill/Osborne
2100 Powell Street, 10th Floor
Emeryville, California 94608
U.S.A.

To arrange bulk purchase discounts for sales promotions, premiums, or fund-raisers, please contact **McGraw-Hill**/Osborne at the above address. For information on translations or book distributors outside the U.S.A., please see the International Contact Information page immediately following the index of this book.

C++ Demystified

1234567890 FGR FGR 01987654

ISBN 0-07-225370-3

Publisher
Brandon A. Nordin

Vice President & Associate Publisher
Scott Rogers

Editorial Director
Wendy Rinaldi

Project Editor
Lisa Wolters-Broder

Acquisitions Coordinator
Athena Honore

Technical Editor
Jim Keogh

Copy Editor
Mike McGee

Proofreader
Susie Elkind

Indexer
Irv Hershman

Composition
Apollo Publishing Services, Lucie Ericksen

Illustrators
Kathleen Edwards, Melinda Lytle

Cover Series Design
Margaret Webster-Shapiro

Cover Illustration
Lance Lekander

This book was composed with Corel VENTURA™ Publisher.

CONTENTS AT A GLANCE

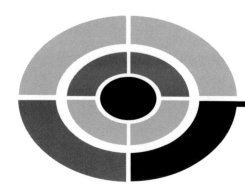

ABOUT THE AUTHOR

Jeff Kent is an Associate Professor of Computer Science at Los Angeles Valley College in Valley Glen, California. He teaches a number of programming languages, including Visual Basic, C++, Java and, when he's feeling masochistic, Assembler, but mostly he teaches C++. He also manages a network for a Los Angeles law firm whose employees are guinea pigs for his applications, and as an attorney gives advice to young attorneys whether they want it or not. He also has written several books on computer programming, including the recent *Visual Basic.NET A Beginner's Guide* for McGraw-Hill/Osborne.

Jeff has had a varied career—or careers. He graduated from UCLA with a Bachelor of Science degree in economics, then obtained a Juris Doctor degree from Loyola (Los Angeles) School of Law, and went on to practice law. During this time, when personal computers still were a gleam in Bill Gates's eye, Jeff was also a professional chess master, earning a third-place finish in the United States Under-21 Championship and, later, an international title.

Jeff does find time to spend with his wife, Devvie, which is not difficult since she also is a computer science professor at Valley College. He also acts as personal chauffeur for his teenaged daughter, Emily (his older daughter, Elise, now has her own driver's license) and in his remaining spare time enjoys watching international chess tournaments on the Internet. His goal is to resume running marathons, since otherwise, given his losing battle to lose weight, his next book may be *Sumo Wrestling Demystified*.

I would like to dedicate this book to my wife, Devvie Schneider Kent. There is not room here to describe how she has helped me in my personal and professional life, though I do mention several ways in the Acknowledgments. She also has been my computer programming teacher in more ways than one; I wouldn't be writing this and other computer programming books if it wasn't for her.

—Jeff Kent

CONTENTS

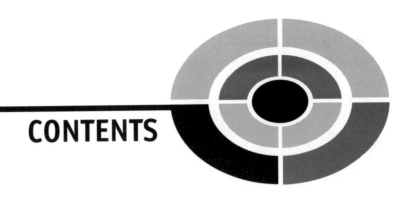

CONTENTS

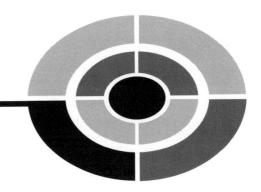

ACKNOWLEDGMENTS

It seems obligatory in acknowledgments for authors to thank their publishers (especially if they want to write for them again), but I really mean it. This is my fourth book for McGraw-Hill/Osborne, and I hope there will be many more. It truly is a pleasure to work with professionals who are nice people as well as very good at what they do (even when what they are good at is keeping accurate track of the deadlines I miss).

I first want to thank Wendy Rinaldi, who got me started with McGraw-Hill/Osborne back in 1998 (has it been that long?). Wendy was also my first Acquisitions Editor. Indeed, I got started on this book through a telephone call with Wendy at the end of a vacation with my wife, Devvie, who, being in earshot, and with an "are you insane" tone in her voice, asked incredulously, "You're writing another book?"

I also must thank my Acquisitions Coordinator, Athena Honore, and my Project Editor, Lisa Wolters-Broder. Both were unfailingly helpful and patient, while still keeping me on track in this deadline-sensitive business (e.g., "I'm so sorry you broke both your arms and legs; you'll still have the next chapter turned in by this Friday, right?").

Mike McGee did the copyediting, together with Lisa. They were kind about my obvious failure during my school days to pay attention to my grammar lessons. They improved what I wrote while still keeping it in my words (that way, if something is wrong, it is still my fault). Mike also indicated he liked some of my stale jokes, which makes him a friend for life.

Jim Keogh was my technical editor. Jim and I had a balance of terror going between us, in that while he was tech editing this book, I was tech editing two books on which he was the main author, *Data Structures Demystified* and *OOP Demystified*. Seriously, Jim's suggestions were quite helpful and added value to this book.

There are a lot of other talented people behind the scenes who also helped get this book out to press, but, as in an Academy Awards speech, I can't list them all. That doesn't mean I don't appreciate all their hard work, because I do.

I truly thank my wife Devvie, who in addition to being my wife, best friend (maybe my only one), and partner (I'm leaving out lover because computer programmers aren't supposed to be interested in such things), also was my personal tech

editor. She is well-qualified for that task, since she has been a computer science professor for 15 years, and also is a stickler for correct English (yes, I know, you can't modify the word "unique"). She made this a much better book.

Finally, I would like to give thanks to my daughters, Elise and Emily, and my mom, Bea Kent, for tolerating me when I excused myself from family gatherings, muttering to myself about unreasonable chapter deadlines and merciless editors (sorry, Athena and Lisa). I also should thank my family in advance for not having me committed when I talk about writing my next book.

INTRODUCTION

C++ was my first programming language. While I've since learned others, I've always thought C++ was the "best" programming language, perhaps because of the power it gives the programmer. Of course, this power is a double-edged sword, being also the power to hang yourself if you are not careful. Nonetheless, C++ has always been my favorite programming language.

C++ also has been the first choice of others, not just in the business world because of its power, but also in academia. Additionally, many other programming languages, including Java and C#, are based on C++. Indeed, the Java programming language was written using C++. Therefore, knowing C++ also makes learning other programming languages easier.

Why Did I Write this Book?

Not as a road to riches, fame, or beautiful women. I may be misguided, but I'm not completely delusional.

To be sure, there are many introductory level books on C++. Nevertheless, I wrote this book because I believe I bring a different and, I hope, valuable perspective.

As you may know from my author biography, I teach computer science at Los Angeles Valley College, a community college in the San Fernando Valley area of Los Angeles, where I grew up and have lived most of my life. I also write computer programs, but teaching programming has provided me with insights into how students learn that I could never obtain from writing programs. These insights are gained not just from answering student questions during lectures. I spend hours each week in our college's computer lab helping students with their programs, and more hours each week reviewing and grading their assignments. Patterns emerge regarding which teaching methods work and which don't, the order in which to introduce programming topics, the level of difficulty at which to introduce a new topic, and so on. I joke with my students that they are my beta testers in my never-ending attempt to become a better teacher, but there is much truth in that joke.

Additionally, my beta testers... err, students, seem to complain about the textbook no matter which book I adopt. Many ask me why I don't write a book they could use to learn C++. They may be saying this to flatter me (I'm not saying it doesn't work), or for the more sinister reason that they will be able to blame the teacher for a poor book as well as poor instruction. Nevertheless, having written other books, these questions planted in my mind the idea of writing a book that, in addition to being sold to the general public, also could be used as a supplement to a textbook.

Who Should Read this Book

Anyone who will pay for it! Just kidding, though no buyers will be turned away.

It is hardly news that publishers and authors want the largest possible audience for their books. Therefore, this section of the introduction usually tells you this book is for you whoever you may be and whatever you do. However, no programming book is for everyone. For example, if you exclusively create game programs using Java, this book may not be for you (though being a community college teacher I may be your next customer if you create a space beasts vs. community college administrators game).

While this book is, of course, not for everyone, it very well may be for you. Many people need or want to learn C++, either as part of a degree program, job training, or even as a hobby. C++ is not the easiest subject to learn, and unfortunately many books don't make learning C++ any easier, throwing at you a veritable telephone book of complexity and jargon. By contrast, this book, as its title suggests, is designed to "demystify" C++. Therefore, it goes straight to the core concepts and explains them in a logical order and in plain English.

What this Book Covers

I strongly believe that the best way to learn programming is to write programs. The concepts covered by the chapters are illustrated by clearly and thoroughly explained code. You can run this code yourself, or use the code as the basis for writing further programs that expand on the covered concepts.

Chapter 1 gets you started. This chapter answers questions such as what is a computer program and what is a programming language. It then discusses the anatomy of a basic C++ program, including both the code you see and what happens "under the hood," explaining how the preprocessor, compiler, and linker work together to translate your code into instructions the computer can understand. Finally, the

chapter tells you how to use an integrated development environment (IDE) to create and run a project.

Being able to create and run a program that outputs "Hello World!" as in Chapter 1 is a good start. However, most programs require the storing of information of different types, such as numeric and text. Chapter 2 first explains the different types of computer memory, including random access memory, or RAM. The chapter then discusses addresses, which identify where data is stored in RAM, and bytes, the unit of value for the amount of space required to store information. Because information comes in different forms, this chapter next discusses the different data types for whole numbers, floating point numbers and text.

The featured star of Chapter 3 is the variable, which not only reserves the amount of memory necessary to store information, but also provides you with a name by which that information later may be retrieved. Because the purpose of a variable is to store a value, a variable without an assigned value is as pointless as a bank account without money. Therefore, this chapter explains how to assign a value to a variable, either at compile time using the assignment operator or at run time using the cin object and the stream extraction operator.

As a former professional chess player, I have marveled at the ability of chess computers to play world champions on even terms. The reason the chess computers have this ability is because they can calculate far more quickly and accurately than we can. Chapter 4 covers arithmetic operators, which we use in code to harness the computer's calculating ability.

As programs become more sophisticated, they often branch in two or more directions based on whether a condition is true or false. For example, while a calculator program would use the arithmetic operators you learned about in Chapter 4, your program first would need to determine whether the user chose addition, subtraction, multiplication, or division before performing the indicated arithmetic operation. Chapters 5 and 6 introduce relational and logical operators, which are useful in determining a user's choice, and the if and switch statements, used to direct the path the code will follow based on the user's choice.

When you were a child, your parents may have told you not to repeat yourself. However, sometimes your code needs to repeat itself. For example, if an application user enters invalid data, your code may continue to ask the user whether they want to retry or quit until the user either enters valid data or quits. The primary subject of Chapters 7 and 8 are loops, which are used to repeat code execution until a condition is no longer true. Chapter 7 starts with the for loop, and also introduces the increment and decrement operators, which are very useful when working with loops. Chapter 8 completes the discussion of loops with the while and do while loops.

Chapter 9 is about functions. A function is a block of one or more code statements. All of your C++ code that executes is written within functions. This chapter will explain why and how you should write your own functions. It first explains how to prototype and define a function, and then how to call the function. This chapter also explains how you use arguments to pass information from the calling function to a called function and a return value to pass information back from the called function to a calling function. Passing by value and by reference also are explained and distinguished. This chapter winds up explaining variable scope and lifetime, and both explaining and distinguishing local, static, and global variables.

Chapter 10 is about arrays. Unlike the variables covered previously in the book, which may hold only one value at a time, arrays may hold multiple values at one time. Additionally, arrays work very well with loops, which are covered in Chapters 7 and 8. This chapter also distinguishes character arrays from arrays of other data types. Finally, this chapter covers constants, which are similar to variables, but differ in that their initial value never changes while the program is running.

Chapter 11 is about pointers. The term pointers often strikes fear in the heart of a C++ student, but it shouldn't. As you learned back in Chapters 2 and 3, information is stored at addresses in memory. Pointers simply provide you with an efficient way to access those addresses. You also will learn in this chapter about the indirection operator and dereferencing as well as pointer arithmetic.

Most information, including user input, is in the form of character, C-string, and C++ string class data types. Chapter 12 shows you functions that are useful in working with these data types, including member functions of the cin object.

Information is stored in files so it will be available after the program ends. Chapter 13 teaches you about the file stream objects, *fstream*, *ifstream*, and *ofstream*, and how to use them and their member functions to open, read, write and close files.

Finally, to provide you with a strong basis to go to the next step after this introductory level book, Chapter 14 introduces you to OOP, Object-Oriented Programming, and two programming concepts heavily used in OOP, structures and classes.

A Quiz follows each chapter. Each quiz helps you confirm that you have absorbed the basics of the chapter. Unlike quizzes you took in school, you also have an answers appendix.

Similarly, this book concludes with a Final Exam in the first appendix, and the answers to that also found in the second appendix.

How to Read this Book

I have organized this book to be read from beginning to end. While this may seem patently obvious, my students often express legitimate frustration about books (or teachers) that, in discussing a programming concept, mention other concepts that are covered several chapters later or, even worse, not at all. Therefore, I have endeavored to present the material in a linear, logical progression. This not only avoids the

frustration of material that is out of order, but also enables you in each succeeding chapter to build on the skills you learned in the preceding chapters.

Special Features

Throughout each chapter are Notes, Tips, and Cautions, as well as detailed code listings. To provide you with additional opportunities to review, there is a Quiz at the end of each chapter and a Final Exam (found in the first appendix) at the end of this book. Answers to both are contained in the following appendix.

The overall objective is to get you up to speed quickly, without a lot of dry theory or unnecessary detail. So let's get started. It's easy and fun to write C++ programs.

Contacting the Author

Hmmm… it depends why. Just kidding. While I always welcome gushing praise and shameless flattery, comments, suggestions, and yes, even criticism also can be valuable. The best way to contact me is via e-mail; you can use jkent@genghiskhent.com (the domain name is based on my students' fond nickname for me). Alternately, you can visit my web site, http://www.genghiskhent.com/. Don't be thrown off by the entry page; I use this site primarily to support the online classes and online components of other classes that I teach at the college, but there will be a link to the section that supports this book.

I hope you enjoy this book as much as I enjoyed writing it.

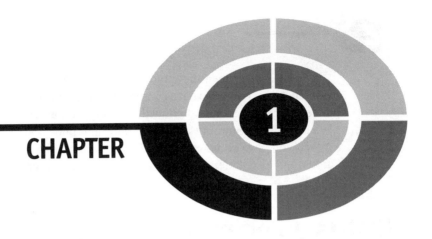

How a C++ Program Works

You probably interact with computer programs many times during an average day. When you arrive at work and find out your computer doesn't work, you call tech support. At the other end of the telephone line, a computer program forces you to navigate a voicemail menu maze and then tortures you while you are on perpetual hold with repeated insincere messages about how important your call is, along with false promises about how soon you will get through.

When you're finally done with tech support, you decide to take a break and log on to your now-working computer to do battle with giant alien insects from the planet Megazoid. Unfortunately, the network administrator catches you goofing off using yet another computer program which monitors employee computer usage. Assuming you are still employed, an accounts payable program then generates your payroll check.

On your way home, you decide you need some cash and stop at an ATM, where a computer program confirms (hopefully) you have enough money in your bank account and then instructs the machine to dispense the requested cash and (unfortunately) deducts that same amount from your account.

Most people, when they interact with computers as part of their daily routine, don't need to consider what a computer program is or how it works. However, a computer programmer should know the answers to these and related questions, such as what is a programming language, and how does a C++ program actually work? When you have completed this chapter, you will know the answers to these questions, and also understand how to create and run your own computer program.

What Is a Computer Program?

Computers are so widespread in our society because they have three advantages over us humans. First, computers can store huge amounts of information. Second, they can recall that information quickly and accurately. Third, computers can perform calculations with lightning speed and perfect accuracy.

The advantages that computers have over us even extend to thinking sports like chess. In 1997, the computer Deep Blue beat the world chess champion, Garry Kasparov, in a chess match. In 2003, Kasparov was out for revenge against another computer, Deep Junior, but only drew the match. Kasparov, while perhaps the best chess player ever, is only human, and therefore no match for the computer's ability to calculate and remember prior games.

However, we have one very significant advantage over computers. We think on our own, while computers don't, at least not yet anyway. Indeed, computers fundamentally are far more brawn than brain. A computer cannot do anything without step-by-step instructions from us telling it what to do. These instructions are called a computer program, and of course are written by a human, namely a computer programmer. Computer programs enable us to harness the computer's tremendous power.

What Is a Programming Language?

When you enter a darkened room and want to see what is inside, you turn on a light switch. When you leave the room, you turn the light switch off.

The first computers were not too different than that light switch. These early computers consisted of wires and switches in which the electrical current followed a path dependent on which switches were in the on (one) or off (zero) position. Indeed, I built such a simple computer when I was a kid (which according to my own children was back when dinosaurs still ruled the earth).

Each switch's position could be expressed as a number: 1 for the on position, 0 for the off position. Thus, the instructions given to these first computers, in the form of the switches' positions, essentially were a series of ones and zeroes.

Today's computers, of course, are far more powerful and sophisticated than these early computers. However, the language that computers understand, called machine language, remains the same, essentially ones and zeroes.

While computers think in ones and zeroes, the humans who write computer programs usually don't. Additionally, a complex program may consist of thousands or even millions of step-by-step machine language instructions, which would require an inordinately long amount of time to write. This is an important consideration since, due to competitive market forces, the amount of time within which a program has to be written is becoming increasingly less and less.

Fortunately, we do not have to write instructions to computers in machine language. Instead, we can write instructions in a programming language. Programming languages are far more understandable to programmers than machine language because programming languages resemble the structure and syntax of human language, not ones and zeroes. Additionally, code can be written much faster with programming languages than machine language because programming languages automate instructions; one programming language instruction can cover many machine language instructions.

C++ is but one of many programming languages. Other popular programming languages include Java, C#, and Visual Basic. There are many others. Indeed, new languages are being created all the time. However, all programming languages have essentially the same purpose, which is to enable a human programmer to give instructions to a computer.

Why learn C++ instead of another programming language? First, it is very widely used, both in industry and in education. Second, many other programming languages, including Java and C#, are based on C++. Indeed, the Java programming language was written using C++. Therefore, knowing C++ makes learning other programming languages easier.

Anatomy of a C++ Program

It seems to be a tradition in C++ programming books for the first code example to output to a console window the message "Hello World!" (shown in Figure 1-1).

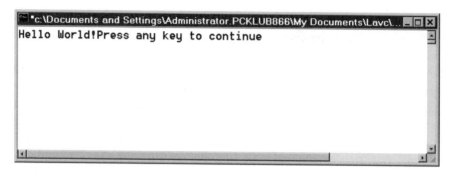

Figure 1-1   C++ program outputting "Hello World!" to the screen

---

NOTE: *The term "console" goes back to the days before Windows when the screen did not have menus and toolbars but just text. If you have typed commands using DOS or UNIX, you likely did so in a console window. The text "Press any key to continue" immediately following "Hello World!" is not part of the program, but instead is a cue for how to close the console window.*

Unfortunately, all too often the "Hello World!" example is followed quickly by many other program examples without the book or teacher first stopping to explain how the "Hello World!" program works. The result soon is a confused reader or student who's ready to say "Goodbye, Cruel World."

While the "Hello World!" program looks simple, there actually is a lot going on behind the scenes of this program. Accordingly, we are going to go through the following code for the "Hello World!" program line by line, though not in top-to-bottom order.

```cpp
#include <iostream>
using namespace std;

int main(void)
{
    cout << "Hello World!";
    return 0;
}
```

NOTE: *The code a programmer writes is referred to as source code, which is saved in a file that usually has a .cpp extension, standing for C++.*

The main Function

As discussed in the "What Is a Programming Language?" section, the purpose of C++, or any programming language, is to enable a programmer to write instructions for a computer. Often, a task is too complex for just one instruction. Instead, several related instructions are required.

A *function* is a group of related instructions, also called statements, which together perform a particular task. The name of the function is how you refer to these related statements. In the "Hello World!" program, *main* is the name of a function. A program may have many functions, and in Chapter 9 I will show you how to create and use functions. However, a program must have one main function, and only one main function. The reason is that the main function is the starting point for every C++ program. If there was no main function, the computer would not know where to start the program. If there was more than one main function, the program would not know whether to start at one or the other.

NOTE: *The main function is preceded by int and followed by void in parentheses. We will cover the meaning of both in Chapter 9.*

The Function Body

Each of the related instructions, or statements, which belong to the main function are contained within the *body* of that function. A function body starts with a left curly brace, {, and ends with a right curly brace, }.

Each statement usually ends with a semicolon. The main function has two statements:

```
cout << "Hello World!";
return 0;
```

Statements are executed in order, from top to bottom. Don't worry, the term "executed" doesn't mean the statement is put to death. Rather, it means that the statement is carried out, or executed, by the computer.

cout

The first statement is

```
cout << "Hello World!";
```

cout is pronounced "C-out." The "out" refers to the direction in which cout sends a stream of data.

A data stream may flow in one of two directions. One direction is input—into your program from an outside source such as a file or user keyboard input. The other direction is output—out from your program to an outside source such as a monitor, printer, or file.

cout concerns the output stream. It sends information to the standard output device. The standard output device usually is your monitor, though it can be something else, such as a printer or a file on your hard drive.

The << following cout is an operator. You likely have used operators before, such as the arithmetic operators +, −, *, and /, for addition, subtraction, multiplication, and division, respectively.

The << operator is known as the stream insertion operator. It inserts the information immediately to its right—in this example, the text "Hello World!" into the data stream. The cout object then sends that information to the standard output device—in this case, the monitor.

NOTE: In Chapter 3, you will learn about the counterparts to the cout object and the << operator, the cin object, which concerns the input stream, and the >> operator used with the cin object.

The return 0 Statement

The second and final statement returns a value of zero to the computer's operating system, whether Windows, UNIX, or another. This tells the operating system that the program ended normally. Sometimes programs do not end normally, but instead crash, such as if you run out of memory during the running of the program. The operating system may need to handle this abnormal program termination differently than normal termination. That is why the program tells the operating system that this time it ended normally.

The #include Directive

Your C++ program "knows" to start at the main function because the main function is part of the core of the C++ language. We certainly did not write any code that told the C++ program to start at *main*.

Similarly, your C++ program seems to know that the cout object, in conjunction with the stream insertion operator <<, outputs information to the monitor. We did not write any code to have the cout object and the << operator achieve this result.

However, the cout object is not part of the C++ core language. Rather, it is defined elsewhere, in a *standard library file*. C++ has a number of standard library files, each defining commonly used objects. Outputting information to the monitor certainly is a common task. While you could go to the trouble of writing your own function that outputs information to the screen, a standard library file's implementation of cout saves you the trouble of "reinventing the wheel."

While C++ already has implemented the cout object for you in a standard library file, you still have to tell the program to include that standard library file in your application. You do so with the #include directive, followed by the name of the library file. If the library file is a standard library file, as opposed to one you wrote (yes, you can create your own), then the file name is enclosed in angle brackets, < and >.

The cout object is defined in the standard library file *iostream*. The "io" in iostream refers to input and output—"stream" to a stream of data. To use the cout object, we need to include the iostream standard library file in our application. We do so with the following include directive:

```
#include <iostream>
```

The include directive is called a *preprocessor directive*. The preprocessor, together with the compiler and linker, are discussed later in this chapter in the section "Translating the Code for the Computer." The preprocessor directive, unlike statements, is not ended by a semicolon.

Namespace

The final statement to be discussed in the Hello World! example is

```
using namespace std;
```

C++ uses *namespaces* to organize different names used in programs. Every name used in the iostream standard library file is part of a namespace called *std*. Consequently, the cout object is really called std::cout. The using namespace std statement avoids the need for putting std:: before every reference to cout, so we can just use cout in our code.

Translating the Code for the Computer

While you now understand the "Hello World!" code, the computer won't. Computers don't understand C++ or any other programming language. They understand only machine language.

Three programs are used to translate your source code into an *executable* file that the computer can run. These programs are, in their order of appearance:

1. Preprocessor
2. Compiler
3. Linker

Preprocessor

The preprocessor is a program that scans the source code for preprocessor directives such as include directives. The preprocessor inserts into the source code all files included by the include directives.

In this example, the iostream standard library file is included by an include directive. Therefore, the preprocessor directive inserts the contents of that standard library file, including its definition of the cout object, into the source code file.

Compiler

The compiler is another program that translates the preprocessed source code (the source code after the insertions made by the preprocessor) into corresponding machine language instructions, which are stored in a separate file, called an object file, having an .obj extension. There are different compilers for different programming languages, but the purpose of the compiler is essentially the same, the translation of a programming language into machine language, no matter which programming language is involved.

The compiler can understand your code and translate it into machine language only if your code is in the proper syntax for that programming language. C++, like other programming languages, and indeed most human languages, has rules for the spelling of words and for the grammar of statements. If there is a syntax error, then the compiler cannot translate your code into machine language instructions, and instead will call your attention to the syntax errors. Thus, in a sense, the compiler acts as a spell checker and grammar checker.

Linker

While the object file has machine language instructions, the computer cannot run the object file as a program. The reason is that C++ also needs to use another code library, called the run-time library, for common operations, such as the translation of keyboard

input or the ability to interact with external hardware such as the monitor to display a message.

NOTE: *The run-time library files may already be installed as part of your operating system. If not, you can download the run-time library files from Microsoft or another vendor. Finally, if you install an IDE as discussed in the next section, the run-time library files are included with the installation.*

The linker is a third program that combines the object file with the necessary parts of the run-time library. The result is the creation of an executable file with an .exe extension. The computer runs this file to display "Hello World!" on the screen.

Using an IDE to Create and Run the "Hello World!" Project

You can use any plain-text editor such as Notepad to write the source code. You also can download a free compiler, which usually includes a preprocessor and linker. You then can compile and run your code from the *command line.* The command line may be, for example, a DOS prompt at which you type a command that specifies the action you want, such as compiling, followed by the name of the file you want to compile.

While there is nothing wrong with using a plain-text editor and command line tools, many programmers, including me, prefer to create, compile, and run their programs in a C++ Integrated Development Environment, known by the acronym IDE. The term "integrated" in IDE means that the text editor, preprocessor, compiler, and linker are all together under one (software) roof. Thus, the IDE enables you to create, compile, and run your code using one program rather than separate programs. Additionally, most IDEs have a graphical user interface (GUI) that makes them easier for many to use than a command line. Finally, many IDEs have added features that ease your task of finding and fixing errors in your code.

The primary disadvantage of using IDEs is you have to pay to purchase them (though there are some free ones). They also require additional hard drive space and memory. Nevertheless, I recommend obtaining an IDE since it enables you to focus on C++ programming issues without distractions such as figuring out the right commands to use on the command line.

There are several good IDEs on the market. Microsoft's, called Visual C++, can be obtained separately or as part of Microsoft's Visual Studio product. Borland offers

C++ Builder, both in a free and commercial version. IBM has a VisualAge C++ IDE. There are a number of others as well.

In this book, I will use Microsoft's Visual C++ .NET 2003 IDE since I happen to have it. However, most IDEs work essentially the same way, and your code will compile and run the same no matter which IDE you use as long as you don't use any library files custom to a particular IDE. The standard library files we will be using, such as iostream, are the same in all C++ IDEs.

Additionally, I am running the code on a Windows 2000 operating system. The results should be similar on other operating systems, not just Windows operating systems, but additional types of operating systems as well, such as UNIX.

Let's now use the IDE to write the source code for the "Hello World!" project, and then compile and run it.

Setting Up the "Hello World!" Project

Once you have purchased and installed Visual C++ .NET 2003, either as a standalone application or as part of Visual Studio .NET 2003, you are now ready to start your first project, which is to create and run the "Hello World!" application.

1. Start Visual C++.

2. Open the New Project dialog box shown in Figure 1-2 using the File | New | Project menu command. (The values in the Name and Location fields will be set in steps 5 and 6.)

3. In the left or list pane of the New Project dialog box, choose Visual C++ Projects from the list of Project Types, and then the Win32 subfolder, as shown in Figure 1-2.

4. In the right or contents pane of the New Project dialog box, choose Win32 Console Project from the list of templates. The word console comes from the application running from a console window. Win32 comes from the Windows 32-bit operating system, such as Windows 9x, 2000, or XP.

5. In the Location field, using the Browse button, choose an existing folder under which you will create the subfolder where you will put your project.

6. In the Name field, type the name you've chosen for your project. This will also be the name of the subfolder created to store your project files. I suggest you use a name that describes your project so you can locate it more easily later.

7. Click the OK button. This will display the Win32 Application Wizard, shown in Figure 1-3.

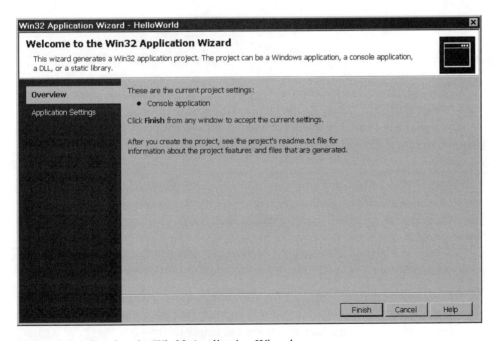

Figure 1-2 Creating a New Project

Figure 1-3 Starting the Win32 Application Wizard

8. Click the Application Settings menu item on the left. The appearance of the Win32 Application Wizard then changes to that shown in Figure 1-4.

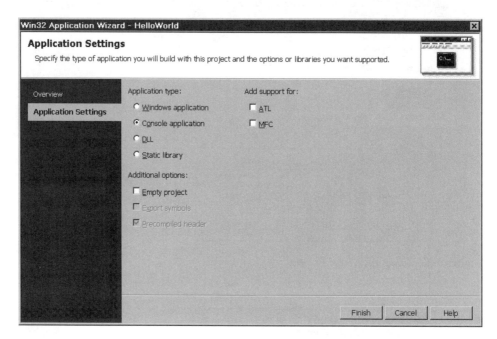

Figure 1-4   Win32 Application Wizard after choosing Application Settings

9. Choose, if necessary, Console Application under Application Type (this is the default) and Empty Project under Additional Options. Choosing Empty Project will disable both checkboxes under Add Support For, which should be disabled anyway.

CAUTION: Make sure you follow this step carefully, particularly choosing Empty Project, which is not the default. Not configuring Application Settings properly is a common mistake and may require you to start over.

---

10. Click the Finish button. Figure 1-5 shows the new subfolder HelloWorld and its parent folder. These were the name and location chosen in steps 5 and 6.

You now have created a project for your application. The project is a shell for your application, containing files that will support the creation and running of your application. However, right now the project is empty of any code you have written, so it won't do anything. Accordingly, the next step is to start writing code.

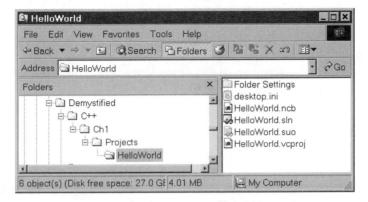

Figure 1-5   Windows Explorer showing newly created subfolder and files

Writing the Source Code

Visual C++ has a view of a project that is similar to Windows Explorer. That view is called Solution Explorer, shown in Figure 1-6. If Solution Explorer is not already displayed, you can display it with the menu command View | Solution Explorer.

Solution Explorer has folders for both source and header files. The file in which the code for the "Hello World!" application will be written is a source file. Source

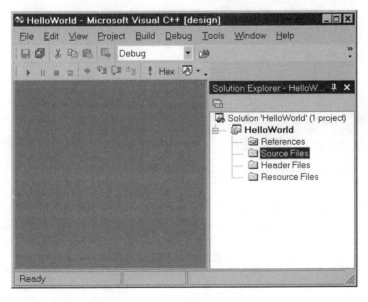

Figure 1-6   Viewing your project with Solution Explorer

files have a .cpp extension, cpp standing for C++. By contrast, the iostream file that is included by the include directive is a header file. Header files have an .h extension—the h standing for header.

We will use Solution Explorer to add a new source file to the project, after which we will write code in that new source file.

You can use the following steps to add a new source file to the project:

1. Right-click Source Files in Solution Explorer. This will display a shortcut menu, shown in Figure 1-7.

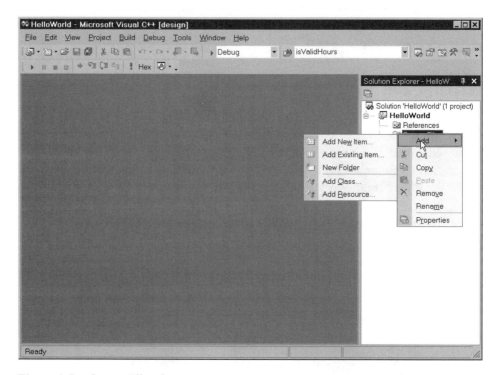

Figure 1-7   Source Files shortcut menu

2. Choose Add | Add New Item from the shortcut menu to add a new source to the project. This will display the Add New Item dialog box, shown in Figure 1-8.

NOTE: *If the source file already exists, you can add it to your project using the Add | Add Existing Item shortcut menu item.*

---

3. Generally, you will not change the Location field, which is the subfolder in which the project files are stored. Type the name of the new source file in the

Name field. You do not need to type the .cpp extension; that extension will be appended automatically since it is a source file. By typing **hello**, as shown in Figure 1-8, the new file will be called hello.cpp.

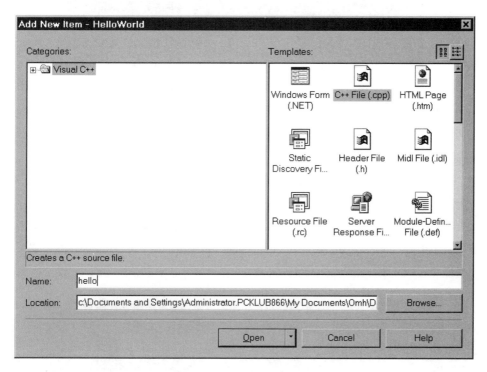

Figure 1-8   Adding a New Source File to your Project

4. When you are done, click the Open button. Figure 1-9 shows the new hello.cpp file in Solution Explorer.

Writing the code is easy. Double-click hello.cpp in Solution Explorer. As shown in Figure 1-10, this will display the hello.cpp file, which at this point is blank.
Now just type your code. When finished, hello.cpp should appear as in Figure 1-11.

CAUTION: You also can use Notepad or any other text editor to write the code. However, do not use Microsoft Word or any other word processing program to write your code. While a word processing program enables you to neatly format your code, it does so using hidden formatting characters that the compiler does not understand and will regard as syntax errors.

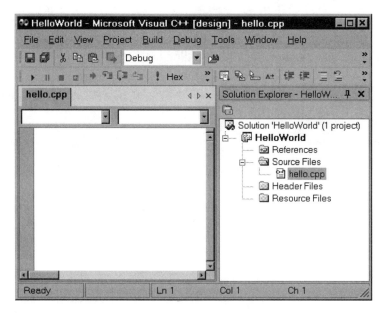

Figure 1-9　Solution Explorer showing the new .cpp file

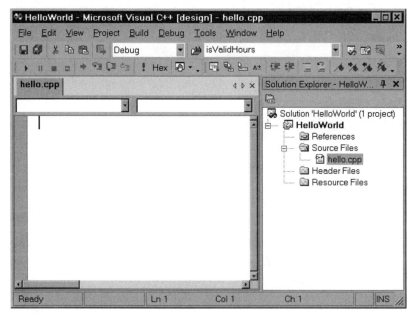

Figure 1-10　The source file before typing code

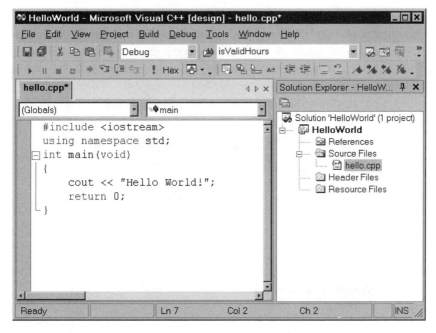

Figure 1-11   The source file after typing code

Save your work, such as by pressing the Save toolbar button. We're now ready to compile.

Building the Project

You compile your code from the Build menu. You may compile your code from any one of the following different menu choices:

- Build | Solution
- Rebuild | Solution
- Build | HelloWorld
- Rebuild | HelloWorld

HelloWorld is the name of your project. A solution may contain more than one project. Here the solution contains only one project, so there is no practical difference between the project and the solution.

Build means to compile changes from the last compilation (if there was one). Rebuild means to start compilation from the beginning. Build therefore is usually faster, but Rebuild is used when there have been extensive changes since the last compilation. As a practical matter, it rarely makes a difference which one you choose.

Before we compile, make one change to the code, changing cout to Cout (capitalizing the C). Then choose one of the four compilation options. A Task List window should display, noting a build error, as shown in Figure 1-12. The error description in the Task List window is "error C2065: 'Cout' : undeclared identifier."

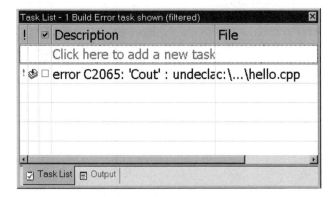

Figure 1-12   The Task List window showing a compilation error

TIP: *If the description column is not wide enough to show the entire error description, you can display the error description in a pop-up window by right-clicking the error description and choosing Show Description Tooltip from the shortcut menu.*

As explained in the earlier section on the Compiler, the compiler can understand your code and translate it into machine language only if your code is in the proper syntax for that programming language. As also explained there, C++ has rules for the spelling of words and for the grammar of statements. If there is a violation of those rules, that is, a syntax error, then the compiler cannot translate your code into machine language instructions, and instead will call your attention to the syntax errors.

In C++, code is case sensitive. That is, a word capitalized is not the same as the word uncapitalized. The correct spelling is cout; Cout is wrong. Since C++ does not know what Cout is, you get the error message that it is an "undeclared identifier."

While here the code is short, if your code is quite lengthy, it is not easy to spot where the error is in the code. If you double-click the error in the Task List window, then a cursor will blink at the line where Cout is, and an icon will display in the margin (as shown in Figure 1-13).

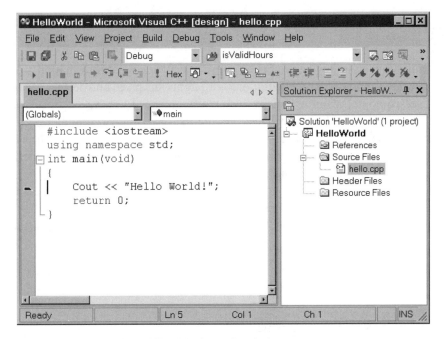

Figure 1-13   The error highlighted in the code window

Now change Cout to cout, and then compile your code again. This time compilation should be successful. Using Windows Explorer, you can now see in the Debug sub-folder of your HelloWorld project folder a file called hello.obj and another file called hello.exe. These are the object and executable files previously discussed in the section "Translating the Code for the Computer." Accordingly, building the project involved the preprocessor, the compiler, and the linker.

Running the Code

The final step is to run the code. You do so from the Debug menu. You may choose either Debug | Start or Debug | Start Without Debugging. The difference is whether you wish to use the debugger, an issue which we will discuss in a later chapter. Since we are not going to use the debugger this time, choose Debug | Start Without Debugging as it is slightly faster. The result is the console window displaying "Hello World!" (shown way back in Figure 1-1).

Summary

Computers can store huge amounts of information, recall that information quickly and accurately, and perform calculations with lightning speed and perfect accuracy. However, computers cannot think by themselves, and need step-by-step instructions from us telling them what to do. These instructions are called a computer program, written by a human computer programmer in a programming language such as C++. A compiler, together with a preprocessor and a linker, translates the computer program into machine language that a computer understands.

We then analyzed a C++ program, which outputs "Hello World!" to the screen. The program looks simple, but much is going on behind the scenes. We analyzed that code, line by line. You then created and ran your own "Hello World!" C++ application.

Quiz

1. What is a computer program?
2. Name several advantages a computer has over humans in processing information?
3. What is a programming language?
4. Why is C++ a good programming language to learn?
5. What is a function?
6. How many main functions should a C++ program have?
7. What is a standard library file?
8. What is the purpose of an include directive?
9. What does a preprocessor do?
10. What does a compiler do?
11. What does a linker do?

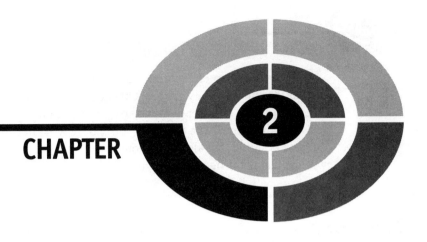

CHAPTER 2

Memory and Data Types

After I wrote my first book, I expectantly waited every day for my mail, hoping to receive requests for my autograph. The result was proof of the adage "be careful what you ask for." My mailbox was stuffed with numerous requests for my autograph. Alas, these requests came from those who wanted to share my money, not my fame. My autograph was requested on checks to pay my mortgage, credit cards, insurance, phone service, electricity; well, you get the picture.

These companies who love sending me bills could not possibly keep track of their thousands of customers by using pencil and paper. Instead, they use computer programs, which harness the computer's ability to store very large amounts of information and to retrieve that stored information very quickly.

We use our memory to store and recall information. So do computers. However, a computer's memory is very different from ours. This chapter will explain how a computer's memory works.

Information, also called data, comes in different forms. Some data is numeric, such as the amount of my gas bill. Other data is text, such as my name on my gas bill. The type of data, whether numeric, text, or something else, quite logically is referred to as the "data type." The data type you choose will affect not only the form in which the data is stored, but also the amount of memory required to store it. This chapter will explain the different data types.

Memory

Computer programs consist of instructions and data. As discussed in Chapter 1, instructions, written in a programming language such as C++ and then translated by the compiler and linker into machine language, give the computer step-by-step directions on what to do. The data is the information that is the subject of the program. For example, if the user of your computer program wants a list of all students with a GPA of 4.0, the data could be a list of all students and their GPAs. The program then would follow instructions to determine and output the list of all students with a GPA of 4.0.

The computer program's instructions and data have to be in the computer's memory for the program to work. This section will explain the different types of computer memory, as well as how and where instructions and data are stored in computer memory.

Types of Memory

There are three principal memory locations on your computer.

- The central processing unit (CPU)
- Random access memory (RAM)
- Persistent storage

Cache Memory

The CPU is the brains of the computer. You may have thought about the CPU when you last considered purchasing a computer, since the CPU's speed often is an important purchase consideration. The faster the CPU's speed, the faster your computer runs.

NOTE: A hertz, named after Heinrich Hertz, who first detected electromagnetic waves, represents one cycle per second. CPU speed is measured in megahertz (MHz), which represents one million cycles per second, or gigahertz (GHz), which represents 1 billion cycles per second. For example, a CPU that runs at 800 MHz executes 800 million cycles per second. Each computer instruction requires a fixed number of cycles, so the CPU speed determines how many instructions per second the CPU can execute.

The CPU, in addition to coordinating the computer's operations, also has memory, called *cache memory*. The CPU's cache memory includes a segment called a *register*. This memory is used to store frequently used instructions and data.

The CPU can access cache memory extremely quickly because it doesn't have far to go; the memory is right on the CPU. However, the amount of available cache memory is quite small; there is only enough room for the most frequently used instructions and data. The remainder of the instructions and data have to be stored somewhere else.

Random Access Memory

That somewhere else is *random access memory,* or RAM. You may also have considered RAM when you last purchased a computer, since the more RAM a computer has, the more programs it can run at one time, and the faster it runs.

The CPU can access RAM almost as quickly as cache memory. Additionally, the amount of RAM available to store instructions and data is much larger than the amount of available cache memory.

However, RAM, like cache memory, is temporary. Instructions and data contained in main memory are lost once the computer is powered down. You may have had the unpleasant experience of losing unsaved data when your computer powered off during a power failure, or had to be rebooted.

Additionally, we would want the data to remain intact after the program ended, even if the computer is rebooted or powered off. That is not possible with RAM.

Furthermore, your computer likely has many other programs, for e-mail, Internet, word processing, and so on, that you may not be using right now, but you may want to use in the future. Likewise, your computer also may have other data files, such as term papers, letters, tax spreadsheets, e-mail messages, and so on, that you also may not be using right now, but that you may want to use in the future. Accordingly, we need another memory location, which unlike cache memory or RAM, is persistent—that is, it will persist even though the computer is rebooted or turned off.

Persistent Storage

That other, persistent type of computer memory is called, naturally enough, *persistent storage*. This usually is a hard drive, but also could be, among other devices, a CD-ROM or DVD-ROM, floppy or zip disk, or optical drive. However, no matter what storage device is used, persistent storage is lasting; instructions and data remain stored even when the computer is powered down. Thus, your computer can be turned off for months, but when it is turned on, the files you previously saved are still there.

Persistent storage, in addition to being lasting, also has a much larger capacity than RAM—about one hundred to one thousand times larger.

Since persistent storage is lasting and has a very large capacity, it is used to store both programs and data. For example, if you installed Microsoft Word on your computer, the files for this program would be stored on your hard drive. If you then prepared documents using that program, those documents likewise would be saved as files on your hard drive.

While persistent storage has the advantages of being lasting and having a large capacity, a computer program cannot execute instructions located in persistent storage. The instructions must be loaded from persistent storage into RAM. Similarly, a computer program cannot manipulate data located in persistent storage. This data likewise must be loaded from persistent storage into RAM.

NOTE: While beyond the scope of this chapter, persistent storage also can serve as a backup to RAM, and when serving this purpose is called virtual memory or swap space.

Generally, computer programs use RAM to store instructions and data, so RAM will be our focus in discussing memory. However, much of the discussion of memory also may apply to persistent storage. CPU cache memory is a different subject, discussed more in connection with programming languages, such as assembly language, that are far closer to machine language than is C++.

Addresses

When someone asks where you live, you may answer 1313 Mockingbird Lane. That is your address.

Addresses are used to locate persons or places. Addresses usually follow a logical pattern. For example, the addresses on one block may be from 1300 to 1399, the next from 1400 to 1499, and so on.

Locations in memory also are identified by address. These addresses often look quite different than the street addresses we're used to, since they usually are expressed as hexadecimal (Base 16) numbers such as 0x8fc1. However, regardless of how the number is written, as shown in Figure 2-1, memory addresses follow the same logical, sequential pattern as do street addresses, one number coming after another.

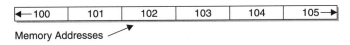

Memory Addresses

Figure 2-1   Sequence of memory addresses

Note: **Hexadecimal Numbers**—*We usually use numbers that are decimal, or Base 10, in which each digit is between 0 and 9. By contrast, memory addresses usually are expressed as hexadecimal, or Base 16, in which each digit is between 1 and 15. Since 10, 11, 12, 13, 14, and 15 are not single digits, 10 is expressed as a, 11 as b, 12 as c, 13 as d, 14 as e, and 15 as f. The number 16 in decimal is expressed as 10 in hexadecimal.*

Memory address numbers can be large values, and thus may be written more compactly in hexadecimal than in decimal. For example, 1,000,000 in decimal is f4240 in hexadecimal.

Converting between hexadecimal and decimal is explained next in the upcoming section, "Converting Between Decimal and Binary or Hexadecimal."

Bits and Bytes

While people live at street addresses, what is stored at each memory address is a *byte*. Don't worry, I have not misspelled Dracula's favorite pastime.

As discussed in Chapter 1, early computers essentially were a series of switches, 1 representing on, 0 representing off. In computer terminology, a *bit* is either a 1 or a 0.

However, while a computer may think in bits, it cannot process information as small as a single bit. Eight bits, or one *byte,* is the smallest unit of information that a computer can process.

Accordingly, each address may store up to one byte of information, represented by a sequence of up to eight ones and zeroes. Thus, just as a street address may be used to locate the persons who live there, a memory address can be used to locate the one byte of information that is stored there. Figure 2-2 shows a sequence of memory addresses, each with a value.

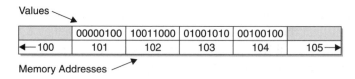

Figure 2-2   A sequence of memory addresses, each with a byte value

Binary Numbering System

The information stored at a memory address, a series of ones and zeroes, probably has little meaning to most of us. However, to a computer, a sequence of ones and zeroes is quite meaningful.

For example, to my computer, I was born in the year 11110100000. Before you tell me that's impossible, I will tell you I was born in the year 1952. How could I have been born both in the year 11110100000 and in the year 1952?

The numbers with which we usually work are decimal, or base 10. Each number in decimal is represented by a digit between 0 and 9. 1952 is a decimal number.

The sequence of ones and zeroes in a byte also is a number, though it may not look like any number you have ever seen. My birth year, expressed as the number 11110100000, is binary, or base 2. Each number in binary is represented by a digit that is either 0 or 1.

The reason both decimal and binary numbers are involved in computer programming is because both humans and computers are involved. While humans think in decimal numbers, computers "think" in binary numbers.

Converting Between Decimal and Binary or Hexadecimal

You can write computer programs without knowing how to convert between binary and decimal numbers. However, knowing how to do so is not difficult and may help your understanding of what happens behind the scenes. If you are interested, read on!

Converting a number from binary to decimal is simple. Going from right to left, the rightmost binary digit is multiplied by 2^0, or 1, the second binary digit from the right is multiplied by 2^1, or 2, the third binary digit from the right is multiplied by 2^2, or 4, and so on, through all of the binary digits. The results of each multiplication are added, and the result is the decimal equivalent of the binary number. Table 2-1 shows this calculation for the binary equivalents of the numbers 1 through 5 in decimal.

Binary	Calculation	Decimal
0	$0 \times 2^0 = 0 \times 1 =$	0
1	$1 \times 2^0 = 1 \times 1 =$	1
10	$(0 \times 2^0) + (1 \times 2^1) = 0 + 2$	2
11	$(1 \times 2^0) + (1 \times 2^1) = 1 + 2$	3
100	$(0 \times 2^0) + (0 \times 2^1) + (1 \times 2^2) = 0 + 0 + 4$	4
101	$(1 \times 2^0) + (0 \times 2^1) + (1 \times 2^2) = 1 + 0 + 4$	5

Table 2-1   Binary Equivalents of the Numbers 1 Through 5 in Decimal

Converting a number from decimal to binary is almost as easy. Let's use 5 in decimal as an example.

1. You find the largest power of 2 that can be divided into 5 with a quotient of 1. The answer is 2^2, or 4.

2. Remember when converting from binary to decimal, the rightmost binary digit is multiplied by 2^0, or 1, the second binary digit from the right is multiplied by 2^1, the third binary digit from the right is multiplied by 2^2, and so on. Since the exponent is 2, a binary 1 goes into the third binary digit from the right, so the binary number now is 1??, the ? representing each binary digit we still need to calculate.

3. When you divide 5 by 4, the remainder is 1. You next try to divide 1 by the next lowest power of 2, 2^1, or 2. The quotient is 0, so a binary 0 goes into the second binary digit from the right. The binary number now is 10?.

4. When you divide 1 by 2, the remainder is still 1. You next try to divide 1 by the next lowest power of 2, 2^0, or 1. The quotient is 1, so a binary 1 goes into the rightmost binary digit. The binary number now is 101, and we're done.

You also can use the same techniques for converting between hexadecimal and decimal. When converting from hexadecimal to decimal, multiply each hexadecimal digit (converting a to 10, b to 11, and so on) by the appropriate power of 16. For example, 5c in hexadecimal is $(12 \times 16^0) + (5 \times 16^1)$, which is $12 + 80$ or 92.

Conversely, when converting from decimal to hexadecimal, the highest power of 16 that can be divided into 92 is 16^1, or 16. The quotient is 5, which goes into the second digit to the right. The remainder is 12, which is c in hexadecimal. This goes into the rightmost digit, resulting in the hexadecimal number 5c.

Data Types

The ones and zeroes that may be stored at a memory address may represent text, such as my name, Jeff Kent. These ones and zeroes instead may represent a whole number, such as my height in inches, 72, or a number with digits to the right of the decimal point, such as my GPA in high school, which I'll say was 3.75 (I honestly don't remember, it was too long ago). Alternatively, the ones and zeroes may represent either true or false, such as whether I am a U.S. citizen.

Data comes in many forms, and is generally either numeric or textual. Additionally, some numeric data uses whole numbers, such as 6, 0, or –7, while other numeric data uses floating-point numbers, such as .6, 7.3, and –6.1.

There are different data types for each of the many forms of data. The data type you choose will affect not only the form in which the data is stored, but also the amount of memory required to store the data. Let's now take a look at these different data types.

Whole Number Data Types

We deal with whole numbers all the time. Think of the answers to questions such as how many cars are in the parking lot, how many classes are you taking, or how many brothers and sisters do you have? Each answer involves a number, with no need to express any value to the right of the decimal point. After all, who has 3.71 brothers and sisters?

Often, you don't need a large whole number. What unfortunate student would be taking 754,361 classes at one time? However, sometimes the whole number needs to be large. For example, if you are studying astronomy, the moon is approximately 240,000 miles from Earth. Indeed, sometimes the whole number may need to be very, very large. Pluto's minimum distance from the Earth is about 2.7 billion miles.

Many times, the whole number won't be negative. No matter how badly you do on a test, chances are you won't score below zero points. However, some whole numbers may be below zero, such as the temperature at the North Pole.

Because of the different needs whole numbers may have to meet, there are several different whole number data types (shown in Table 2-2). The listed sizes and ranges are typical, but may vary depending on the compiler and operating system. In the *sizeof* operator project later in this chapter, you will determine through code the size of different data types on your compiler and operating system.

Data Type	Size (in Bytes)	Range
short	2	−32,768 to 32,767
unsigned short	2	0 to 65,365
int	4	−2,147,483,648 to 2,147,483,647
unsigned int	4	0 to 4,294,987,295
long	4	−2,147,483,648 to 2,147,483,647
unsigned long	4	0 to 4,294,987,295

Table 2-2   Whole Number Data Types, Sizes, and Ranges

NOTE: You may be wondering about the purpose of the long data type, since its size and range is the same as an int in Table 2-2. However, as noted just before that table, the actual size, and, therefore, range of a particular data type varies depending on the compiler and operating system. On some combinations of compilers and operating systems, short may be 1 byte, int may be 2 bytes, and long may be 4 bytes.

Beginning programmers sometimes see information like that shown in Table 2-2 and panic that they can't possibly memorize all of it. The good news is you don't have to. To be sure, some memorization is necessary for almost any task. However, since there really is too much information to memorize, programmers frequently resort to online help or reference books. Believe me, I do.

Far more important to a programmer than rote memorization is to understand how and why a program works as it does. Therefore, this section will go into some detail as to how data types work. Some arithmetic necessarily is involved, but it is not difficult, and if you follow the arithmetic, you will have a good understanding of data types that will help you in your programming in the following chapters.

Unsigned vs. Signed Data Type

Table 2-2 lists three data types: short, int, and long. Each of these three data types has either the word unsigned in front of it or nothing at all—as in unsigned short and short.

Unsigned means the number is always zero or positive, never negative. *Signed* means the number may be negative or positive (or zero). If you don't specify signed or unsigned, the data type is presumed to be signed. Thus, signed short and short are the same.

Since an unsigned data type means its value is always 0 or positive, never negative, in Table 2-2 the smallest value of an unsigned short is therefore zero; an unsigned short cannot be negative. By contrast, the smallest value of a short is −32767, since a signed data type may be negative, positive, or zero.

Size

Each of the whole number data types listed in Table 2-2 has a size. Indeed, all C++ data types have a size. However, unlike people, the size of a data type is not expressed in inches or in pounds (a sore subject for me), but in bytes.

Since a byte is the smallest unit of information that a computer can process, no data type may be smaller than one byte. Most data types are larger than one byte; all the whole number data types listed in Table 2-2 are. However, regardless of the size, the number of bytes is always a whole number. You cannot have a data type whose size is 3.5 bytes because .5 bytes, or 4 bits, is too small for the computer to process.

Generally, the number of bytes for a data type is the result of a power of 2 since computers use a binary number system. Thus, typical data type sizes are 1 byte (2^0), 2 bytes (2^1), four bytes (2^2), or eight bytes (2^3).

The size of a data type matters in two related respects: (1) the *range* of different values that the data type may represent and (2) the amount of memory required to store the data type.

Range

Range means the highest and lowest value that may be represented by a given data type. For example, the range of the unsigned short data type is 0 to 65,365. These lowest and highest values are not arbitrary, but instead can be calculated.

The number of different values that a data type can represent is 2^n, n being the number of bits in the data type. The size of a short data type is 2 bytes, or 16 bits. Therefore, the number of different whole numbers that the short data type can represent is 2^{16}, which is 65,356.

However, the highest value that an unsigned short can represent is 65,355, not 65,356, because the unsigned short data type starts at 0, not 1. Therefore, the highest number that an unsigned data type may represent is $2^n − 1$; n again being the number of bits in the data type, and the minus 1 being used because we are starting at 0, not 1.

Signed data types involve an additional issue. Since the range of a signed data type includes negative numbers, there needs to be a way of determining if a number is positive or negative. We determine if a decimal number is positive or negative by looking to see if the number is preceded by a negative sign (–). However, a bit can be only 1 or 0; there is no option for a negative sign in a binary number.

There are several different explanations in computer science for the representation of negative numbers, such as *signed magnitude, one's complement,* and *two's complement.* However, we don't need to get into the complexities of these explanations.

For example, a signed short data type, like an unsigned short data type, can represent 2^{16} or 65,356 different numbers. However, with a signed data type, these different numbers must be split evenly between those starting at zero and going up, and those starting at zero and going down. To do this, the two ranges would be 0 to 32,767 and –1 to –32,768. This can be confirmed by Table 2-2, which shows the range of a signed data type as –32,768 to 32,767.

Another way of explaining the high and low numbers of the range of the signed short data type is that one of the bits is used to store the sign, positive or negative. That leaves 15 bits. The highest number in the range is $2^{15} - 1$, or 32,767; the minus 1 being used because we are starting at 0, not 1. The lowest number in the range is $-(2^{15})$, or –32,768; there's no minus 1 because we are starting at –1, not 0.

Storage

In binary, 65365 as an unsigned short is represented by sixteen ones: 1111111111111111. You cannot fit 16 bits into a single memory address. A memory address can hold only 8 bits, or a byte. How then can you store this value in memory?

The answer is you need two memory addresses to store 65365 in decimal. This provides two bytes of storage, sufficient to store this value. This is why the short data type requires 2 bytes of storage. Figure 2-3 shows how this value would be stored as a short data type.

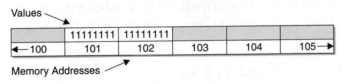

Figure 2-3   Storage in memory of 65365 in decimal as an unsigned short data type

The int data type requires 4 bytes of storage. Figure 2-4 shows how 65365 in decimal would be stored as an unsigned int data type.

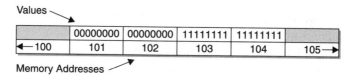

Figure 2-4   Storage in memory of 65365 in decimal as an unsigned int data type

You may legitimately wonder why 65365 in decimal as an unsigned int data type requires four bytes of storage when 65365 in decimal as an unsigned short data type requires only two bytes of storage. In other words, if you specify int instead of short as the data type, four bytes of storage will be reserved, even if you could store the number in less bytes. The reason is that it is not known, when memory is reserved, what value will be stored there. Additionally, the value could change. Accordingly, enough bytes of storage are reserved for the maximum possible value of that data type.

Why Use a Smaller Size Data Type?

Given that an int can store a far wider range of numbers than a short, you also may be wondering why you ever would use a short rather than an int. The answer is that the wider range of an int comes at a price; it requires twice as much RAM as a short—four instead of two bytes.

However, computers these days come with hundreds of megabytes of RAM, each megabyte being 1,048,576 bytes; you still may wonder why you should care about two measly extra bytes. If it *was* just 2 extra bytes, you wouldn't care. However, if you are writing a program for an insurance company that has one million customers, you won't be talking about 2 extra bytes, but instead 2 *million* extra bytes. Therefore, you should not just reflexively choose the largest data type.

All this said, as a general rule, of the six whole number data types, you most often will use int. However, it is good to know about the other choices.

Floating-Point Data Types

I was nearsighted my entire adult life until I had lasik surgery on my eyes. In this surgery, the eye surgeon programs information that the laser used to reshape my eyeball by shaving off very thin slices of my cornea, measuring only thousandths of an inch, in certain areas of my eyeball, leaving untouched other areas, again only thousandths of an inch away.

Can you imagine my reaction if the eye surgeon had told me his philosophy was "close enough for government work," so he was using only whole numbers, ignoring any values to the right of the decimal point? You next would have seen my silhouette through the wall after I ran through it to escape. (Since I still go to my eye surgeon, who, by the way, earned his way through college as a computer programmer, and it is not in my best interest to get on his bad side, let me hasten to add that he was very precise and the surgery was successful.)

Whole numbers work fine for certain information where fractions don't apply. For example, who would say they have 2 ¾ children? Whole numbers also work fine for certain information where fractions do apply but are not important. For example, it would be sufficient normally to say the location is 98 miles away; precision such as 98.177 miles usually is not necessary.

However, other times fractions, expressed as numbers to the right of the decimal point, are very important. My lasik surgery is an extreme example, but there are many other more common ones. If you had a 3.9 GPA, you probably would not want the school to just forget about the .9 and say your GPA was 3. Similarly, a bank that kept track of dollars but not cents with deposits and withdrawals would, with potentially millions of transactions a day, soon have very inaccurate information as to how much money it has, and its depositors have.

Accordingly, there are floating-point data types that you can use when a value to the right of the decimal point is important. The term *floating point* comes from the fact that there is no fixed number of digits before and after the decimal point; that is, the decimal point can float. Floating-point numbers also are sometimes referred to as real numbers.

Table 2-3 lists each of the floating-point number data types. As with the whole number data types, the listed sizes and ranges are typical, but may vary depending on the compiler and operating system.

Data Type	Size (in Bytes)	Range (in E notation)
float	4	±3.4E-38 to ±3.4E38
double	8	±1.7E-308 to ±1.7E308
long double	10	±3.4E-4932 to ±3.4E4932

Table 2-3   Floating-point Number Data Types, Sizes, and Ranges

Note: *The size of a long double on many combinations of compilers and operating systems may be 8 bytes, not 10.*

Scientific and E Notations

The range column in Table 2-3 may not look like any number you have ever seen before. That is because these are not usual decimal numbers, but instead numbers expressed in *E notation*, the letter *E* standing for exponent.

The float data types can store very large numbers, such as (in decimal) 1000000000000000000000000000000000000, which could be a distance across the universe. The float data types also can store very small numbers, such as .0000000000000000000000000000000000001, which could be the diameter of a subatomic particle.

Rather than having digits running across the page, the number can be expressed more compactly. One way is with *scientific notation,* another is with E notation. Table 2-4 shows how certain floating-point numbers are represented in both notations.

Decimal Notation	Scientific Notation	E Notation
123.45	1.2345×10^2	1.2345E2
0.0051	5.1×10^{-3}	5.1E-3
1,200,000,000	1.2×10^9	1.2E9

Table 2-4 Scientific and E Notation Representations of Floating Point Values

In scientific notation, the number before the multiplication operator, called the *mantissa*, always is expressed as having a single digit to the left of the decimal point, and as many digits as necessary to the right side of the decimal point to express the number. The number after the multiplication operator is a power of 10, which may be positive for very large numbers or negative for very small fractions. The value of the expression is the mantissa multiplied by the power of 10.

E notation is very similar to scientific notation. The only difference is the multiplication operator, followed by 10 and an exponent, is replaced by an E followed by the exponent.

Storage of Floating-Point Numbers

Since only ones and zeroes can be stored in memory, complex codes, well beyond the scope of this book, are required to store floating-point numbers. Even with complex codes, a computer can only approximately represent many floating-point values. Indeed, in certain programs the programmer has to take care to ensure that small discrepancies in each of a number of approximations don't accumulate to the point where the final result is wrong.

NOTE: Because mathematics with floating-point numbers requires a great deal of computing power, many CPUs come with a chip specialized for performing floating-point arithmetic. These chips often are referred to as math coprocessors.

Text Data Types

There are two text data types. The first is *char,* which stands for character. It usually is 1 byte, and can represent any single character, including a letter, a digit, a punctuation mark, or a space.

The second text data type is *string.* The string data type may store a number of characters, including this sentence, or paragraph, or page. The number of bytes required depends on the number of characters involved.

NOTE: Unlike char and the other data types we have discussed, the string type is not a data type built into C++. Instead, it is defined in the standard library file string, which therefore must be included with an include directive (#include <string>) to use the string data type. Chapter 1 covers the include directive, which in the "Hello World!" program was #include <iostream>.

Storage of Character Values

There is a reason why the size of a character data type usually is 1 byte.

ANSI (American National Standards Institute) and ASCII (American Standards Committee for Information Interchange) adopted for the English language a set of 256 characters, which includes all alphabetical characters (upper- and lowercase), digits and punctuation marks, and even characters used in graphics and line drawing. Each of these 256 different characters is represented by a number between 0 and 255 that it corresponds to. Table 2-5 lists the ASCII values of commonly used characters.

Each of the 256 different values can be represented by different combinations of 8 bits, or one byte. This is true because 2^8 equals 256. Thus, 00000000 is equal to 0, the smallest ASCII value, and 11111111 is equal to 255, the largest ASCII value.

For example, the letter J has the ASCII code 74. The binary equivalent of 74 is 1001010. Thus, 1001010 at a memory address could indicate the letter J.

Characters	Values	Comments
0 through 9	48–57	0 is 48, 9 is 57
A through Z	65–90	A is 65, Z is 90
a through z	97–122	a is 97, z is 122

Table 2-5   ASCII Values of Commonly Used Characters

NOTE: 1001010 also could indicate the number 74; you wouldn't know which value was being represented unless you knew the data type associated with that memory address. In the next chapter, you will learn about variables, which enable you to associate a particular data type with a specific memory address.

Storage of Strings

The amount of memory required for a string depends on the number of characters in the string. However, each memory address set aside for the string would store one character of the string.

The bool Data Type

There is one more data type, *bool.* This data type has only two possible values, true and false, and its size usually is one byte. The term "bool" is a shortening of Boolean, which is usually used in connection with Boolean Algebra, named after the British mathematician, George Boole.

The *bool* data type is mentioned separately since it does not neatly fit into either the number or text categories. It could be regarded as a numeric data type in that zero is seen as false, and one (or any other non-zero number) as true. While it may not seem intuitive why zero would be false and one would be true, remember that computers essentially store information in switches, where 1 is on, and 0 is off.

Project: Determining the Size of Data Types

As discussed in the previous Data Types section, the size of each data type depends on the compiler and operating system you are using. In this project, you will find out the size of each data type on your system by using the *sizeof* operator.

The sizeof Operator

The *sizeof* operator is followed by parentheses, in which you place a data type. It returns the size in bytes of that data type.

For example, on my computer, the expression sizeof(int) returns 4. This means that on my compiler and operating system, the size of an int data type is 4 bytes.

Changing the Source File of Your Project

Try creating and running the next program using the steps you followed in Chapter 1 to create the "Hello World!" program. While you could start a new project, in this example, you will reuse the project you used in Chapter 1. It is good to know both how to create a new project and how to reuse an existing one.

1. Start Visual C++.

2. Use the File | Open Solution menu command to display the Open Solution dialog box shown in Figure 2-5.

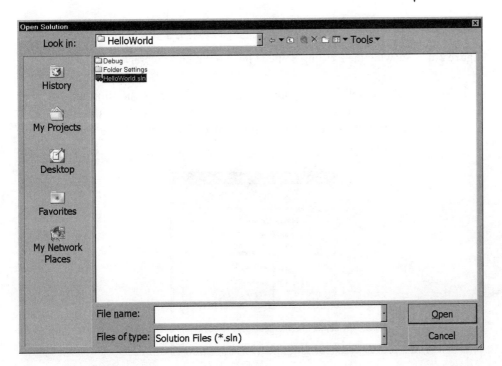

Figure 2-5   Opening the Existing Solution

3. Navigate to the folder where you saved the project (C:\temp\helloworld on my computer) and find the solution file. It has the extension .sln, which stands for solution. The solution file is helloworld.sln in Figure 2-5.

4. Open the solution file. This should open your project.

5. Display Solution Explorer using the View | Solution Explorer menu command, and then click the Source Files folder to show the hello.cpp file, as depicted in Figure 2-6.

Figure 2-6   Showing the Existing Source File in Solution Explorer

6. Right-click the hello.cpp file and choose Remove from the shortcut menu (shown in Figure 2-7). Don't worry, this will not delete the file, but instead simply remove it from the project. You still will be able to use it later if you wish.

Figure 2-7   Remove option on Shortcut Menu

7. Right-click the Source Files folder and choose Add New Item from the shortcut menu. This will display the Add New Item dialog box, shown in Figure 2-8.

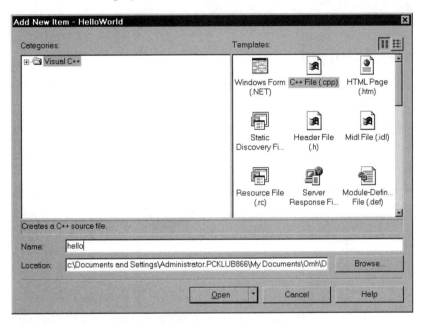

Figure 2-8   Adding a New Source File to your Project

8. Don't change the Location field, which holds the subfolder in which the project files are stored. Type the name of the new source file in the Name field, such as **sizeof.cpp**.

9. When you are done, click the Open button. Figure 2-9 shows the new sizeof.cpp file in Solution Explorer.

Figure 2-9   Solution Explorer showing the new .cpp file

Double-click sizeof.cpp in Solution Explorer to display the sizeof.cpp file in the code editing window. At this point, the sizeof.cpp is blank. In the next section, you will add code.

Code and Output

Write the following code in the source file you have created. I will explain the code in the following sections.

```cpp
#include <iostream>
using namespace std;
int main(void)
{
   cout << "Size of short is " << sizeof(short) << "\n";
   cout << "Size of int is " << sizeof(int) << "\n";
   cout << "Size of long is " << sizeof(long) << "\n";
   cout << "Size of float is " << sizeof(float) << "\n";
   cout << "Size of double is " << sizeof(double) << "\n";
   cout << "Size of long double is
         " << sizeof(long double) << "\n";
   cout << "Size of char is " << sizeof(char) << "\n";
   cout << "Size of bool is " << sizeof(bool) << "\n";
return 0;
}
```

Next, build and run the project, following the same steps you did for the "Hello World!" Project in Chapter 1. The resulting output on my computer is

```
Size of short is 2
Size of int is 4
Size of long is 4
Size of float is 4
Size of double is 8
Size of long double is 8
Size of char is 1
Size of bool is 1
```

NOTE: *The numbers displayed on your computer may be different, because the size of a data type depends on the particular compiler and operating system you are using, and yours may not be the same as mine.*

Expressions

The line of code

```
cout << "Size of int is " << sizeof(int) << "\n";
```

displays the following output:

```
Size of int is 4
```

In essence, the code sizeof(int) is replaced by 4 in the output.

The code sizeof(int) is called an *expression*. An expression is a code statement that has a value, usually a value that has to be evaluated when the program runs. An example of an expression is 4 + 4, which has a value, 8, that would be evaluated when the program runs.

When the code runs, the expression sizeof(int) is evaluated as having the value 4, which then is outputted.

By contrast, the portion of the statement within double quotes, "Size of int is ," is outputted literally as "Size of int is 4." There is no need for an evaluation. Instead, this is considered a *literal string*. The term string refers to the data type, a series of characters, and the term literal refers to the fact that the string is outputted literally, without evaluation. The string "Hello World!" in the cout statement in Chapter 1 also was a literal string.

Outputting an Expression

The expression sizeof(int) is separated by the stream insertion operator (<<) from the literal string "Size of int is ." If the code statement instead were

```
cout << "Size of int is sizeof(int)\n";
```

then the output would be quite different:

```
Size of int is sizeof(int)
```

The reason is sizeof(int), being encased inside the double quotes, would be treated as a literal string, not an expression, and therefore would not be evaluated, but instead displayed as is.

Since "Size of int is" is a literal string and sizeof(int) is an expression, they need to be differentiated before being inserted into the output stream. This differentiation is done by placing a stream insertion operator between the literal string and the expression.

NOTE: *The string "Size of int is" ends with a space between "is" and the following 4. Without that space, the output would be "Size of int is4." You, as the programmer, have the responsibility to ensure proper spacing; C++ won't do it for you.*

Escape Sequences

The string "\n" following the expression sizeof(int) is also a literal string, so it, too, is separated by a stream insertion operator from the sizeof(int) expression. However, "\n" is a special type of string called an *escape sequence.*

C++ has many escape sequences, though this may be the commonest one. This particular escape sequence causes the cursor to go to the next line for further printing. Without it, all the output would be on one line.

The "\n" in a string is not displayed literally by cout even though it is encased in double quotes. The reason is that the backslash signals cout that this is an escape sequence.

Table 2-6 shows some of the most common escape sequences.

Escape Sequence	Name	What It does
\a	Alarm	Causes the computer to beep
\n	newline	Causes the cursor to go to the next line
\t	Tab	Causes the cursor to go to the next tab stop
\\	Backslash	Causes a backslash to be printed
\'	Single quote	Causes a single quote to be printed
\"	Double quote	Causes a single quote to be printed

Table 2-6   Common Escape Sequences

Summary

A computer program's instructions and data have to be in the computer's memory for the program to work. There are three principal memory locations on your computer: the central processing unit (CPU), random access memory (RAM), and persistent storage. Computer programs usually use RAM to store instructions and data.

Instructions and data are stored at addresses, represented by a sequential series of numbers. A computer stores information in a series of ones and zeroes. Each one or zero is a bit. However, a computer cannot process information as small as a single bit. Eight bits, or one *byte,* is the smallest unit of information that a computer can process. Therefore, each address stores one byte of information.

Some information is numeric; other data is textual. Each type of information is referred to as a data type. The principal data type categories are whole numbers, floating-point numbers, and text. However, all data types have in common a characteristic of size, which is the number of bytes required to store information of that data type. A data type's size also determines its range, which is the highest and lowest number that can be stored by that data type.

The size of a data type varies depending on the compiler and operating system. You may use the sizeof operator to determine the size of a data type on your particular system.

Quiz

1. From which of the following types of memory can the CPU most quickly access instructions or data: cache memory, RAM, or persistent storage?

2. Which of the following types of memory is not temporary: cache memory, RAM, or persistent storage?

3. What is the amount of information that may be stored at a particular memory address?

4. Is the size of a data type always the same no matter which computer you may be working on?

5. What is meant by the range of a data type?

6. What is the difference between an unsigned and signed data type?

7. What decimal number is represented by 5.1E-3 in E notation?

8. What is an ASCII value?

9. What does the sizeof operator do?

10. What is a literal string?

11. What is an expression?

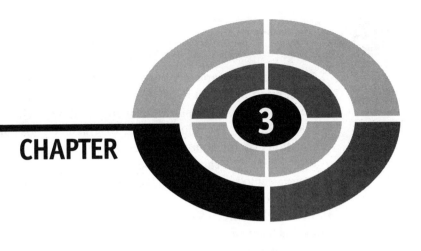

Variables

Recently, while in a crowded room, someone yelled "Hey, you!" I and a number of other people looked up, because none of us could tell to whom the speaker was referring. Had the speaker instead yelled "Hey, Jeff Kent!," I would have known he was calling me (unless of course there happened to be another Jeff Kent in the room).

We use names to refer to each other. Similarly, when you need to refer in code to a particular item of information among perhaps thousands of items of information, you do so by referring to the name of that information item.

You name information by creating a variable. A variable not only gives you a way of referring later to particular information, but also reserves the amount of memory necessary to store that information. This chapter will show you how to create variables, store information in them, and retrieve information from them.

Declaring Variables

You learned in Chapter 2 that the information a program uses while it is running first needs to be stored in memory. You need to reserve memory before you can store information there. You reserve memory by *declaring* a variable.

Declaring a variable not only reserves memory, but also gives you a convenient way of referring to that reserved memory when you need to do so in your program. You also learned in Chapter 2 that memory addresses have hexadecimal values such as 0012FED4. These values are hard to remember. It is much easier to remember information that, for example, relates to a test score by the name testScore. By declaring a variable, you can refer to the reserved memory by the variable's name, which is much easier to remember and identify with the stored information than is the hexadecimal address.

While declaring a variable is relatively simple, requiring only one line of code, much is happening behind the scenes. The program at the end of this section will show you how to determine the address and size of the memory reserved by declaring a variable.

Syntax of Declaring Variables

You have to *declare* a variable before you can use it. Declaring a variable involves the following syntax:

```
[data type] [variable name] ;
```

The data type may be any of the ones discussed in Chapter 2, including int, float, bool, char, or string. The data type tells the computer how much memory to reserve. As you learned in Chapter 2, different data types have different sizes in bytes. If you specify a data type with a size (on your compiler and operating system) of 4 bytes, then the computer will reserve 4 bytes of memory.

You choose the variable name; how you name a variable is discussed later in the section "Naming the Variable." The name is an alias by which you can refer in code to the area of reserved memory. Thus, when you name a variable that relates to a test score *testScore,* you can refer in code to the reserved memory by the name *testScore* instead of by a hexadecimal value such as 0012FED4.

Finally, the variable declaration ends with a semicolon. The semicolon tells the compiler that the statement has ended. You can declare a variable either within a function, such as main, or above all functions, just below any include directives. Since for now our programs have only one function, main, we will declare all variables within main. When our programs involve more than one function, we will revisit the issue of where to declare variables.

The following statement declares in main an integer variable named *testScore.*

```
int main(void)
{
```

```
    int testScore;
    return 0;
}
```

NOTE: *Unlike the code in Chapters 1 and 2, there is no include directive such as*
#include <iostream> in this code because this code does not use cout or another
function defined in a standard library file.

You will receive a compiler error if you refer to a variable before declaring it. In
the following code, the reference to *testScore* will cause the compiler error "undeclared identifier."

```
int main(void)
{
    testScore;
    int testScore;
    return 0;
}
```

This compiler error will occur even though the variable is declared in the very next
statement. The reason is that the compiler reads the code from top to bottom, so when
it reaches the first reference to *testScore,* it has not seen the variable declaration.

This "undeclared identifier" compiler error is similar to the one in the "Hello
World!" project in Chapter 1 when we (deliberately) misspelled cout as Cout. Since
testScore is not a name built into C++, like main and int, the compiler does not recognize it. When you declare a variable, then the compiler recognizes further references
to the variable name as referring to the variable that you declared.

Declaring Multiple Variables of the Same Data Type

If you have several variables of the same data type, you could declare each variable
in a separate statement.

```
    int testScore;
    int myWeight;
    int myHeight;
```

However, if the variables are of the same data type, you don't need to declare each
variable in a separate statement. Instead, you can declare them all in one statement, separated by commas. The following one statement declares all three integer variables:

```
    int testScore, myWeight, myHeight;
```

The data type int appears only once, even though three variables are declared. The reason is that the data type qualifies all three variables, since they appear in the same statement as the data type.

However, the variables must all be of the same data type to be declared in the same statement. You cannot declare an int variable and a float variable in the same statement. Instead, the int and float variables would have to be declared in separate statements.

```
int testScore;
float myGPA;
```

Naming the Variable

Variables, like people, have names, which are used to identify the variable so you can refer to it in code. There are only a few limitations on how you can name a variable.

- The variable name cannot begin with any character other than a letter of the alphabet (A–Z or a–z) or an underscore (_). Secret agents may be named 007, but not variables. However, the second and following characters of the variable name may be digits, letters, or underscores.
- The variable name cannot contain embedded spaces, such as *My Variable,* or punctuation marks other than the underscore character (_).
- The variable name cannot be the same as a word reserved by C++, such as main or int.
- The variable name cannot have the same name as the name of another variable declared in the same scope. Scope is an issue that will be discussed in Chapter 8. For present purposes, this rule means you cannot declare two variables in main with the same name.

Besides these limitations, you can name a variable pretty much whatever you want. However, it is a good idea to give your variables names that are meaningful. If you name your variables *var1, var2, var3,* and so on, up through *var17,* you may find it difficult to later remember the difference between *var8* and *var9.* And if you find it difficult, imagine how difficult it would be for a fellow programmer, who didn't even write the code, to figure out the difference.

In order to preserve your sanity, or possibly your life in the case of enraged fellow programmers, I recommend you use a variable name that is descriptive of the purpose of the variable. For example, *testScore* is descriptive of a variable that represents a test score.

The variable name *testScore* is a combination of two names: test and score. You can't have a variable name with embedded spaces such as *test score.* Therefore, the two words are put together, and differentiated by capitalizing the first letter of the second word. By the convention I use, the first letter of a variable name is not capitalized.

Naming Conventions

A naming convention is simply a consistent method of naming variables. There are a number of naming conventions. In addition to the one I described earlier, another naming convention is to name a variable with a prefix, usually all lowercase and consisting of three letters, that indicate its data type, followed by a word with its first letter capitalized, that suggests its purpose. Some examples:

- *intScore*   Integer variable representing a score, such as on a test.
- *strName*   String variable representing a name, such as a person's name.
- *blnResident*   Boolean variable, representing whether or not someone is a resident.

It is not particularly important which naming convention you use. What is important is that you use one and stick to it.

The Address Operator

Declaring a variable reserves memory. You can use the *address operator* (&) to learn the address of this reserved memory. The syntax is

```
&[variable name]
```

For example, the following code outputs 0012FED4 on my computer. However, the particular memory address for *testScore* on your computer may be different than 0012FED4. Indeed, if I run this program again some time later, the particular memory address for *testScore* on my computer may be different than 0012FED4.

```
#include <iostream>
using namespace std;
int main(void)
{
   int testScore;
   cout << &testScore;
   return 0;
}
```

The address 0012FED4 is a hexadecimal (Base 16) number. As discussed in Chapter 2, memory addresses usually are expressed as a hexadecimal number.

The operating system, not the programmer, chooses the address at which to store a variable. The particular address chosen by the operating system depends on the data type of the variable, how much memory already has been reserved, and other factors.

You really do not need to be concerned about which address the operating system chose since your code will refer to the variable by its name, not its address. However, as you will learn in Chapter 11 when we discuss pointers, the address operator can be quite useful.

Using the Address and sizeof Operators with Variables

The amount of memory reserved depends on a variable's data type. As you learned in Chapter 2, different data types have different sizes.

In Chapter 2, you used the sizeof operator to learn the size (on your compiler and operating system) of different data types. You also can use the sizeof operator to determine the size (again, on your compiler and operating system) of different variables.

The syntax for using the sizeof operator to determine the size of a variable is almost the same as the syntax for using the sizeof operator to determine the size of a data type. The only difference is that the parentheses following the sizeof operator refers to a variable name rather than a data type name.

The following code outputs the address and size of two variables:

```
#include <iostream>
using namespace std;
int main(void)
{
    short testScore;
    float myGPA;
    cout << "The address of testScore is "
            << &testScore << "\n";
    cout << "The size of testScore is "
            << sizeof(testScore) << "\n";
    cout << "The address of myGPA is " << &myGPA << "\n";
    cout << "The size of myGPA is "
            << sizeof(myGPA) << "\n";
    return 0;
}
```

The output when I ran this program (yours may be different) is

```
The address of testScore is 0012FED4
The size of testScore is 2
The address of myGPA is 0012FEC8
The size of myGPA is 4
```

Figure 3-1 shows how memory is reserved for the two variables. Due to the different size of the variables, the short variable, *testScore,* takes up two bytes of memory, and the float variable, *myGPA,* takes up four bytes of memory.

float myGPA					short testScore	
0012FEC8	0012FEC9	0012FECA	0012FEFB	....	0012FED4	0012FED5

Figure 3-1   Memory reserved for declared variables

As Figure 3-1 depicts, the addresses of the two variables are near each other. The operating system often attempts to do this. However, this is not always possible, depending on factors such as the size of the variables and memory already reserved. There is no guarantee that two variables will even be near each other in memory.

In Figure 3-1, the value for both memory addresses is unknown. That is because we have not yet specified the values to be stored in those memory locations. The next section shows you how to do this.

Assigning Values to Variables

The purpose of a variable is to store information. Therefore, after you have created a variable, the next logical step is to specify the information that the variable will store. This is called *assigning* a value to a variable.

A variable can be assigned a value supplied by the programmer in code. A variable also can be assigned a value by the user, usually via the keyboard, when the program is running.

You may use the assignment operator, which is discussed in the next section, to specify the value to be stored in a variable. You use the cin object (discussed in the upcoming section "Using the cin Object") after the assignment operator, to obtain the user's input, usually from the keyboard, and then store that input in a variable.

Assignment Operator

You use the assignment operator to assign a value to a variable. The syntax is

```
[variable name] = [value];
```

The assignment operator looks like the equal sign. However, in C++ the = sign is not used to test for equality; it is used for assignment. As you will learn in Chapter 5, in C++ the equal sign is ==, also called the equality operator.

The variable must be declared either before, or at the same time, you assign it a value, not afterwards. In the following example, the first statement declares the variable, and the second statement assigns a value to that variable:

```
int testScore;
testScore = 95;
```

The next example concerns *initialization,* which is when you assign a value to a variable as part of the same statement that declares that variable:

```
int testScore = 95;
```

However, the variable cannot be declared after you assign it a value. The following code will cause the compiler error "undeclared identifier" at the line testScore = 95:

```
testScore = 95;
int testScore;
```

As mentioned earlier in the "Declaring Variables" section, this compiler error will occur even though the variable is declared in the very next line because the compiler reads the code from top to bottom, so when it reaches the line testScore = 95, it has not seen the variable declaration.

The value assigned need not be a literal value, such as 95. The following code assigns to one integer variable the value of another integer variable.

```
int a, b;
a = 44;
b = a;
```

The assignment takes place in two steps:

- First, the value 44 is assigned to the variable *a.*
- Second, the value of *a,* which now is 44, is assigned to the variable *b.*

You also can assign a value to several variables at once. The following code assigns 0 to three integer variables:

```
int a, b, c;
a = b = c = 0;
```

The assignment takes place in three steps, from right to left:

1. The value 0 is assigned to the variable *c*.

2. The value of the variable *c*, which now is 0, is next assigned to the variable *b*.

3. The value of the variable *b*, which now is 0, is assigned to the variable *a*.

Finally, you can assign a value to a variable after it has already been assigned a value. The word "variable" means likely to change or vary. What may change or vary is the variable's value. The following code demonstrates a change in the value of a variable that was previously assigned a value:

```
#include <iostream>
using namespace std;
int main(void)
{
    int testScore;
    testScore = 95;
    cout << "Your test score is " << testScore << "\n";
    testScore = 75;
    cout << "Your test score now is " << testScore << "\n";
    return 0;
}
```

The output is

```
Your test score is 95
Your test score now is 75
```

Assigning a "Compatible" Data Type

The value assigned to a variable must be compatible with the data type of the variable that is the target of the assignment statement. Compatibility means, generally, that if the variable that is the target of the assignment statement has a numeric data type, then the value being assigned must also be a number.

The following code is an example of incompatibility. If it is placed in a program, it will cause a compiler error.

```
int testScore;
testScore = "Jeff";
```

The description of the compiler error is "cannot convert from 'const char [5]' to 'int'." This is the compiler's way of telling you that you are trying to assign a string to an integer, which of course won't work; "Jeff" cannot represent an integer.

The value being assigned need not necessarily be the exact same data type as the variable to which the value is being assigned. In the following code, a floating-point value, 77.83, is being assigned to an integer variable, *testScore.* The resulting output is "The test score is 77."

```
#include <iostream>
using namespace std;
int main(void)
{
    int testScore;
    testScore = 77.83;
    cout << "The test score is " << testScore << "\n";
    return 0;
}
```

While the code runs, data is lost, specifically the value to the right of the decimal point, .83. The fractional part of the number cannot be stored in *testScore,* that variable being a whole number.

Overflow and Underflow

You may recall from Chapter 2 that the short data type has a range from –32768 to 32767. You can run the following program to see what happens when you attempt to assign to a variable a value that is compatible (here a whole number for a short data type) but that is outside its range.

```
#include <iostream>
using namespace std;
int main(void)
{
    short testScore;
    testScore = 32768;
    cout << "Your test score is " << testScore << "\n";
    return 0;
}
```

The output is "Your test score is –32768." That's right, not 32768, but –32768.

This is an example of *overflow.* Overflow occurs when a variable is assigned a value too large for its range. The value assigned, 32768, is 1 too large for the short data type. Therefore, the value overflows and wraps around to the data type's lowest possible value, –32768.

Similarly, an attempt to assign to testScore 32769, which is 2 too large for the short data type, would result in an output of –32767, an attempt to assign to testScore 32770, which is 3 too large for the short data type, would result in an output of –32766, and so on. Figure 3-2 illustrates how the overflow value is reached.

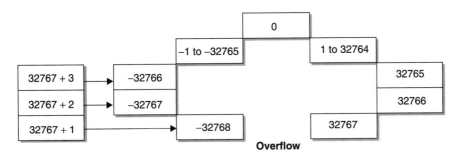

Figure 3-2   Overflow

The converse of overflow is *underflow*. Underflow occurs when a variable is assigned a value too small for its range. The output of the following code is "Your test score is 32767." The value assigned, –32769, is 1 too small for the short data type. Therefore, the value underflows and wraps around to the data type's highest possible value, 32767.

```
#include <iostream>
using namespace std;
int main(void)
{
    short testScore;
    testScore = -32769;
    cout << "Your test score is " << testScore << "\n";
    return 0;
}
```

Similarly, an attempt to assign to testScore –32770, which is 2 too small for the short data type, would result in an output of 32766, an attempt to assign to testScore –32771, which is 3 too small for the short data type, would result in an output of 32765, and so on. Figure 3-3 illustrates how the underflow value is reached.

NOTE: *Floating-point variables, of the float or double data type, also may overflow or underflow. However, the result depends on the compiler used, and may be a run-time error stopping your program, or instead an incorrect result.*

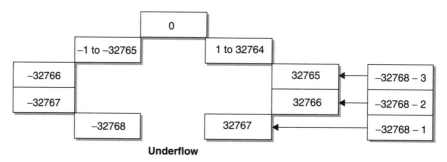

Figure 3-3 Underflow

Using the cin Object

Thus far, the programmer has supplied the values that are assigned to variables. However, most programs are interactive, asking the user to provide information, which the user then inputs, usually via the keyboard.

In Chapter 1, we used the cout object to output information to a standard output, usually the monitor. Now we will use the *cin* object to obtain information from standard input, which usually is the keyboard. The cin object, like the cout object, is defined in the standard library file <iostream>, which therefore must be included (with an include directive) if your code uses cin.

The syntax of a cin statement is

```
cin >> [variable name];
```

The cin object is followed by >>, which is the stream extraction operator. It obtains the input, usually from the keyboard, and assigns that input to the variable to its right.

TIP: *Knowing when to use >> instead of << can be confusing. It may be helpful to remember that the >> and << operators each point in the direction that data is moving. For example in the expression cin >> var, data is moving from standard input into the variable var. By contrast, in the expression cout >> var, the << indicates that data is moving from the variable var to standard output.*

When your program reaches a cin statement, its execution halts until the user types something at the keyboard and presses the ENTER key. Try running the following program. You will see a blinking cursor until you type a number. Once you type a number and press ENTER, the program will output "Your test score is" followed by the number you inputted. For example, if you inputted 100, the output will be "Your test score is 100."

```
#include <iostream>
using namespace std;
int main(void)
{
    int testScore;
    cin >> testScore;
    cout << "Your test score is " << testScore << "\n";
    return 0;
}
```

This program is not very user friendly. Unless the user happened to know what your program did, they would not know what information is being asked of them. Accordingly, a cin statement usually is preceded by a cout statement telling the user what to do. This is called a *prompt.* The following code adds a prompt:

```
#include <iostream>
using namespace std;
int main(void)
{
    int testScore;
    cout << "Enter your test score: ";
    cin >> testScore;
    cout << "Your test score is " << testScore << "\n";
    return 0;
}
```

The program input and output could be

```
Enter your test score: 78
Your test score is 78
```

Assigning a "Compatible" Data Type

As with the assignment operator, the value being assigned by the cin operator need not necessarily be the exact same data type as that of the variable to which the value is being assigned. In the previous program, entering a floating-point value, 77.83, at the prompt for entry of the test score results in the following output: "The test score is 77." Data is lost, though, specifically the part of the number to the right of the decimal point. The cin statement will not read the part of the number to the right of the decimal point because it cannot be stored in a whole number variable.

However, the value being assigned by the cin operator must be compatible with the data type of the variable to which the value is being assigned. In the preceding program, typing "Jeff" at the prompt for entry of the test score results in the following output: "Your test score is –858993460."

Obviously, –858993460 is not a test score anyone would want. Less obvious is the reason why that number is outputted.

The string literal "Jeff" cannot be assigned to an integer variable such as *testScore*. Therefore, the cin operator will not assign "Jeff" to that integer variable. Therefore, when the cout statement attempts to output the value of *testScore,* that variable has not yet been assigned a value.

When *testScore* was declared, there was some value at its memory address left over from programs previously run on the computer. The cout statement, when trying to output the value of *testScore,* does the best it can and attempts to interpret this leftover value. The result of that interpretation is –858993460.

NOTE: *Compile Time vs. Run-Time Difference When Incompatible Data Types Are Assigned—Earlier in this chapter, the attempt to assign "Jeff" to testScore (testScore = "Jeff";) resulted in a compiler error. Here, the attempt to assign "Jeff" to testScore using a cin statement instead results in an incorrect value. The reason that this time there is no compiler error is because the value the user would input could not be known at compile time, but instead would be known only at run time. Therefore, there would be no compile error, since at the time of compilation there was no attempt to assign an incompatible value.*

Inputting Values for Multiple Variables

If you are inputting values for several variables, you could input them one line at a time.

```
#include <iostream>
using namespace std;
int main(void)
{
    int myWeight, myHeight;
    string myName;
    cout << "Enter your name: ";
    cin >> myName;
    cout << "Enter your weight in pounds: ";
    cin >> myWeight;
    cout << "Enter your height in inches: ";
    cin >> myHeight;
    cout << "Your name score is " << myName << "\n";
    cout << "Your weight in pounds is " << myWeight << "\n";
    cout << "Your height in inches is " << myHeight << "\n";
    return 0;
}
```

The output of the program, with the input of "Jeff" for the name, 200 for the pounds, and 72 for the height, is

```
Enter your name: Jeff
Enter your weight in pounds: 200
Enter your height in inches: 72
Your name is Jeff
Your weight in pounds is 200
Your height in inches is 72
```

Instead of having separate prompts and cin statements for each variable, you can have one cin statement assign values to all three variables. The syntax is

```
cin >> [first variable] >> [second variable] >>
        [third variable];
```

The same syntax would work when using one cin statement to assign values to four or more variables. The variables are separated by the stream extraction operator >>.

When you use one cin statement to assign values to multiple variables, the user separates each input by one or more spaces. The space tells the cin object that you have finished assigning a value to one variable and the next input should be assigned to the next variable in the cin statement. As before, the user finishes input by choosing the ENTER key.

The following program uses one cin statement to assign values to three variables:

```
#include <iostream>
using namespace std;
#include <string>
int main(void)
{
    int myWeight, myHeight;
    string name;
    cout << "Enter your name, weight in pounds and height
            in inches\n";
    cout << "The three inputs should be separated by a
            space\n";
    cin >> name >> myWeight >> myHeight;
    cout << "Your name is " << name << "\n";
    cout << "Your weight in pounds is " << myWeight << "\n";
    cout << "Your height in inches is " << myHeight << "\n";
    return 0;
}
```

The interaction between user input and the cin statement could be as follows:

- The user would type "Jeff," followed by a space.

- The space tells the cin object that the first input has ended, so the cin object will assign "Jeff" to the first variable in the cin statement, *name.*
- The user would type 200, followed by a space.
- The space tells the cin object the second input has ended, so the cin object will assign 200 to the next variable in the cin statement, *myWeight.*
- The user would type 200, and then press the ENTER key.
- The ENTER key tells the cin object that the third and final input has ended, so the cin object will assign 72 to the remaining variable in the cin statement, *myHeight,* which completes execution of the cin statement.

The resulting program output would be

```
Enter your name, weight in pounds and height in inches
The three inputs should be separated by a space
Jeff 200 72
Your name is Jeff
Your weight in pounds is 200
Your height in inches is 72
```

Assigning a "Compatible" Data Type

The data types in the cin statement may be different. In this example, the data type of the first variable is a string, whereas the data type of the second and third variables is an integer.

What is important is that the order of the input matches the order of the data types of the variables in the cin statement. The input order "Jeff," 200, and 72 is assigned to the variables in the order of their appearance in the cin statement, *myName, myWeight,* and *myHeight.* Therefore, "Jeff" is assigned to the string variable *myName,* 72 to the integer variable *myWeight,* and 200 to the integer variable *myHeight.*

The importance of the order of the input matching the order of the data types of the variables in the cin statement is demonstrated by changing the order of the user's input from "Jeff," 200, and 72, to 200, "Jeff," and 72. The program output then would be

```
Enter your name, weight in pounds and height in inches
The three inputs should be separated by a space
200 Jeff 72
Your name is 200
Your weight in pounds is -858993460
Your height in inches is -858993460
```

While I would like to lose weight, –858993460 seems a bit extreme. Also, while it is understandable why "Jeff" cannot be assigned to my weight, 72 was not assigned to my height either.

The one output that is correct is the name. Any characters, including digits, can be part of a string. Therefore, while 200 may be an unusual name to us, it is perfectly OK for cin, which therefore assigns 200 to the string variable *name*.

Why –858993460 was outputted for myWeight also has been explained earlier in the example in which the user entered "Jeff" at the prompt to enter a test score.

However, 72 would be a valid value for assignment to the integer variable *myHeight*. Why then isn't 72 the output for height?

The reason is that the next value for cin to assign is not 72, but instead "Jeff." Since cin was unable to assign "Jeff" to *myWeight,* the value "Jeff" remains next in line for assignment, this time to the variable *myHeight.* Unfortunately, cin is unable to assign "Jeff" to *myHeight* either, so the value of *myHeight,* like *myWeight,* also is outputted as –858993460.

Inputting Multiple Words into a String

Finally, cin will only take the first word of a string. If in the following program you input "Jeff Kent" at the prompt, the output will be "Your name is Jeff" not "Your name is Jeff Kent."

```
#include <iostream>
using namespace std;
#include <string>
int main(void)
{
    string name;
    cout << "Enter your name: ";
    cin >> name;
    cout << "Your name is " << name;
    return 0;
}
```

The reason why the value of name is outputted only as "Jeff," omitting "Kent," is that the cin object interprets the space between "Jeff" and "Kent" as indicating that the user has finished inputting the value of the name variable.

The solution involves using either the get or getline method of the cin object. These methods will be covered in Chapter 10.

Overflow and Underflow

The consequences of an overflow or underflow of whole number variables is more unpredictable with cin than with the assignment operator. Inputting either 32768, which is 1 more than the highest number in the range of a short data type, or –32769, 1 less than the lowest number in that range, results on my computer in the output "Your test score is –13108."

```
#include <iostream>
using namespace std;
int main(void)
{
    short testScore;
    testScore = 32768;
    cout << "Your test score is " << testScore << "\n";
    return 0;
}
```

Summary

A variable serves two purposes. It provides you with a way of referring to particular information, and also reserves the amount of memory necessary to store that information.

You must create a variable before you can start using it. You create a variable by declaring it. You may declare multiple variables of the same type in one statement.

You can use the address operator, &, to determine the address of a variable, and the sizeof operator to determine the size of a variable.

The purpose of a variable is to store information. Therefore, after you have created a variable, the next logical step is to specify the information that the variable will store. This is called *assigning* a value to a variable.

A variable can be assigned a value either by the programmer in code or by the user, usually via the keyboard, when the program is running. You use the assignment operator to assign a value supplied by code. You use the cin object to assign a value supplied by the user.

In the next chapter, you will learn how to use variables to perform arithmetic.

Quiz

1. What is the effect of declaring a variable?

2. Can you refer to a variable before declaring it as long as you declare it later?

3. Can you declare several variables in the same statement?

4. What is a "naming convention" with respect to variables?

5. What is the difference between the address and sizeof operators?

6. What is initialization?

7. What is overflow?

8. What is the consequence of using an assignment operator to assign a string value to an integer variable?

9. Do you use the cin object for compile time or run-time assignment of values to variables?

10. Can you use one cin statement to assign values to several variables of different data types?

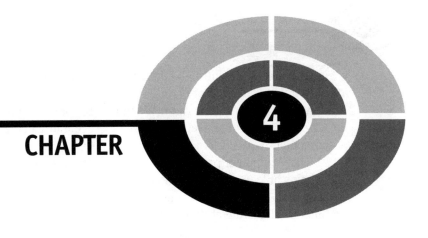

Arithmetic Operators

When I went to elementary school, which as far as my kids are concerned was when dinosaurs roamed the earth, I had to perform arithmetic calculations by hand or in my head. There were no calculators, only slide rules. (Warning: You may date yourself by even admitting you know what a slide rule is!)

When it was my kids' turn to go to school, and I'd ask them to perform an arithmetic calculation while going over their homework or tests, they would whip out a calculator. When I asked them to perform the calculation by hand or in their head, they

would look at me with mixed amazement and pity and exclaim "Aw, Dad, no one does it that way anymore."

Maybe my kids were right. When I write computer programs, I don't do it "that way" anymore either. I let the fastest, most accurate calculator I own do the work: my computer.

Many computer programs need to perform calculations. Computers, in addition to being able to store vast amounts of data, also can calculate far more quickly and accurately than we can. Thus, you use arithmetic operators to harness your computer's calculating ability, something which we will explore in this chapter.

Arithmetic Operators

An operator is a symbol that represents a specific action. We have discussed and used operators in prior chapters, including the assignment operator, =. C++ also supports operators for arithmetic, specifically addition, subtraction, multiplication, and division. Operators used for arithmetic are called, naturally enough, arithmetic operators. Table 4-1 summarizes them.

Operator	Purpose	Example	Result
+	Addition	5 + 2	7
-	Subtraction	5 – 2	3
*	Multiplication	5 * 2	10
/	Division (Quotient)	5 / 2	2
%	Division (Remainder)	5 % 2	1

Table 4-1   Arithmetic Operators

The % operator, also called the *modulus* operator, may look unfamiliar. It returns the remainder in division, and will be explained in the "Division Operators" section later in this chapter.

Arithmetic operators are binary operators because they operate on two *operands*, binary being a reference to 2, and operand referring to each of the two values that is in the arithmetic expression. For example, in the expression *5 + 2,* the + sign is the operator, and the 5 and 2 each is an operand.

NOTE: Not all operators are binary. For example, in the expression –3, the negative sign, or negation operator, is a unary operator because it operates on only one operand, which is the integer 3 in this example. There also are ternary operators, which operate on 3 operands. However, all arithmetic operators involve two operands—no more, no less.

The arithmetic operators work with negative as well as positive numbers, and, with the exception of the modulus operator, floating point numbers (numbers with values to the right of the decimal point) as well as whole numbers. The addition operator also works with strings as well as with numbers.

This chapter will demonstrate each of the arithmetic operators in a working program which tracks student enrollment in a course. The scenarios in the program are real world, based on my experience teaching computer science at a community college in the San Fernando Valley area of Los Angeles.

The Addition Operator

At the community college where I teach computer science, students often will pre-register, enrolling in a course before the semester starts. However, some students will add a course during the first few weeks of the semester.

The following program has two integer variables, *total* and *added*. The program first assigns to *total* the value inputted by the user for the number of preregistered students. The program then assigns to *added* the value inputted by the user for the number of students adding the course. Afterward, the program uses the addition operator to add two operands, *total* and *added*. The resulting sum is then assigned to *total,* which now reflects the number of all students in the course, both preregistered and added. That sum then is outputted.

```
#include <iostream>
using namespace std;
int main(void)
{
    int total, added;
    cout << "Enter number of pre-registered students: ";
    cin >> total;
    cout << "Enter number of students adding the course: ";
    cin >> added;
    total = total + added;
    cout << "Total number of students: " << total;
    return 0;
}
```

The input and output of the program could be

```
Enter number of registered students: 30
Enter number of students adding the course: 3
Total number of students: 33
```

Combined Assignment and Arithmetic Operator

New programmers sometimes are confused by statements such as *total = total + added* because, in *mathematics,* a variable cannot *equal* itself plus another number. However, this statement is not made in mathematics, but in C++ programming, in which the = operator is not used for equality, but instead for assignment.

Nevertheless, there also is another way to express *total = total + added:*

```
total += added;
```

To the compiler, it makes no difference whether you use *total = total + added* or *total += added.* However, many programmers prefer *total += added,* some because it looks more elegant, others because it seems more readable, and still others for the practical reason that it requires less typing.

This compact form of combining arithmetic and assignment operators is not limited to the addition operator. As Table 4-2 shows, it also can be used with the other arithmetic operators. In that table, it is assumed *a* is a previously declared integer variable.

Statement	Combining Operators
a = a + 2;	a +=2;
a = a − 2;	a −=2;
a = a * 2;	a *=2;
a = a / 2;	a /=2;
a = a % 2;	a %=2;

Table 4-2   Combining Arithmetic and Assignment Operators

Precedence Between Arithmetic and Assignment Operators

The statement *total = total + added* uses two operators, assignment and arithmetic. The arithmetic operation has *precedence* over the assignment operation. This means the addition is performed before the assignment. This makes more sense intuitively than the other order. However, as I will explain in detail later in this chapter, precedence also arises when more than one arithmetic operator is used in a statement, and there the correct order is less intuitive.

Overflow and Underflow

Overflow and underflow applies to the results of addition. The range of the int data type on my compiler and operating system is –2,147,483,648 to 2,147,483,647. Here is the result of my class starting with a very large preregistration, 2,147,483,647, and then adding one more student:

```
Enter number of preregistered students: 2147483647
Enter number of students adding the course: 1
Total number of students: -2147483648
```

While negative inputs make no sense in this program since you can't have a negative number of students enroll in or add a class, other programs may use negative numbers, such as for below zero temperatures. Therefore, the following input uses negative numbers to illustrate underflow with the addition operator.

```
Enter number of preregistered students: -2147483648
Enter number of students adding the course: -1
Total number of students: 2147483647
```

Adding Strings

While we think of addition as involving numeric operands, the addition operator also can be used with string operands. The output of the following code is: "Your name is JeffKent."

```cpp
#include <iostream>
#include <string>
using namespace std;
int main(void)
{
    string firstName = "Jeff";
    string lastName = "Kent";
    cout << "Your name is " << firstName + lastName;
    return 0;
}
```

Adding two strings has the effect of *appending* the second string operand to the first string operand. Appending means adding the contents of the second string to the end of the first string.

While you can add numbers and numbers, or strings and strings, attempting to add a number and a string will cause a compiler error. The addition operator may perform arithmetic addition with two numeric operands, or appending with two string operands, but it does not know how to add a numeric operand and a string operand.

The Subtraction Operator

At the community college where I teach, students leave the class as well as join it. Some of the preregistered students never show up. Other students who show up later decide to drop the course.

The following program builds on the one we used with the addition operator by adding one integer variable, *dropped* for students who I dropped because they never showed up, or who dropped themselves from the course. The *dropped* variable is assigned a value by the user. The program then uses the subtraction operator to update *total*.

```
#include <iostream>
using namespace std;
int main(void)
{
    int total, added, dropped;
    cout << "Enter number of pre-registered students: ";
    cin >> total;
    cout << "Enter number of students adding the course: ";
    cin >> added;
    total = total + added;
    cout << "How many students dropped? ";
    cin >> dropped;
    total -= dropped;
    cout << "Total number of students: " << total << endl;
    return 0;
}
```

The input and output of the program could be

```
Enter number of pre-registered students: 30
Enter number of students adding the course: 3
How many students dropped? 5
Total number of students: 28
```

In this example, we used the combined assignment and arithmetic operator −= in the expression *total −= dropped*, rather than *total = total − dropped*. As explained with the addition operator, either alternative will work the same way.

The effect of overflow and underflow are the same with the subtraction operator as with the addition operator. However, unlike the addition operator, the subtraction operator will not work with string operands.

The Multiplication Operator

Returning to my community college course example, all students who enroll in a course owe a tuition of $72, even if they don't show up or later drop the course.

The following program builds on the one we used with the addition operator by adding the following statement:

```
cout << "Total tuition owed: $" << (total + dropped) * 72
     << endl;
```

The program now reads

```
#include <iostream>
using namespace std;
int main(void)
{
    int total, added, dropped;
    cout << "Enter number of pre-registered students: ";
    cin >> total;
    cout << "Enter number of students adding the course: ";
    cin >> added;
    total = total + added;
    cout << "How many students dropped? ";
    cin >> dropped;
    total -= dropped;
    cout << "Total number of students: " << total << endl;
    cout << "Total tuition owed:
   $" << (total + dropped) * 72
        << endl;
    return 0;
}
```

The input and output of the program could be

```
Enter number of preregistered students: 30
Enter number of students adding the course: 3
How many students dropped? 5
Total number of students: 28
Total tuition owed: $2376
```

The variables *total* and *dropped* are added so that *total* reflects all students ever enrolled, even if they are no longer in the class, because all students owe tuition even if they don't show up or later drop the course.

The effect of overflow and underflow are the same with the multiplication operator as with the addition and subtraction operators. Unlike the addition operator, but like the subtraction operator, the multiplication operator will not work with string operands.

Precedence Between Arithmetic Operators

The statement we added has two arithmetic operators, for addition and multiplication. The order in which the two arithmetic operations are performed makes a difference. If addition is performed first, 28 + 5, and then the sum, 33, is multiplied by 72, the result is 2376. However, if multiplication is performed first, 5 * 72, and then the product, 360, is added to 28, the result would be 388.

C++ has rules, called *precedence,* for determining which operation is performed first. Precedence was discussed earlier in this chapter in the section on the addition operator concerning the precedence of arithmetic operators over the assignment operator. However, here the issue is precedence between arithmetic operators.

Table 4-3 lists the precedence between arithmetic operators.

Precedence	Operator
Highest	– (unary negation)
Middle	* / %
Lowest	+ –

Table 4-3   Precedence of Arithmetic Operators

When there is more than one operator in a row in Table 4-3, those operators have equal precedence. Thus, the multiplication operator and the two division operators have equal precedence. Similarly, the addition and subtraction operators have equal precedence.

Table 4-4 shows the results of applying precedence to several arithmetic expressions. We have not reviewed the division operators yet, but in the examples in Table 4-4 the / operator works exactly as it does in arithmetic.

Expression	Result
2 + 3 * 4	14, not 20
8 / 2 – 1	3, not 8

Table 4-4   Precedence in Action

C++ also has rules called *associativity* for determining which operation is performed first when two operators have equal precedence. Table 4-5 describes those rules.

Operator	Associativity
(unary negation)	Right to left
* / %	Left to right
+ −	Left to right

Table 4-5   Associativity of Arithmetic Operators

Therefore, the result of the expression 8 / 2 * 4 is 16, not 1, because division, being the leftmost operator, is performed first.

However, there are times when you want to override the default precedence. For example, in our program, in calculating tuition, the default precedence would be to multiply *dropped* by 72, after which the product would be added to *total*. However, we want to change the order of operations so that *dropped* is first added to *total,* and the sum then multiplied by 72.

You can override the default precedence with parentheses. This is done in the statement:

```
cout << "Total tuition owed: $" << (total + dropped) * 72
    << endl;
```

Expressions in parentheses are done first. As a result of the parentheses, the expression *(total + dropped) * 72* is evaluated so that dropped is first added to *total,* and the sum is then multiplied by 72.

Division Operators

Addition, subtraction, and multiplication each have one operator. However, division has two. The / operator gives you the quotient, while the % (or modulus operator) gives you the remainder.

Quotient and remainder, along with dividend and divisor, are terms that I first learned in elementary school and then did not use very much again until many years later. If you are rusty on your arithmetic terminology like I was, this example may help. In the problem 7 divided by 2, 7 is the dividend and 2 is the divisor. The result of this division is that 3 is the quotient and 1 is the remainder.

The Division Operator

The division operator returns the quotient. However, the value of the quotient depends on whether at least one of the operands is a floating point data type.

For example, the value of 10 / 4 is 2.5. However, in C++, the value is 2 because, when both operands are an integer or other whole number data type, then the result is an integer as well, and the remainder is not part of the quotient. This is true even if the result is assigned to a floating point variable. The output of the following program is 10 / 4 = 2.

```
#include <iostream>
using namespace std;
int main(void)
{
    int firstOp = 10, secondOp = 4;
    float result = firstOp / secondOp;
    cout << firstOp << " / " << secondOp << " = " << result;
    return 0;
}
```

However, the value of 10.0 / 4 is 2.5 in C++. When at least one of the operands is a floating point data type, and 10.0 would be interpreted as floating point, then the result is a floating point as well. The output of the following program is 10 / 4 = 2.5 because we changed the data type of *firstOp* from int to float:

```
#include <iostream>
using namespace std;
int main(void)
{
    float firstOp = 10, result;
    int secondOp = 4;
    result = firstOp / secondOp;
    cout << firstOp << " / " << secondOp << " = " << result;
    return 0;
}
```

Going back to the first example, if you want the result of the division of two integer variables to be a float, then you have to *cast* one of the variables to a float. A cast does not change the data type of the variable, just the data type of the *value* of the variable during the completion of the operation. You cast the variable by putting the desired data type in front of it in an expression, and placing either the desired data type or the variable in parentheses. This is how the first example could be changed to make the result of integer division a float:

```
#include <iostream>
using namespace std;
int main(void)
{
   int firstOp = 10, secondOp = 4;
   float result = (float) firstOp / secondOp;
   cout << firstOp << " / " << secondOp << " = " << result;
   return 0;
}
```

All of the following expressions would work

```
float result = (float) firstOp / secondOp;
float result = float (firstOp) / secondOp;
float result = firstOp / (float) secondOp;
float result = firstOp / float (secondOp);
```

However, in some programs you may want integer division so that the quotient will ignore the fractional value. The Change Machine project later in the chapter is an example.

Let's now put this into practice with the student enrollment program. In the last modification to this program, tuition was calculated based on all students who ever enrolled in the course, even if they no longer were in the course. The addition to the program calculates and displays the average tuition per student still enrolled. An integer variable *tuition* is added to store the total tuition collected, which is calculated using the expression *(total + dropped) * 72*. The average tuition per student still enrolled then is calculated and displayed with the statement:

```
cout << "Average tuition per enrolled student: $"
   << (float)
        tuition / total;
```

The code now reads

```
#include <iostream>
#include <string>
using namespace std;
int main(void)
{
   int total, added, dropped, tuition;
   cout << "Enter number of preregistered students: ";
   cin >> total;
   cout << "Enter number of students adding the course: ";
   cin >> added;
   total = total + added;
   cout << "How many students dropped? ";
   cin >> dropped;
```

```
    total -= dropped;
    cout << "Total number of students: " << total << endl;
    tuition = (total + dropped) * 72;
    cout << "Total tuition owed: $" << tuition << endl;
    cout << "Average tuition per enrolled student: $"
         << (float) tuition / total;
    return 0;
}
```

The input and output could be

```
Enter number of preregistered students: 30
Enter number of students adding the course: 3
How many students dropped? 5
Total number of students: 28
Total tuition owed: $2376
Average tuition per enrolled student: $84.8571
```

The casting of one of the operands to a float is necessary. Otherwise, the average tuition would be $84 instead of $84.8571.

The Modulus Operator

The modulus operator also involves division, but returns only the remainder. For example, the result of *7 % 2* is not the quotient, 3, but the remainder, 1.

The modulus operator works only with whole number operands. The result of an attempt to use it with a floating point operand is undefined. The result often is a compiler error, but this is compiler dependent.

The modulus operator will be used in the Change Machine project later in this chapter.

CAUTION: *Whether you use the / or the % operator, you cannot divide by zero. The result is an error.*

Exponents

C++, unlike some other programming languages, does not have an exponent operator. Instead, it has a built-in function named *pow*, which is defined in the standard library *cmath*. The name *pow* is shorthand for power, since with exponents one number is raised to the power of another.

The *pow* function has two arguments. The first argument is the number that is being raised to a certain power. The second argument is the power the first argument

is being raised to. Therefore, the expression *pow (4, 2)* would be used to raise 4 to the power of 2, the result being 16.

While in the example 4 to the power of 2, the result is a whole number, the *pow* function returns a double data type. Floating point numbers also can be raised to a power, resulting in another floating point number. Additionally, whole numbers can be raised to a negative power, which also may result in a floating point number.

The *pow* function is useful for solving math problems. The formula for the area of a circle is *area* = πr^2. Assuming a value of π of 3.14159, two double variables *area* and *radius,* and that radius has already been assigned a value, the code for determining the circle's area is

```
area = 3.14159 * pow(radius, 2);
```

The following program calculates the area of a circle based on a radius inputted by the user.

```
#include <iostream>
#include <cmath>
using namespace std;
int main(void)
{
    double radius, area;
    cout << "Enter radius of circle: ";
    cin >> radius;
    area = 3.14159 * pow(radius, 2);
    cout << "The area is " << area << endl;
    return 0;
}
```

The input and output could be

```
Enter radius of circle: 6
The area is 113.097
```

The Change Machine Project

My mother was not above using a change machine to distract cranky or mischievous young grandchildren. The youngsters poured hundreds of pennies into the top of the machine, and watched with fascination (fortunately, youngsters are easily fascinated) as the machine sorted the pennies into amounts of change that could be taken to the bank and exchanged for dollars, quarters, and bigger loot. The youngsters were motivated as well as fascinated, since guess who got to keep the quarters?

Program Description

This program will ask the user to input the number of pennies. You may assume the user will input a positive whole number. The code then will output the number of dollars, quarters, dimes, nickels, and pennies. The input and output could be

```
Enter number of pennies to make change for: 387
Dollars: 3
Quarters: 3
Dimes: 1
Nickels: 0
Pennies: 2
```

The next section will reproduce the code, and the section following will explain the code. However, as a programming challenge, first try to write the code yourself. If you can, great! If not, no problem; you still will learn more from the code and the explanation if you first try to write this program.

As a hint (you don't have to look), here are the first three lines of code in *main:*

```
int total, dollars, quarters, dimes, nickels, leftover;
cout << "Enter number of pennies to make change for: ";
cin >> total;
```

The variable *total* will be assigned the total number of pennies entered by the user. The variable *dollar* will be assigned the number of dollars in the pennies, 3 in the preceding sample run for 387 total pennies. The variables *quarters, dimes,* and *nickels* will be assigned the number of quarters, dimes, and nickels in the change, 3, 1, and 0, respectively, in the previous sample run for 387 total pennies. The variable *leftover* ultimately will be assigned the number of pennies in the change (2 in the prior sample run for 387 total pennies), but also will be used for other purposes. Of course, you could write this program with a few more, or a few less, variables.

The Code

There is more than one way to write this program. Here is how I wrote it:

```
#include <iostream>
#include <string>
using namespace std;
int main(void)
{
    int total, dollars, quarters, dimes, nickels, leftover;
    cout << "Enter number of pennies to make change for: ";
    cin >> total;
```

```
dollars = total / 100;
leftover = total % 100;
quarters = leftover / 25;
leftover %= 25;
dimes = leftover / 10;
leftover %= 10;
nickels = leftover / 5;
leftover %= 5;
cout << "Dollars: " << dollars << endl;
cout << "Quarters: " << quarters << endl;
cout << "Dimes: " << dimes << endl;
cout << "Nickels: " << nickels << endl;
cout << "Pennies: " << leftover << endl;
return 0;
}
```

The Algorithm

You learned in Chapter 1 that in a computer program a computer programmer gives instructions to a computer. These instructions are in a programming language such as C++. However, before you can write code, you need to formulate the instructions in English or whatever other language you think in.

An algorithm, pronounced "Al Gore rhythm," is a step-by-step logical procedure for solving a problem. You frequently will need to create and implement algorithms. Implementing algorithms in your code is computer programming. Creating algorithms is a skill that can be developed from any field that requires analytical thinking, including, but not limited to, mathematics as well as computer programming.

Let's say you were given a number of pennies, such as 387, and you had to determine, in your head, how many dollars, quarters, dimes, nickels, and pennies to give as change. How would you do it?

A logical approach is to start with dollars. There are 100 pennies in a dollar. If 387 is divided by 100, the quotient is the number of dollars in the pennies: 3.

One problem is that 387 divided by 100 could be 3.87, not 3. However, as discussed earlier in this chapter in the "Division Operators" section, when an integer is divided by an integer, then the result always is an integer unless one of the integer operands first is cast to a float. We want the result of the division to be an integer, so we will not cast either of the integer operands to a float.

Since the beginning number of pennies (387) is stored in the integer variable *total*, if *total* is divided by 100, also regarded as an integer, the quotient is the number of dollars in the pennies, 3.

```
dollars = total / 100;
```

After you take out 300 pennies (3 dollars) from the pile of 387 pennies, 87 pennies are left over. 87 is the remainder of the division *total / 100*. We obtain this remainder with the modulus operator, and assign it to the integer variable *leftover:*

```
leftover = total % 100;
```

Next, you follow the same procedure to determine the number of quarters in the 87 pennies left over. The only differences are that the divisor is 25 instead of 100 and the number of pennies left is represented by *leftover* instead of *total.*

```
quarters = leftover / 25;
leftover %= 25;
```

The same process is followed for determining the number of dimes and nickels:

```
dimes = leftover / 10;
leftover %= 10;
nickels = leftover / 5;
leftover %= 5;
```

The number of pennies left over after division by 5 cannot be converted into higher change. Accordingly, there is no need for further division. There also is no need for a separate variable for pennies because *leftover* stores the number of pennies left.

All that remains is to output the values of the variables representing the dollars, quarters, dimes, nickels, and pennies.

This method of solving the problem by dividing the total number of pennies by the number of pennies in a dollar, storing the quotient in a variable holding the number of dollars, and dividing the remainder by the number of pennies in a quarter and so on, is an algorithm. We will be discussing many algorithms in this book.

Summary

Many computer programs need to perform calculations. Computers, in addition to being able to store vast amounts of data, also can calculate far faster and more accurately than we can. You use arithmetic operators to harness the computer's calculating ability.

C++ supports arithmetic operators for addition, subtraction, multiplication, and division. While addition, subtraction, and multiplication each have one operator, division has two. The / operator gives you the quotient, while the % (or modulus operator) gives you the remainder.

The arithmetic operators all work with whole number operands. All but the modulus operator also work with floating number operands. The addition operator also works with string operands, appending one string to another.

C++, unlike some other programming languages, does not have an exponent operator. Instead, it has a built-in function named *pow* which is defined in the standard library *cmath*.

In the next chapter, you will learn about relational and logical operators and control structures, which enable your program to take different actions depending on choices the user makes while the program is running.

Quiz

1. Which of the four arithmetic operations has more than one operator?
2. Which of the arithmetic operators can operate on string as well as numeric operands?
3. Which of the arithmetic operators cannot have a floating point operand?
4. Which of the arithmetic operators cannot have a zero as a second operand?
5. Assuming *total* is a variable, how else could you express in code *total = total + 2?*
6. What is the result of 2 + 3 * 4?
7. What is the result of the expression 8 / 2 * 4?
8. What is the result of the expression 10 / 4?
9. What operator or function do you use to raise a number to a certain power?
10. What is an algorithm?

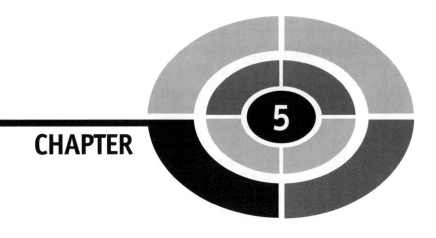

Making Decisions: if and switch Statements

The famous poem "The Road Not Taken" by Robert Frost begins: "Two roads diverged in a yellow wood, and sorry I could not travel both." This poem illustrates that life, if nothing else, presents us with choices.

Similarly, computer programs present their users with choices. So far, for the sake of simplicity, the flow of each program has followed a relatively straight line, taking a predetermined path from beginning to end. However, as programs become more sophisticated, they often branch in two or more directions based on a choice a user makes. For example, when I am buying books online, I am presented with choices such as adding another item to my shopping cart, recalculating my total, or checking out. The program does something different if I add another item to my shopping cart rather than check out.

The program determines the action it takes by comparing my choice with the various alternatives. That comparison is made using a relational operator. There are relational operators to test for equality, inequality, whether one value is greater (or less) than another, and other comparisons.

The code then needs to be structured so different code executes depending on which choice was made. This is done using either the if statement or the switch case statement, both of which we'll discuss in this chapter.

We'll also discuss flowcharting, which enables you to visually depict the flow of a program. Flowcharting becomes increasingly helpful as we transition from relatively simple programs that flow in a straight line to more complex programs that branch in different directions.

Relational Operators

We make comparisons all the time, and so do programs. A program may need to determine whether one value is equal to, greater than, or less than another value. For example, if a program calculates the cost of a ticket to a movie in which children less than 12 get in free, it needs to find out if the customer's age is less than 12.

Programs compare values by using a relational operator. Table 5-1 lists the relational operators supported by C++:

Operator	Meaning
>	Greater than
<	Less than
>=	Greater than or equal to
<=	Less than or equal to
==	Equal to
!=	Not equal to

Table 5-1   Relational Operators

Relational Expressions

Like the arithmetic operators discussed in the last chapter, the relational operators are binary—that is, they compare two operands. A statement with two operands and a relational operator between them is called a *relational expression*.

The result of a relational expression is a Boolean value, depicted as either true or false. Table 5-2 lists several relational expressions, using different relational operators and their values.

Relational Expression	Value
4 == 4	true
4 < 4	false
4 <= 4	true
4 > 4	false
4 != 4	false
4 == 5	false
4 < 5	true
4 <= 5	true
4 >= 5	false
4 != 5	true

Table 5-2   Relational Expressions and Their Values

Table 5-2 uses operands that have literal values. A literal value is a value that cannot change. 4 is a literal value, and cannot have a value other than the number 4.

Operands may also be variables (which were discussed in Chapter 3). The following program outputs the results of several variable comparisons.

```
#include <iostream>
using namespace std;
int main(void)
{
    int a = 4, b = 5;
    cout << a << " > " << b << " is " << (a > b) << endl;
    cout << a << " >= " << b << " is " << (a >= b) << endl;
    cout << a << " == " << b << " is " << (a == b) << endl;
```

```
    cout << a << " <= " <<  b << " is " << (a <= b) << endl;
    cout << a << " < " <<  b << " is " << (a < b) << endl;
    return 0;
}
```

The program's output is

```
4 > 5 is 0
4 >= 5 is 0
4 == 5 is 0
4 <= 5 is 1
4 < 5 is 1
```

In the output, 0 is false and 1 is true. 0 is the integer value of Boolean false, while 1 is the usual integer value of Boolean true. As you may recall from Chapter 1, early computers consisted of wires and switches in which the electrical current followed a path that depended on which switches were in the on position (corresponding to the value one) or the off position (corresponding to the value zero). The on position corresponds to Boolean true, the off position to Boolean false.

CAUTION: *While the usual integer value of logical true is 1, any non-zero number may be logical true. Therefore, in a Boolean comparison, do not compare a value to 1, compare it to true.*

The data types of the two operands need not be the same. For example, you could change the data type of the variable *b* in the preceding program from an int to a float and the program still would compile and provide the same output. However, the data types of the two operands need to be compatible. As you may recall from Chapter 3, compatibility means, generally, that if one of the variable operands in the relational expression is a numeric data type, then the expression's other variable operand must also be a numeric data type.

For example, the program would not compile if you changed the data type of the variable *b* in the preceding program from an int to a string.

Precedence

Relational operators have higher precedence than assignment operators and lower precedence than arithmetic operators. Table 5-3 lists precedence among relational operators.

Precedence	Operator
Highest	> >= < <=
Lowest	== !=

Table 5-3   Precedence of Relational Operators

Operators in the same row have equal precedence. The associativity of relational operators of equal precedence is from left to right.

Flowcharting

A program, like a river, flows from beginning to end. Programmers may find it helpful, both in writing code and in understanding someone else's code, to visually depict the flow of the program. After all, as the adage goes, a picture is worth a thousand words. The ability to visualize the flow of a program becomes even more helpful as we transition from relatively simple programs that flow in a straight line to more complex varieties that branch in different directions based on the value of a relational expression.

Programmers use a flowchart to visually depict the flow of a program. Flowcharts use standardized symbols prescribed by the American National Standard Institute (ANSI), which prescribes other standards we will be using in this book. These flowcharting symbols represent different aspects of a program, such as the start or end of a program, user input, how it displays on a monitor, and so on. These symbols are joined by arrows and other connectors which show the connections between different parts of the program and the direction of the program flow. Figure 5-1 shows several commonly used flowchart symbols. Others will be introduced later in this book as they are used.

The following program from Chapter 4 can be depicted with a flowchart. As you may recall, this program first assigns to the integer variable *total* the value inputted by the user for the number of preregistered students. The program then assigns to the integer variable *added* the value inputted by the user for the number of students adding the course. The program then uses the addition operator to add two operands, *total* and *added.* The resulting sum is then assigned to *total,* which now reflects the

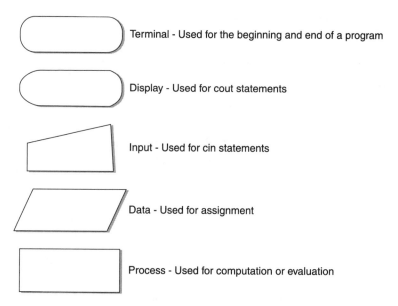

Terminal - Used for the beginning and end of a program

Display - Used for cout statements

Input - Used for cin statements

Data - Used for assignment

Process - Used for computation or evaluation

Figure 5-1   Commonly used flowchart symbols

total number of students in the course, both preregistered and added. That sum then is outputted.

```cpp
#include <iostream>
using namespace std;
int main(void)
{
    int total, added;
    cout << "Enter number of pre-registered students: ";
    cin >> total;
    cout << "Enter number of students adding the course: ";
    cin >> added;
    total = total + added;
    cout << "Total number of students: " << total;
    return 0;
}
```

Figure 5-2 shows a flowchart of this program.

This program was relatively linear. By contrast, the following programs will branch in different directions based on the value the user inputs. We will use flowcharts in later sections of this chapter to help explain how different code executes depending on the result of comparisons with the user's input.

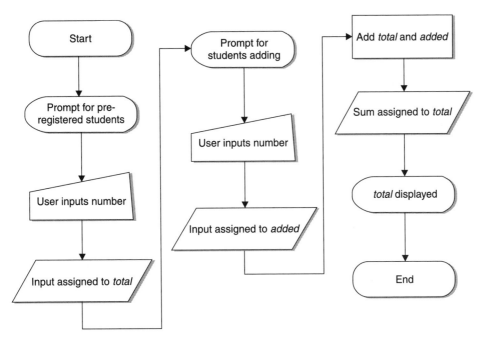

Figure 5-2   Flowchart of the program adding preregistered and added students

The if Statement

The if statement is used to execute code only when the value of a relational expression is true. The syntax of an if statement is

```
if (Boolean value)
   statement;
```

Both lines together are called an if statement. The first line consists of the if keyword followed by an expression, such as a relational expression, that evaluates to a Boolean value, true or false. The relational (or other Boolean) expression must be in parentheses, and should not be terminated with a semicolon.

The next line is called a conditional statement. As you may recall from Chapter 1, a statement is an instruction to the computer, directing it to perform a specific action. The statement is conditional because it executes only if the value of the relational expression is true. If the value of the relational expression is false, then the conditional statement is not executed—meaning, it's essentially skipped.

The following program, which tests if a whole number entered by the user is even, illustrates the use of an if statement.

```
#include <iostream>
using namespace std;
int main(void)
{
    int num;
    cout << "Enter a whole number: ";
    cin >> num;
    if ( num % 2 == 0 )
        cout << "The number is even" << endl;
    return 0;
}
```

If the user enters an even number, then the program outputs that the number is even.

```
Enter a whole number: 16
The number is even
```

However, if the user enters an odd number, then there is no output that the number is even.

```
Enter a whole number: 17
```

Figure 5-3 is a flowchart of this program. This flowchart has one new symbol: a diamond. It's used to represent the true/false statement being tested.

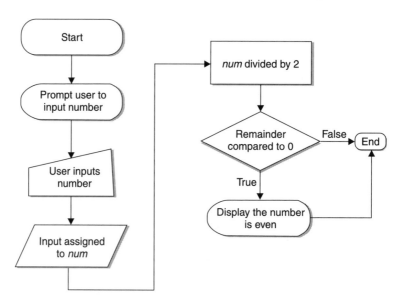

Figure 5-3   Flowchart of a program that determines whether a number is even

Let's now analyze how the program works. You may find the flowchart a helpful visual aid in following this textual explanation.

The program first prompts the user to enter a number. It then stores that input in the integer variable *num*.

The program next evaluates the relational expression *num % 2 == 0,* which is enclosed in parentheses following the *if* keyword. That expression involves two operators, the arithmetic modulus operator (%) and the relational equality operator (===). Since arithmetic operators have higher precedence than relational operators, the expression *num % 2* will be evaluated first, with the result then compared to zero.

A number is even if, when divided by two, the remainder equals zero. You learned in Chapter 4 that the modulus operator will return the remainder from integer division. Accordingly, the expression *num % 2* will divide the number entered by the user by two, and return the remainder. That remainder then will be compared to zero using the relational equality operator.

If the relational expression is true, which it would be if the number inputted by the user is even, then the conditional statement executes, outputting "The number is even." If the relational expression is false, which it would be if the number inputted by the user is odd, then the conditional statement is skipped, and it will not execute.

Indenting

It is good practice to indent the conditional statement.

```
if ( num % 2 == 0 );  // don't put a semicolon here!
    cout << "The number is even" << endl;
```

While the compiler doesn't care whether you indent or not, indentation makes it easier for you, the programmer, to see that the statement is conditional.

Common Mistakes

During several years of teaching C++ in an introductory programming class, I have noticed several common mistakes in the writing of if statements. Some of these mistakes may result in compiler errors and therefore are easy to spot. However, other mistakes are harder to pick out since they do not cause an error, either at compile time or run-time, but instead give rise to illogical results.

Don't Put a Semicolon after the Relational Expression!

The first common mistake is to place a semicolon after the relational expression:

```cpp
if ( num % 2 == 0 );   // don't put a semicolon here!
    cout << "The number is even" << endl;
```

Since the compiler generally ignores blank spaces, the following if statement would be the same, and better illustrates visually the problem:

```cpp
if ( num % 2 == 0 )
    ;   // don't put a semicolon here!
cout << "The number is even" << endl;
```

No compiler error will result. The compiler will assume from the semicolon that it is an empty statement. An empty statement does nothing, and though it is perfectly legal in C++, and indeed sometimes has a purpose, here it is not intended.

One consequence will be that the empty statement will execute if the relational expression is true. If this comes about, nothing will happen. So far, there is no harm done.

However, there is an additional consequence, an illogical result. The cout statement "The number is even" will execute whether or not the relational expression is true. In other words, even if an odd number is entered, the program will output "The number is even."

```
Enter a whole number: 17
The number is even
```

The reason the cout statement will execute whether or not the relational expression is true is that the cout statement no longer is part of the if statement. Unless you use curly braces as explained in the next section, only the first statement following the if keyword and relational expression is conditional. That first conditional statement is the empty statement, by virtue of the semicolon following the if expression.

Curly Braces Needed for Multiple Conditional Statements

As just discussed, unless you use curly braces (explained later in this section), only the first statement following the if keyword and relational expression is conditional. For example, in the following code, only the first cout statement is conditional. The second cout statement is not, so it will execute whether the relational expression is true or false:

```cpp
if ( num % 2 == 0 )
    cout << "The number is even" << endl;
cout << "And the number is not odd" << endl;
```

NOTE: *The indentation tells the programmer which statement is conditional and which is not. The compiler ignores indentation.*

Thus, if the user enters an odd number such as 17, the cout statement "The number is even" will not display because the relational expression is false. However, the following statement "And the number is not odd" will display because that statement does not belong to the if statement.

```
Enter a whole number: 17
And the number is not odd
```

If you want more than one statement to be part of the overall if statement, you must encase these statements in curly braces:

```
if ( num % 2 == 0 )
{
    cout << "The number is even" << endl;
    cout << "And the number is not odd" << endl;
}
```

Now the second cout statement will execute only if the if expression is true.

Forgetting these curly braces when you want multiple statements to be conditional is another common syntax error.

Don't Mistakenly Use the Assignment Operator!

The third most common syntax error is to use the assignment operator instead of the relational equality operator because the assignment operator looks like an equal sign:

```
if ( num % 2 = 0 )   // wrong operator!
    cout << "The number is even" << endl;
```

The result is that the if expression will not evaluate as the result of a comparison. Instead, it will evaluate the expression within the parentheses as the end result of the assignment, with a non-zero value being regarded as true, a zero value being regarded as false.

NOTE: *Some compilers will treat this mistake as a compiler error.*

The if / else Statement

One problem with the program that tests whether a number is even is that there is no output if the number is odd. While there is a conditional statement if the relational expression is true, there is no corresponding conditional statement (cout << "The number is odd") if the relational expression is false.

The solution is to add an else part to the if statement. The result is an if / else statement. The syntax of an if / else statement is

```
if (relational expression)
   conditional statement;
else
   conditional statement;
```

Accordingly, the program may be modified to add an else part to the if statement:

```
#include <iostream>
using namespace std;
int main(void)
{
   int num;
   cout << "Enter a whole number: ";
   cin >> num;
   if ( num % 2 == 0 )
      cout << "The number is even" << endl;
   else
      cout << "The number is odd" << endl;
   return 0;
}
```

Run this code. If the inputted number is even, then the output once again is "The number is even." However, if the number is now odd, instead of no output, the output is "The number is odd."

```
Enter a whole number: 17
The number is odd
```

Figure 5-4 uses a flowchart to illustrate this program.

Conditional Operator

This program could be rewritten using the conditional operator.

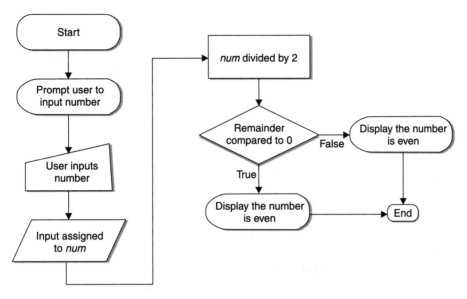

Figure 5-4   Flowchart of program output if number is even or odd

```cpp
#include <iostream>
using namespace std;
int main(void)
{
   int num;
   cout << "Enter a whole number: ";
   cin >> num;
   cout << "The number is " << ( num % 2 == 0 ? "even" :
         "odd") << endl;
   return 0;
}
```

The syntax of the conditional operator is

```
[Relational expression] ? [statement if true] :
[statement if false]
```

In this example, the relational expression is *num % 2 == 0*. If the value of the relational expression is true, then the output is "even." However, if the value of the relational expression is false, then the output is "odd."

The conditional operator requires three operands, the relational expression and the two conditional statements. Therefore, it is considered a ternary operator.

Common Mistakes

Just as with the if statement, I noticed several common syntax mistakes with the else statement while teaching C++ in introductory programming classes.

No else Without an if

You can have an if expression without an else part. However, you cannot have an else part without an if part. The else part must be part of an overall if statement. This requirement is logical. The else part works as "none of the above"; without an if part there is no "above."

As a consequence, placing a semicolon after the Boolean expression following the if keyword will result in a compiler error. Since curly braces are not used, the if statement ends after the empty statement created by the incorrectly placed semicolon. The cout statement "The number is even" is not part of the if statement. Consequently, the else part is not part of the if statement, and therefore will be regarded as an else part without an if part.

```
if ( num % 2 == 0 ); // don't put a semicolon here
    cout << "The number is even" << endl;
else ( num % 2 == 1 )
    cout << "The number is odd" << endl;
```

Don't Put a Relational Expression after the else Keyword!

Another common mistake is to place a relational expression in parentheses after the else keyword. This will not cause a compiler or run-time error, but it will often cause an illogical result.

```
if ( num % 2 == 0 )
    cout << "The number is even" << endl;
else ( num % 2 == 1 )
    cout << "The number is odd" << endl;
```

The program will not compile, and the cout statement following the else expression will be highlighted with an error description such as "missing ';' before identifier 'cout'."

Actually, the error description is misleading. There is nothing wrong with the cout statement. Instead, no relational expression should follow the else keyword. The reason is that the else acts like "none of the above" in a multiple choice test.

If the if expression is not true, then the conditional statements connected to the else part execute.

Don't Put a Semicolon after the Else!

Another common mistake is to place a semicolon after the else expression. This too will not cause a compiler or run-time error, but often will cause an illogical result.

For example, in the following code, the cout statement "The number is odd" will output even if the number that's input is even.

```
if ( num % 2 == 0 )
    cout << "The number is even" << endl;
else;  // don't put a semicolon here!
    cout << "The number is odd" << endl;
```

The result of inputting an even number will be

```
Enter a whole number: 16
The number is even
The number is odd
```

The cout statement "The number is odd" will execute whether or not the relational expression is true because the cout statement no longer is part of the if statement. Unless you use curly braces as explained already in connection with the if statement, only the first statement following the else keyword is conditional. That first, conditional statement is the empty statement by virtue of the semicolon following the if expression. Therefore, the cout statement "The number is odd" is not part of the if statement at all.

Curly Braces Are Needed for Multiple Conditional Statements

As with the if expression, if you want more than one conditional statement to belong to the else part, then you must encase the statements in curly braces. For example, in the following code fragment, the cout statement "This also belongs to the else part" will always display whether the number is even or odd since it does not belong to the if statement.

```
if ( num % 2 == 0 )
    cout << "The number is even" << endl;
else
    cout << "The number is odd" << endl;
cout << "This also belongs to the else part";
```

The sample input and output could be

```
Enter a whole number: 16
The number is even
This also belongs to the else part
```

Encasing the multiple conditional statements in curly braces solves this issue.

```
if ( num % 2 == 0 )
     cout << "The number is even" << endl;
else
{
     cout << "The number is odd" << endl;
     cout << "This also belongs to the else part";
}
```

The if /else if /else Statement

The program we used to illustrate the if/else statement involved only two alternatives. Additionally, these alternatives were mutually exclusive; only one could
be chosen, not both. A whole number is either even or odd; it can't be both and
there is no third alterative. There are many other examples of only two mutually
exclusive alternatives. For example, a person is either dead or alive, male or fe-
male, child or adult.

However, there are other scenarios where there are more than two, mutually exclusive alternatives. For example, if you take a test, your grade may be one of five
types: A, B, C, D, or F. Additionally, these grades are mutually exclusive; you can't
get an A and a C on the same test.

Since you can have only one if expression and only one else expression in an if
statement, you need another expression for the third and additional alternatives.
That expression is else if.

You use the if / else if / else statement when there are three or more mutually exclusive alternatives. The if / else if / else statement has an if part and an else part, like
an if/else statement. However, it also has one or more else if parts.

NOTE: *While the if part is required, the else part is not. Without it, the statement
would be named an if / else if statement.*

The else if part works similarly to an if expression. The else if keywords are followed by a relational expression. If the expression is true, then the conditional statement or statements "belonging" to the else if part execute. Otherwise, they don't.

While an if statement may include only one if part and one else part, it may include multiple else if parts.

The following program shows the if/else if/else statement in action in a program that determines your grade based on your test score.

```cpp
#include <iostream>
using namespace std;
int main(void)
{
    int testScore;
    cout << "Enter your test score: ";
    cin >> testScore;
    if (testScore >= 90 )
        cout << "Your grade is an A" << endl;
    else if (testScore >= 80 )
        cout << "Your grade is a B" << endl;
    else if (testScore >= 70 )
        cout << "Your grade is a C" << endl;
    else if (testScore >= 60 )
        cout << "Your grade is a D" << endl;
    else
        cout << "Your grade is an F" << endl;
    return 0;
}
```

Here are several sample runs, each separated by a dotted line:

```
Enter your test score: 77
Your grade is a C
------
Enter your test score: 91
Your grade is an A
------
Enter your test score: 55
Your grade is an F
```

Figure 5-5 uses a flowchart to illustrate this program.

In this program, if your test score is 90 or better, then the conditional statement belonging to the if part executes, displaying that you received an A. The relational expressions of each of the following else if parts also are true; if your score is 90 or better, it also is 80 or better, 70 or better, and so on. However, in an if/else if/else statement, only the conditional statements in the first part whose relational expression is true will execute; the remaining parts are skipped.

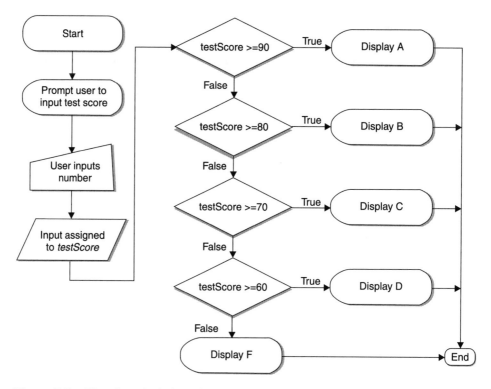

Figure 5-5   Flowchart depiction of grading program

Common Syntax Errors

The common syntax errors for the if part discussed earlier in this chapter apply to the else if part also. Don't put a semicolon after the relational expression, and multiple conditional statements must be enclosed in curly braces.

Additionally, just as you cannot have an else part without a preceding if part, you cannot have an else if part without a preceding if part. However, you may have an if part and one or more else if parts without an else part. The downside in omitting the else part is you will not have code to cover the "none of the above" scenario in which none of the relational expressions belonging to the if part and else if parts is true.

The switch Statement

The switch statement is similar to an if /else if /else statement. It evaluates the value of an integer expression and then compares that value to two or more other values to determine which code to execute.

The following program shows a switch statement in action in a program that determines your average based on your grade:

```cpp
#include <iostream>
using namespace std;
int main(void)
{
   char grade;
   cout << "Enter your grade: ";
   cin >> grade;
   switch (grade)
   {
   case 'A':
      cout << "Your average must be between 90 - 100"
           << endl;
      break;
   case 'B':
      cout << "Your average must be between 80 - 89"
           << endl;
      break;
   case 'C':
      cout << "Your average must be between 70 - 79"
           << endl;
      break;
   case 'D':
      cout << "Your average must be between 60 - 69"
           << endl;
      break;
   default:
      cout << "Your average must be below 60" << endl;

   }
  return 0;
}
```

Here are several sample runs, each separated by a dotted line:

```
Enter your grade: C
Your average must be between 70 - 79
------
Enter your grade: A
Your average must be between 90 - 100
------
Enter your grade: F
Your average must be below 60
```

Figure 5-6 uses a flowchart to illustrate this program.

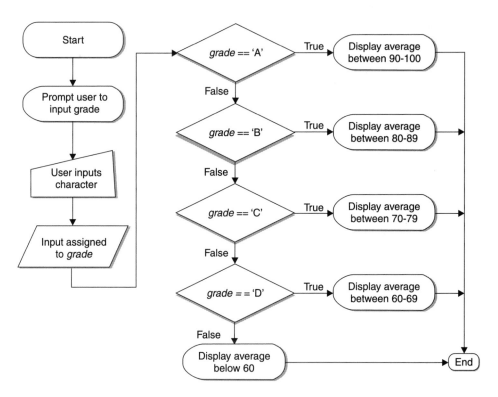

Figure 5-6   Flowchart depiction of the grade determination program

Let's now analyze the program.

The *switch* keyword evaluates an integer expression, *grade*. While grade is a character variable, every character has a corresponding integer value.

Earlier in this chapter, we discussed flowchart symbols prescribed by the American National Standard Institute (ANSI), and mentioned that ANSI also prescribes other standards that we will be using in this book. One of those other standards is the ANSI character set, which includes 256 characters, each having an integer value between 0 and 255. These values also are called ASCII values, since values 0 to 127 of the ANSI character set are the same as in the ASCII (American Standard Code for Information Interchange) character set.

Table 5-4 lists the ANSI/ASCII values for commonly used characters. Note that digits also can be characters, and that the ANSI/ASCII value of an uppercase character is different than the value of the corresponding lowercase character.

Character	Value
0	48
9	57
A	65
Z	90
a	97
z	122

Table 5-4   Selected ANSI/ASCII Values

Each *case* keyword is followed by an integer expression that must be constant, that is, it cannot change in value during the life of the program. Therefore, a variable cannot follow a case keyword. In this program, the constant is a character literal, such as A, B, and so on. Each character's ANSI value is an integer value, and the integer expression is followed by a colon.

CAUTION: *A common mistake is to follow the integer expression not with a colon but with a semicolon, which is typically used to terminate statements. This will cause a compiler error.*

The default keyword serves the same purpose as an else part in an if/else if/else statement, and therefore is not followed by an integer expression.

The integer expression following the switch keyword is evaluated and compared with the integer constant following each case keyword, from top to bottom. If there is a *match*—that is, the two integers are equal—then the statements belonging to that case are executed. Otherwise, they are not. Thus, the statements belonging to a case are conditional, just as are statements in an if, else if, or else part. However, unlike an if/else if/else statement, multiple conditional statements belonging to a case do not need to be enclosed in curly braces.

Differences Between switch and if /else if /else Statements

While a switch statement is similar to an if/else if/else statement, there are important differences.

One difference is that in an if/else if/else statement, the comparison following the if part may be independent of the comparison following an else if part. The following example, while perhaps a bit silly, is illustrative of this concept:

```
if (apples == oranges)
    do this;
else if (sales >= 5000)
    do that;
```

By contrast, in a switch statement, the constant integer expression following a case keyword must be compared with the value following the switch keyword, and nothing else. The next chapter on logical operators discusses other differences between switch and if/else if/else statements. However, two differences can be discussed now. One is commonly known as "falling through." The other concerns ranges of numbers.

Falling Through

In an if/else if/else statement, each part is separate from all the others. By contrast, in a switch statement (once a matching case statement is found), unless a break statement is reached, execution "falls through" to the following case statements that execute their conditional statements without checking for a match. For example, if you removed the break statements from the program, you could have the following sample run:

```
Enter your grade: A
Your average must be between 90 - 100
Your average must be between 80 - 89
Your average must be between 70 - 79
Your average must be between 60 - 69
Your average must be below 60
```

This "falling through" behavior is not necessarily bad. In the following modification of the grade program, the falling-through behavior permits the user to enter a lowercase grade in addition to an uppercase grade.

```
#include <iostream>
using namespace std;
int main(void)
{
    char grade;
    cout << "Enter your grade: ";
    cin >> grade;
    switch (grade)
```

```
    {
    case 'a':
    case 'A':
        cout << "Your average must be between 90 - 100"
            << endl;
        break;
    case 'b':
    case 'B':
        cout << "Your average must be between 80 - 89"
            << endl;
        break;
    case 'c':
    case 'C':
        cout << "Your average must be between 70 - 79"
            << endl;
        break;
    case 'd':
    case 'D':
        cout << "Your average must be between 60 - 69"
            << endl;
        break;
    default:
        cout << "Your average must be below 60" << endl;

    }
return 0;
}
```

Another example occurs in the following program. Since the "D" (for deluxe) option includes the feature in the "L" (for leather) option, case 'D' deliberately falls through the case 'L.'

```
#include <iostream>
using namespace std;
int main(void)
{
    char choice;
    cout << "Choose your car\n";
    cout << "S for Standard\n";
    cout << "L for Leather Seats\n";
    cout << "D for Leather Seats + Chrome Wheels\n";
    cin >> choice;
    cout << "Extra features purchased\n";
    switch (choice)
    {
```

```
    case 'D':
        cout << "Chrome wheels\n";
    case 'L':
        cout << "Leather seats\n";
        break;
    default:
        cout << "None selected\n";}
    return 0;
}
```

The sample run could be

```
Choose your car
S for Standard
L for Leather Seats
D for Leather Seats + Chrome Wheels
D
Extra features purchased
Chrome wheels
Leather seats
```

Ranges of Numbers

Another difference between switch and if/else ifelse statements concerns the handling of ranges of numbers. For example, earlier in this chapter we used an if /else if /else statement to output the user's grade based on the test score that was input by the user. The issued grade was an A if the test score was between 90 and 100, a B if the test score was between 80 and 89, and so on. The if/else if/else statement in that program was

```
if (testScore >= 90 )
    cout << "Your grade is an A" << endl;
else if (testScore >= 80 )
    cout << "Your grade is a B" << endl;
else if (testScore >= 70 )
    cout << "Your grade is a C" << endl;
else if (testScore >= 60 )
    cout << "Your grade is a D" << endl;
else
    cout << "Your grade is an F" << endl;
```

By contrast, a case statement cannot be followed by an expression such as testScore >= 90 because the case statement keyword has to be followed by an integer constant. Instead, a case statement would be necessary for each possible test score. The following code fragment shows only the code for an A or B grade to avoid the code example being unduly long, but the code for a C or D grade would be essentially a repeat (an F grade would be handled with the default keyword).

```
switch (testScore)
{
case 100:
case 99:
case 98:
case 97:
case 96:
case 95:
case 94:
case 93:
case 92:
case 91:
case 90:
    cout << "Your grade is an A";
    break;
case 89:
case 88:
case 87:
case 86:
case 85:
case 84:
case 83:
case 82:
case 81:
case 80:
    cout << "Your grade is an A";
    break;
}
```

This code example illustrates that the switch statement is more cumbersome than the if /else if /else structure in dealing with ranges of numbers.

Summary

Computer programs usually do not take a preordained path from beginning to end. Instead, different code executes based on choices made by the user. Relational operators are used to compare the user's choice with various alternatives. The if, if/else, if /else if /else, and switch statements are used to structure the code so different code executes depending on which choice was made. You also learned about flowcharts, which help make programs more understandable by visually depicting the program components and flow.

In this chapter, only one comparison was made at a time. However, sometimes more than one comparison needs to be made. For example, you are eligible to vote in the U.S. only if you are a citizen and are at least 18 years old. You cannot vote unless both are true. However, you may get into a movie free if you are either a senior citizen (65 years or older) or a child (12 or under). Thus, you get in free if either is true. In the next chapter, you will learn about how to use logical operators to combine comparisons.

Quiz

1. How many operands are in a relational expression?
2. What is the purpose of a flowchart?
3. What is the data type of the expression following the if keyword?
4. In an if /else if /else statement, which part must you have one, but only one, of?
5. In an if /else if /else statement, which part may you have more than one of?
6. In an if /else if /else statement, which part may you omit?
7. In a switch statement, what is the required data type of expression following the switch keyword?
8. In a switch statement, may an expression of the character data type follow the switch keyword?
9. In a switch statement, may the expression following a case keyword be a variable?
10. Which keyword in a switch statement corresponds to the else keyword in an if /else if /else statement?

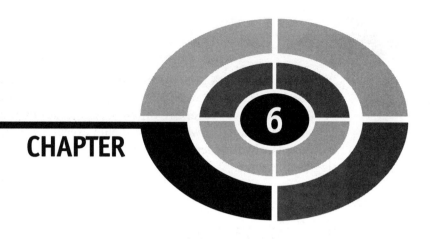

CHAPTER

6

Nested if Statements and Logical Operators

Chapter 5 began with the opening words of the famous poem "The Road Not Taken" by Robert Frost: "Two roads diverged in a yellow wood, and sorry I could not travel both."

Not to be a poetry critic, but often there are more than two roads.

In Chapter 5, we evaluated only one Boolean expression at a time, and chose which of the two roads our code would travel down depending on whether the expression was true or false. However, sometimes two (or more) Boolean expressions need to be evaluated to determine the path the code will travel.

For example, you are eligible to vote only if you are a citizen *and* you are at least 18 years old. You cannot vote unless both conditions are true. Other times with Boolean expressions, you are testing if either of two comparisons is true.

For example, you may get into a movie free if you are either a senior citizen (65 years or older) *or* a child (12 or under). Thus, you get in free if either condition is true.

This chapter will cover two different approaches to evaluating two Boolean expressions to determine which code should execute. The first approach nests one if statement inside another. The second approach introduces another type of operator: logical operators.

Nested if Statements

An if statement may appear inside another if statement. When this is done, the inner if statement is said to be "nested" inside the outer if statement.

You can nest if statements to determine if both of two Boolean expressions are true, or if either of the expressions is true.

Testing if Both Boolean Expressions Are True

The following program shows the use of nested if statements in determining if both of two Boolean expressions are true. If the user's input is that they are at least 18 years old *and* a citizen, the program outputs that they are eligible to vote. Otherwise, the program outputs that they are not eligible to vote.

```
#include <iostream>
using namespace std;
int main(void)
{
    int age;
    char choice;
    bool citizen;
    cout << "Enter your age: ";
    cin >> age;
    cout << "Are you a citizen (Y/N): ";
    cin >> choice;
    if (choice == 'Y')
       citizen = true;
    else
       citizen = false;
    if (age >= 18)
       if(citizen == true)
          cout << "You are eligible to vote";
       else
```

```
         cout << "You are not eligible to vote";
   else
      cout << "You are not eligible to vote";
   return 0;
}
```

The following are several sample runs, each separated by ===:

```
Enter your age: 18
Are you a citizen (Y/N): Y
You are eligible to vote
===
Enter your age: 18
Are you a citizen (Y/N): N
You are not eligible to vote
===
Enter your age: 17
Are you a citizen (Y/N): Y
You are not eligible to vote
===
Enter your age: 17
Are you a citizen (Y/N): N
You are not eligible to vote
===
```

Figure 6-1 depicts a flowchart of this program.
The nested if portion of the program is

```
if (age >= 18)
   if(citizen == true)
      cout << "You are eligible to vote";
   else
      cout << "You are not eligible to vote";
else
   cout << "You are not eligible to vote";
```

NOTE: *The statement if(citizen == true) could be rewritten as if(citizen). The parentheses following the if keyword requires only an expression that evaluates to a Boolean value. Since citizen is a Boolean variable, it evaluates to a Boolean value without the need for any comparison.*

The if/else structure comparing whether the user is a citizen is nested within the if/else structure comparing whether the user is at least 18 years old. By this nesting, the comparison of whether the user is a citizen is made only if the user is at least

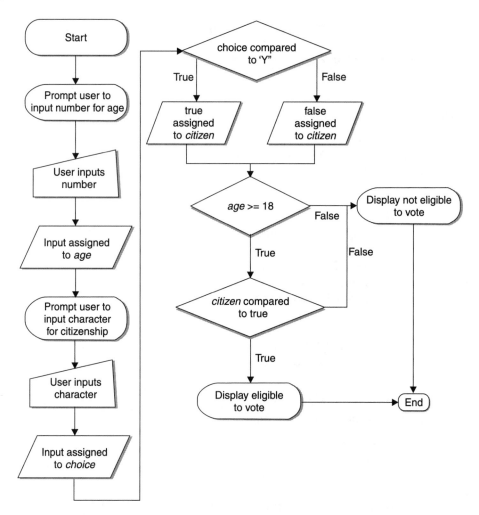

Figure 6-1   Flowchart of the voting eligibility program

18 years old. This approach is logical, since if the user is not at least 18 years old, they will not be eligible to vote even if they are a citizen.

The if / else structure comparing whether the user is a citizen is referred to as the "inner" if / else structure. The if / else structure comparing whether the user is at least 18 years old is referred to as the "outer" if / else structure.

The entire inner if / else structure (comparing whether the user is a citizen) is nested within the if part of the outer if / else structure (comparing whether the user is at least 18 years old). You also can nest an if / else structure (or an if structure, or an if /else if /else structure) within the else if or else part of an outer if else/if else if else/if else structure.

This program illustrates a good use of nested if statements. It would be difficult to rewrite this program using an if / else if / else structure without nested if statements. However, later in this chapter we will cover another, equally good alternative: logical operators.

Testing if Either Boolean Expression Is True

The following program shows the use of the nested if statements in determining if either of two Boolean expressions are true. If the user's input indicates that they are either no more than 12 years old *or* at least 65 years old, the program outputs that their admission is free. Otherwise, the program outputs that they have to pay.

```
#include <iostream>
using namespace std;
int main(void)
{
    int age;
    cout << "Enter your age: ";
    cin >> age;
    if (age > 12)
        if (age >= 65)
            cout << "Admission is free";
        else
            cout << "You have to pay";
    else
        cout << "Admission is free";
    return 0;
}
```

The following shows several sample runs:

```
Enter your age: 12
Admission is free
===
Enter your age: 13
You have to pay
===
Enter your age: 65
Admission is free
```

Figure 6-2 depicts a flowchart of this program.

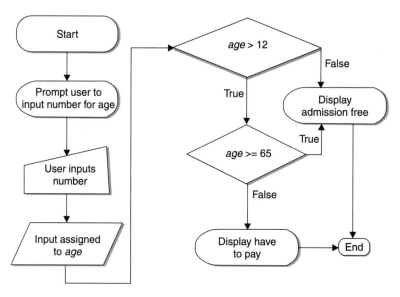

Figure 6-2 Flowchart of the movie admission program

The nested if portion of the program is

```
if (age > 12)
   if (age >= 65)
      cout << "Admission is free";
   else
      cout << "You have to pay";
else
   cout << "Admission is free";
```

The inner if/else structure, comparing whether the user is at least 65 years old, is nested within the outer if/else structure, comparing whether the user is over 12 years old. By this nesting, the comparison of whether the user is at least 65 years old is made only if the user is over 12 years old. This approach is logical, since if the user is no more than 12 years old, they will be admitted free (and also could not possibly be 65 years or older).

This program also could have been written using the following if / else if / else structure in place of the nested if statements:

```
if (age <= 12)
   cout << "Admission is free";
else if (age >= 65)
```

```
      cout << "Admission is free";
  else
      cout << "You have to pay";
```

Each of these two alternatives, the nested if statements and the if / else if / else structure, have disadvantages. Nesting one if statement inside another by its very nature may be somewhat difficult to write and understand. However, the if / elseif/else if / else structure has the disadvantage of repeating the same cout statement for both the if and else if parts. While this is just one line of repetitive code in this program, in more complex programs the repetitive code could be many lines long.

C++ has a third and perhaps better alternative, the use of logical operators, which we will discuss next.

Logical Operators

C++ has logical operators that enable you to combine comparisons in one if or else if statement. Table 6-1 lists the logical operators supported by C++ and describes what each does.

Operator	Name	What It Does
&&	And	Connects two relational expressions. Both expressions must be true for the overall expression to be true.
||	Or	Connects two relational expressions. If either expression is true, the overall expression is true.
!	Not	Reverses the "truth" of an expression, making a true expression false, and a false expression true.

Table 6-1   Logical Operators

The && Operator

The && operator also is known as the logical And operator. It is a binary operator; it takes two Boolean expressions as operands. It returns true only if both expressions are true. If either expression is false, the overall expression is false. Of course, if both expressions are false, the overall expression is false. Table 6-2 illustrates this.

Expression #1	Expression #2	Expression #1 && Expression #2
true	true	true
true	false	false
false	true	false
false	false	false

Table 6-2   The Logical And Operator

The following program shows the use of the logical And operator in determining whether the user is eligible to vote, the criteria being that the user must be at least 18 years old and a citizen.

```cpp
#include <iostream>
using namespace std;
int main(void)
{
    int age;
    char choice;
    bool citizen;
    cout << "Enter your age: ";
    cin >> age;
    cout << "Are you a citizen (Y/N): ";
    cin >> choice;
    if (choice == 'Y')
        citizen = true;
    else
        citizen = false;
    if (age >= 18 && citizen == true)
        cout << "You are eligible to vote";
    else
        cout << "You are not eligible to vote";
    return 0;
}
```

The following are several sample runs, separated by ===:

```
Enter your age: 18
Are you a citizen (Y/N): Y
You are eligible to vote
===
```

```
Enter your age: 18
Are you a citizen (Y/N): N
You are not eligible to vote
===
Enter your age: 17
Are you a citizen (Y/N): Y
You are not eligible to vote
===
Enter your age: 17
Are you a citizen (Y/N): N
You are not eligible to vote
```

The part of the program that uses the logical And operator is

```
if (age >= 18 && citizen == true)
    cout << "You are eligible to vote";
else
    cout << "You are not eligible to vote";
```

The comparison *age >= 18* is referred to as the left part of the expression since it is to the left of the logical And operator. Similarly, the comparison *citizen == true* is referred to as the right part of the expression because it is to the right of the logical And operator.

If the user's age is at least 18 years, then the program makes the second comparison, whether the user is a citizen. If the user's age is not at least 18 years of age, the second comparison is not even made before the else part is executed. The reason is to avoid wasting CPU time, since if the left expression is false, the overall expression is false regardless of the result of the evaluation of the right expression.

Because the second comparison of whether the user is a citizen is made only if the user's age is at least 18, the flowchart in Figure 6-1 of this program using nested if statements also applies to this program using the logical And operator.

The || Operator

The || operator is also known as the logical Or operator. Like the logical And operator, the logical Or operator also is a binary operator, taking two Boolean expressions as operands. It returns true if either expression is true. It returns false only if both expressions are false. Of course, if both expressions are true, the overall expression is true. Table 6-3 illustrates this.

The following program shows the use of the logical Or operator in determining whether you get into a movie free, the criteria being that the user must be either no more than 12 or at least 65 years old.

Expression #1	Expression #2	Expression #1 || Expression #2
true	true	true
true	false	true
false	true	true
false	false	false

Table 6-3   The Logical Or Operator

```
#include <iostream>
using namespace std;
int main(void)
{
    int age;
    cout << "Enter your age: ";
    cin >> age;
    if (age <= 12 || age >= 65)
        cout << "Admission is free";
    else
        cout << "You have to pay";
    return 0;
}
```

The following shows several sample runs:

```
Enter your age: 12
Admission is free
===
Enter your age: 18
You have to pay
===
Enter your age: 65
Admission is free
```

The part of the program that uses the logical Or operator is

```
if (age <= 12 || age >= 65)
    cout << "Admission is free";
else
    cout << "You have to pay";
return 0;
```

As with the logical And operator, the comparison *age <= 12* is referred to as the left part of the expression and the comparison *age >= 65* is referred to as the right part of the expression.

If the user's age is over 12 years, then the program makes the second comparison, whether the user is at least 65 years of age. If the user is no more than 12 years of age, the second comparison is not even made before the else part is executed. The reason, as with the logical And operator, once again is to avoid wasting CPU time, since if the left expression is true, the overall expression is true regardless of the result of the evaluation of the right expression.

Because the second comparison of whether the user is at least 65 years old is made only if the user's age is over 12, the flowchart in Figure 6-2 of this program using nested if statements also applies to this program using the logical Or operator.

The ! Operator

The ! operator also is known as the logical Not operator. My daughters have been using the logical Not operator for years, telling me "Dad, you look just like Tom Cruise ... not!"

The logical Not operator inverts the value of the Boolean expression, returning false if the Boolean expression is true, and true if the Boolean expression is false. Table 6-4 illustrates this.

Expression	!Expression
true	true
false	true

Table 6-4   The Logical Not Operator

Unlike the logical And and Or operators, the logical Not operator is a unary operator; it takes only one Boolean expression, not two.

The following program shows the use of the logical Not operator, combined with the logical And operator, in determining whether you get into a movie for free.

```
#include <iostream>
using namespace std;
int main(void)
{
    int age;
    cout << "Enter your age: ";
    cin >> age;
    if (!(age > 12 && age < 65))
        cout << "Admission is free";
```

```
   else
      cout << "You have to pay";
   return 0;
}
```

This program is almost identical to the one used to illustrate the logical Or operator. The only difference is that the statement

```
   if (age <= 12 || age >= 65)
```

is replaced by the statement

```
   if (!(age > 12 && age < 65))
```

NOTE: *This change is an illustration of DeMorgan's law, which is a rule of inference pertaining to the logical And, Or, and Not operators that are used to distribute a negative to a conjunction or disjunction. In this book, it is only referred to and not covered, but in case you hear DeMorgan's law mentioned in a programming class or another book, you heard it here first!*

The Not operator permits you to state a Boolean expression a different way that may be more intuitive for you. In this example, expressing the condition for free admission as being that the age is not between 13 and 64 may be more intuitive than expressing that condition as being that the age is either no more than 12 or 65 or over.

Precedence

Table 6-5 lists precedence, from highest to lowest, among logical operators and between them and the relational operators.

Operator (from highest to lowest)
!
Relational operators (>, >=, <, <=, ==. !=)
&&
||

Table 6-5   The Precedence of Logical and Relational Operators

Precedence and the Logical Not Operator

Since the logical Not operator has a higher precedence than the relational operators, the program used to illustrate the logical Not operator uses an extra set of parentheses.

```
if (!(age > 12 && age < 65))
```

Had the extra set of parentheses been omitted as follows, the result would always be that the user has to pay. Thus, admission would never be free regardless of the age.

```
if (!age > 12 && age < 65)
```

The reason why the user always has to pay regardless of age is that since the logical Not operator has a higher precedence than the relational operators, the logical Not operator operates on *age,* not the expression *age > 12 && age < 65.* If *age* is non-zero, then *!age* is zero. Since 0 is not greater than 12, the left part of the logical And expression is false, so the overall expression is false.

The result of the user always having to pay regardless of age is the same even if *age* is zero. If *age* is zero, then *!age* is logical true, the integer equivalent of which usually is 1. Since 1 is not greater than 12, once again the left part of the logical And expression is false, so the overall expression is false.

Precedence and the Logical And and Or Operators

In contrast to the logical Not operator, the logical And and Or operators rank lower in precedence than the relational operators. Therefore, parentheses normally are not necessary to separate the logical And and Not operators from the relational operators. For example, the following two statements (the first taken from the program that illustrated the logical And operator) are equivalent.

```
if (age >= 18 && citizen == true)
if ( (age >= 18) && (citizen == true) )
```

However, parentheses are necessary when logical And and Or operators are used together in one statement and you want the Or done before the And since the logical And operator has higher precedence than the logical Or operator. This issue often arises when you have more than two Boolean expressions.

For example, assume the voting rules were changed so legal residents (represented by the Boolean variable *resident* having a value of true) as well as citizens who are at least 18 years old could vote. Given that assumption, the statement

```
if (resident == true || citizen == true && age >= 18)
```

would be the same as the following since the logical And operator has higher precedence than the logical Or operator.

```
if (resident == true || (citizen == true && age >= 18 ))
```

In this expression, a resident under 18 years old would be able to vote. The reason is that even if the expression (*citizen == true && age >= 18*) is false, as long as *resident* is true, the overall expression is true, since with a logical Or operator only one of the two Boolean expressions needs to be true for the overall expression to be true.

A resident under 18 years old being able to vote is not a correct result for this program. To avoid this logic error, parentheses would be necessary, so the logical Or operation is performed first.

```
if ( (resident == true || citizen == true) && age >= 18)
```

Using the switch Statement with Logical Operators

The switch statement was discussed at some length in Chapter 5. However, so far in this chapter it has been conspicuous by its absence.

In Chapter 5, we discussed how the switch statement was cumbersome when dealing with a range of numbers. The reason was that the case keyword cannot be followed by a range of numbers because it must instead be followed by a single integer constant.

However, the switch statement may be used with expressions that use the logical And or Or operator. The reason is that these expressions have only one of two possible values, true or false. True and false are both constants; the value of true is always true and the value of false is always false. While true and false are Boolean values, each has a corresponding integer value: 1 and 0. Therefore, the case keyword may be followed by true or false, just as in Chapter 5 where the case keyword can be followed by a character since a character has a corresponding integer ANSI or ASCII value.

For example, earlier in this chapter the logical And operator was used in the following if/else structure in determining whether the user is eligible to vote, the criteria being that the user must be at least 18 years old and a citizen.

```
if (age >= 18 && citizen == true)
   cout << "You are eligible to vote";
else
   cout << "You are not eligible to vote";
```

The corresponding switch statement is

```
switch (age >= 18 && citizen == true)
{
case true:
   cout << "You are eligible to vote";
   break;
case false:
   cout << "You are not eligible to vote";
}
```

Also earlier in this chapter, the logical Or operator was used in the following if/else structure in determining whether the user gets into a movie free, the criteria being that the user must be either under 18 or at least 65 years old.

```
if (age <= 12 || age >= 65)
   cout << "Admission is free";
else
   cout << "You have to pay";
```

The corresponding switch statement is

```
switch (age <= 12 || age >= 65)
{
   case true:
      cout << "Admission is free";
      break;
   case false:
      cout << "You have to pay";
}
```

These examples illustrate that the switch statement can be employed as an alternative to an if/else or if/else if/else structure in programs that evaluate Boolean expressions using logical operators. However, it is not common for the switch statement to be employed in this manner because, with Boolean expressions, there are always just two alternatives, true and false, and switch statements generally are used when there are many more alternatives than two.

Summary

In Chapter 5, we evaluated only one Boolean expression at a time to determine which of two alternative blocks of code should execute. However, often two (or more) Boolean expressions need to be evaluated to determine which block of code should execute. In the example in which you are eligible to vote only if the user is

a citizen *and* at least 18 years old, both Boolean expressions must be true in order for the program to output that the user is eligible to vote. In another example, in which you get into a movie free if the user is either a senior citizen (65 years or older) *or* a child (12 or under), the program outputs that the user gets into the movie free if either Boolean expression is true.

This chapter covered two different approaches of evaluating two Boolean expressions to determine which code should execute. The first approach nested one if statement inside another. The second approach introduced three logical operators. The logical && (And) operator is used when both Boolean expressions must be true. The logical || (Or) operator is used when either Boolean expression must be true. Finally, the logical ! (Not) operator inverts the value of a Boolean expression, from true to false, or false to true.

Finally, this chapter showed how you can use the switch statement as an alternative to an if / else or if / else if /else structure in programs that evaluate Boolean expressions using logical operators.

Quiz

1. Can you use nested if statements as an alternative to the logical And and Or operators?

2. Can an if statement be nested in the else if or else part of an if / else if / else statement, or just the if part?

3. For which of the logical operators do both Boolean expressions have to be true for the overall Boolean expression to be true?

4. For which of the logical operators do both Boolean expressions have to be false for the overall Boolean expression to be false?

5. Which of the logical operators reverses the "truth" of a Boolean expression, making a true expression false and a false expression true?

6. Assuming *resident* is a Boolean variable, is *if(resident)* the same as *if(resident == true)*?

7. Which of the logical operators is a unary rather than binary operator?

8. Which of the logical operators has a higher precedence than the relational operators?

9. Which logical operator has a higher precedence, And or Or?

10. Can a Boolean value of either true or false be used following the case keyword in a switch statement?

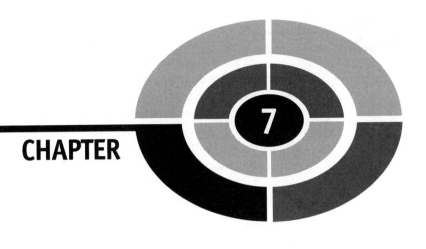

The For Loop

Parents customarily remind their children not to repeat themselves. Indeed, parents often illustrate another saying ("Do as I say, not as I do") by continually repeating that reminder.

This is my nifty way of introducing the idea that, in the world of computers, sometimes you want your code to repeat itself, too. For example, if the user enters invalid data, you may want to ask the user whether they want to retry or quit. If they retry and still enter invalid data, you again would ask the user whether they want to retry or quit. This process keeps repeating until the user either enters valid data or quits.

You use a loop to repeat the execution of code statements. A loop in C++ is a structure that repeats the execution of code until a condition becomes false. In the preceding example, the condition is that the data is invalid and the user wants to retry, thus the repeating code is the prompt asking the user whether they want to retry or quit.

This chapter will show you how to use one type of loop: the for loop. However, before discussing the for loop, I'll show you how to use increment and decrement operators, which are used in for and other types of loops. The next chapter will then show you how to use two other kinds of loops: the while loop and the do while loop.

Increment and Decrement Operators

Increment means to increase a value by one. Conversely, decrement means to decrease a value by one. C++ has an increment operator that you can use to increase a value by one and a decrement operator that you can use to decrease a value by one. This section will show you how to use both, something that will be useful in the next section on the for loop, which uses increment and decrement operators.

The Increment Operator

In the following program, the statement *num += 1* increases the value of the integer variable *num,* which was initialized to the value 2, by 1, so the output will be 3.

```
#include <iostream>
using namespace std;
int main(void)
{
    int num = 2;
    num += 1;
    cout << num;
    return 0;
}
```

Another way to accomplish the same result is by using the increment operator, ++. The increment operator is unary—that is, it operates on one operand. That operand generally is a whole number variable, such as an int. We can use the increment operator simply by changing the program we just ran by replacing the statement *num += 1* with the statement *num++*:

```
#include <iostream>
using namespace std;
int main(void)
```

```
{
    int num = 2;
    num++;
    cout << num;
    return 0;
}
```

The same output would occur if you substituted the statement ++*num* for *num*++:

```
#include <iostream>
using namespace std;
int main(void)
{
    int num = 2;
    ++num;
    cout << num;
    return 0;
}
```

Placing the ++ before the variable *num* is called prefix incrementing—the "pre" indicating that the increment operator precedes its operand. Placing the ++ before the variable *num* is called postfix incrementing—the "post" indicating that the increment operator follows its operand.

In this example, it makes no difference to the output of the program whether you use prefix or postfix incrementing. The reason is that the statement ++*num* has only one operator; the same is true of the statement *num*++. However, there is a difference between prefix and postfix incrementing when the statement has more than one operator. This is discussed later in this chapter in the section "The Difference Between Prefix and Postfix."

The Decrement Operator

In the following program, the statement *num* −= *1* decreases the value of the integer variable *num,* which was initialized to the value 2, by 1, so the output will be 1.

```
#include <iostream>
using namespace std;
int main(void)
{
    int num = 2;
    num -= 1;
    cout << num;
    return 0;
}
```

Another way to accomplish the same result is by using the decrement operator, --. The decrement operator, like the increment operator, is unary, operating on one op erand which generally is a whole number variable, such as an int. We can use the decrement operator simply by changing the program we just ran and replacing the statement *num −= 1* with the statement *num--*:

```cpp
#include <iostream>
using namespace std;
int main(void)
{
    int num = 2;
    num--;
    cout << num;
    return 0;
}
```

The same output would occur if you substituted the statement *--num* for *num--*:

```cpp
#include <iostream>
using namespace std;
int main(void)
{
    int num = 2;
    --num;
    cout << num;
    return 0;
}
```

As with the increment operator, placing the -- before the variable *num* is called prefix decrementing, while placing the -- after the variable *num* is called postfix decrementing.

Also, as with the example of the increment operator, in this example it makes no difference to the output of the program whether you use prefix or postfix decrementing because the statement *--num* (or *num--*) has only one operator. However, as discussed in the next section, "The Difference Between Prefix and Postfix," there is a difference between prefix and postfix decrementing (or incrementing) when the statement has more than one operator.

The Difference Between Prefix and Postfix

The following program is similar to the previous program that illustrated the increment operator.

```
#include <iostream>
using namespace std;
int main(void)
{
    int num = 2;
    cout << num++;
    return 0;
}
```

However, instead of two statements:

```
num++;
cout << num;
```

This program uses one statement:

```
cout << num++;
```

There are two operators in this cout statement: the increment operator ++ and the stream insertion operator <<. The issue is one of precedence; which operation occurs first.

The output of this program is 2. The reason is that when an increment or decrement operator is postfix, that operation is the *last* to occur. Therefore, the output of *num* occurs first while the variable's value is still 2, and then the value of *num* is incremented from 2 to 3.

Now, change the line:

```
cout << num++;
```

to the line:

```
cout << ++num;
```

so the program now reads

```
#include <iostream>
using namespace std;
int main(void)
{
    int num = 2;
    cout << ++num;
    return 0;
}
```

This time, the output of this program is 3 instead of 2. The reason is that when an increment or decrement operator is prefix, that operation is the *first* to occur. Therefore, *num* first is incremented from 2 to 3 before the value of *num* is outputted.

The distinction between prefix and postfix also arises frequently with arithmetic operators. In the following code fragment, the value of *result* is 15, not 18, because *op2* is incremented from 5 to 6 after the multiplication and assignment occurs.

```
int op1 = 3, op2 = 5, result;
result = op1 * op2++;
```

If prefix incrementing instead were used, as in the following code fragment, the value of *result* is 18, not 15, because *op2* is incremented from 5 to 6 before the multiplication and assignment occurs.

```
int op1 = 3, op2 = 5, result;
result = op1 * ++op2;
```

The distinction between prefix and postfix arises as well with relational operators. In the following code fragment, the output is 1 (the integer representation of Boolean true) because the integer variable *num* is compared to 5 for equality before *num* is incremented from 5 to 6.

```
int num = 5;
cout << (num++ == 5);
```

If prefix incrementing instead were used, as in the following code fragment, then the output would be 0 (the integer representation of Boolean false) because the integer variable *num* is incremented from 5 to 6 before it is compared to 5 for equality.

```
int num = 5;
cout << (++num == 5);
```

The increment and decrement operators generally are not used by themselves, but in conjunction with loops. The next section covers one type of loop: the for loop.

The For Loop

If you wanted to output the numbers between 1 and 10, you could write a program such as the following:

```
#include <iostream>
using namespace std;
int main(void)
{
    int num = 1;
    cout << num++;
    cout << num++;
    cout << num++;
```

```
    cout << num++;
    cout << num++;
    cout << num++;
    cout << num++;
    cout << num++;
    cout << num++;
    cout << num++;
    return 0;
}
```

However, you could write the same program with far less code by using a for loop:

```
#include <iostream>
using namespace std;
int main(void)
{
    for (int num = 1; num <= 10; num++)
        cout << num << " ";
    return 0;
}
```

The difference between the two programs becomes more pronounced if you change the specification from outputting the numbers between 1 and 10 to outputting the numbers between 1 and 100. I won't rewrite the first program because it would take up too many pages; suffice it to say, you would have to add 90 more cout statements. However, the same program using a for loop would be:

```
#include <iostream>
using namespace std;
int main(void)
{
    for (int num = 1; num <= 100; num++)
        cout << num << " ";
    return 0;
}
```

Indeed, by using the for loop, the same code could output the numbers between 1 and 1000 or even 1 and 10000; you just would need to change the 100 in the code to 1000 or 10000.

The for loop is one of three types of loops; the other two (while and do while) will be covered in the next chapter. A loop is a structure that repeats the execution of code until a condition becomes false. Each repetition is called an *iteration*.

In the example that printed out the numbers between 1 and 10, the output of the value of *num* was repeated as long as the condition—the value of *num* being less than or equal to 10—remained true. There were ten iterations of this loop; that is, the current value of *num* was outputted ten times.

The Syntax of the For Loop

Let's discuss the syntax of the for loop. The for keyword is followed by parentheses that contain three expressions that will be discussed in a moment. This line of code is followed by one or more statements.

The three expressions contained in the parentheses following the for keyword are separated by semicolons; there is no semicolon after the third expression since no expression follows it.

The first expression usually is used to initialize the value of a variable, typically referred to as a counter, to provide that variable with a starting value. In this example, the integer variable *num* is initialized to the starting value of 0. This initialization is the first action performed by the loop, and is only performed once.

The second expression is the condition, which must be true for the code inside the loop to execute. In this example, the condition is whether the current value of *num* is less than or equal to 10.

The third expression usually is used to update the value of the counter. In this example, the integer variable *num* is incremented. This expression executes at the end of each iteration, and only executes if the condition was true at the beginning of the iteration.

NOTE: *Postfix incrementing was used in this example and generally is employed by convention. However, the result would be the same if prefix incrementing were used, as only one operator is involved in this expression.*

Therefore, the order of execution in the first iteration of the loop is

1. The integer variable *num* is initialized to 1.
2. The current value of *num,* 1, is compared to 10.
3. Since the comparison is true, the current value of *num,* 1, is outputted.
4. The value of *num* is incremented, becoming 2.

The order of execution in the second iteration of the loop is

1. The current value of *num,* 2, is compared to 10.
2. Since the comparison is true, the current value of *num,* 2, is outputted.
3. The value of *num* is incremented, becoming 3.

Note that the initialization that occurred during the first iteration of the loop did not occur during the second iteration of the loop. As discussed previously, initialization occurs only once, in the first iteration of the loop.

This order of execution in the second iteration of the loop repeats during the third and following executions of the loop, each time incrementing the value of *num* through the tenth iteration of the loop, which executes in the following order:

1. The current value of *num,* 10, is compared to 10.

2. Since the comparison is true (10 is less than or equal to 10), the current value of *num,* 10, is outputted.

3. The value of *num* is incremented, becoming 11.

In the next iteration of the loop, the current value of *num,* 11, is compared to 10. Since the comparison is false (11 is not less than or equal to 10), the for loop ends. The code inside the for loop does not execute, the value of num is not incremented, and the code following the for loop executes. In this example, the code following the for loop is the return 0 statement, so the program ends.

Note: The preceding examples used the increment operator. However, you also can use the decrement operator. Changing the parentheses following the keyword to (int num = 10; num >= 1; num--) would result in the numbers between 1 and 10 being outputted in reverse. Note that the relational operator is changed from >= to <=.

In the example of outputting the numbers between 1 and 10, only one statement belonged to the for loop. However, as with the if structure, if more than one statement belongs to the for loop, then the statements must be contained within curly braces.

```
for (int num = 1; num <= 10; num++)
{
    cout << num << " ";
    cout << "Next loop ";
}
```

Also, as with the if structure, the statement or statements following the for keyword and parentheses will not execute if the parentheses are followed by a semi-colon since that would be interpreted as an empty statement. Accordingly, in the following code fragment, the only number that would output is 11:

```
for (int num = 1; num <= 10; num++);
    cout << num << " ";
```

The reason the output would be 11 is that the loop continues, and the empty statement executes, until the condition fails when *num* is 11. The cout statement is not part of the for loop, so it executes when the for loop completes, outputting 11, the value of *num* after the loop finishes.

The expressions do not need be inside the parentheses following the for loop. In the following program, *num* is initialized before the for loop, and is incremented inside the body of the loop.

```cpp
#include <iostream>
using namespace std;
int main(void)
{
    int num = 1;
    for (; num <= 10;)
    {
        cout << num << " ";
        num++;
    }
    return 0;
}
```

Even though initialization and incrementing are not done within the parentheses, two semicolons are nevertheless within the parentheses to separate where the three expressions would be. While an expression may be empty, the semicolon nevertheless is necessary.

Beware the Infinite Loop

In the preceding program, if the statement num++ was omitted, the loop would never stop:

```cpp
#include <iostream>
using namespace std;
int main(void)
{
    int num = 1;
    for (; num <= 10;)
    {
        cout << num << " ";
    }
    return 0;
}
```

The reason is that the condition *num <= 10* would never become false since *num* would start at 0 and its value would never change because the statement *num++* was omitted.

This loop that never stops executing is called an *infinite loop*. Usually, it manifests itself by a character or characters appearing in rapid succession in your console window, with the application never ending.

You would not intend an infinite loop in your code, but mistakes do happen; I have made this mistake a lot more than once. If it happens to you, don't panic. You can use the CTRL-BREAK keyboard combination to end the program. Knowing you have encountered an infinite loop, you then can correct the code error that caused it.

A Factorial Example

So far, use of the for loop has been relatively trivial, counting numbers in ascending or descending order. However, the for loop can be used for more sophisticated programs.

The following program calculates the factorial of a number inputted by the user. A factorial is the product of all the positive integers from 1 to that number. For example, the factorial of 3 is 3 * 2 * 1, which is 6, while the factorial of 5 is 5 * 4 * 3 * 2 * 1, which is 120.

```
#include <iostream>
using namespace std;
int main(void)
{
    int num, counter, total = 1;
    cout << "Enter a number: ";
    cin >> num;
    cout << "The factorial of " << num << " is ";
    for (int counter = 1; counter <= num; counter++)
        total *= counter;
    cout << total;
    return 0;
}
```

Input and output could be

```
Enter a number: 4
The factorial of 4 is 24
```

Breaking Out of a Loop

We previously used the break keyword in a switch statement. You also can use the break keyword in a for loop. The break keyword is used within the code of a for loop, commonly within an if / else structure. If the break keyword is reached, the for loop terminates, even though the condition still is true.

For example, in the following program, the user is given three tries to guess a number (which happens to be 3) between 1 and 10. However, if the user guesses the number on their first or second try, it would be pointless to ask them again to guess the number. Accordingly, if the user guesses the number, the break statement is used to break out of the loop.

```cpp
#include <iostream>
using namespace std;
int main(void)
{
    int num, counter, secret = 3;
    cout << "Guess a number between 1 and 10\n";
    cout << "You have 3 tries\n";
    for (int counter = 1; counter <= 3; counter++)
    {
        cout << "Enter the number now: ";
        cin >> num;
        if (num == secret)
        {
            cout << "You guessed the secret number!";
            break;
        }
    }
    cout << "Program over";
    return 0;
}
```

Here are two sample inputs and outputs. In the first one, the user tried three times without guessing correctly. In the second one, the user guessed correctly on their second try, so there was no third iteration of the loop due to the break keyword.

```
Guess a number between 1 and 10
You have 3 tries
Enter the number now: 2
Enter the number now: 4
Enter the number now: 6
Program over
-------------------
Guess a number between 1 and 10
You have 3 tries
Enter the number now: 2
Enter the number now: 3
You guessed the secret number!
Program over
```

While the break keyword is part of the C++ language, I recommend you use it sparingly. Normally, the for loop has one exit point, the condition when it becomes false. However, when you use one or more break statements, the for loop has multiple exit points. This makes your code more difficult to understand, and can result in logic errors.

In the following program, the logical && (And) operator is an alternative to using the break keyword.

```cpp
#include <iostream>
using namespace std;
int main(void)
{
    int num, counter, secret = 3;
    cout << "Guess a number between 1 and 10\n";
    cout << "You have 3 tries\n";
    bool keepgoing = true;
    for (int counter = 1; counter <= 3 && keepgoing == true;
        counter++)
    {
        cout << "Enter the number now: ";
        cin >> num;
        if (num == secret)
        {
            cout << "You guessed the secret number!";
            keepgoing = false;
        }
    }
    cout << "Program over";
    return 0;
}
```

Before leaving the discussion of the break keyword, one additional use of it (in conjunction with the parentheses following the for keyword being empty of all three expressions) deserves mention simply because you may encounter it. The following program is a variant of the one that outputs numbers between 1 and 10 with the first and third expressions inside the parentheses being empty because *num* is initialized before the for loop and incremented inside the body of the loop. In this program, the second expression—the condition—is missing as well. Instead, the break keyword inside the if/else structure substitutes for that condition.

```cpp
#include <iostream>
using namespace std;
int main(void)
{
    int num = 1;
    for (;;)
    {
        if (num > 10)
            break;
        else
        {
```

```
            cout << num << " ";
            num++;
        }
    }
    return 0;
}
```

Without the break keyword, the for loop would be infinite due to the lack of a second expression. Again, however, I do recommend against this use of the break keyword, and point it out simply because other programmers believe differently—thus, you're likely to encounter it at some point in time.

The Continue Keyword

You also can use the continue keyword in a for loop. The continue keyword, like the break keyword, is used within the code of a for loop, commonly within an if/else structure. If the continue statement is reached, the current iteration of the loop ends, and the next iteration of the loop begins.

For example, in the following program, the user is charged $3 an item, but not charged for a "baker's dozen." In other words, every 13th item is free—in other words, the user is charged for only a dozen items, instead of 13.

```
#include <iostream>
using namespace std;
int main(void)
{
    int num, counter, total = 0;
    cout << "How many items do you want to buy: ";
    cin >> num;
    for (int counter = 1; counter <= num; counter++)
    {
        if (counter % 13 == 0)
            continue;
        total += 3;
    }
    cout << "Total for " << num << " items is $" << total;
    return 0;
}
```

Here are three sample inputs and outputs, illustrating that the price for 12 or 13 items is the same, but on the 14th item the user again is charged an additional $3. The reason why the code charges the user no additional price for the 13th item is that the continue statement is reached, preventing three dollars from being added to the total.

```
How many items do you want to buy: 12
Total for 12 items is $36
---------------
How many items do you want to buy: 13
Total for 13 items is $36
-----------------
How many items do you want to buy: 14
Total for 14 items is $39
```

While the continue keyword is part of the C++ language, I recommend, as I do with the break keyword, that you use it sparingly. Normally, each iteration of a for loop has one end point. However, when you use a continue statement, each iteration has multiple end points. This makes your code more difficult to understand, and can result in logic errors.

In the following program, the logical ! (Not) operator is an alternative to using the continue keyword.

```cpp
#include <iostream>
using namespace std;
int main(void)
{
    int num, counter, total = 0;
    cout << "How many items do you want to buy: ";
    cin >> num;
    bool keepgoing = true;
    for (int counter = 1; counter <= num; counter++)
    {
        if (! (counter % 13 == 0 ))
            total += 3;
    }
    cout << "Total for " << num << " items is $" << total;
    return 0;
}
```

NOTE: *You also could use the relational != (not equal) operator, changing the if statement to if (counter % 13 != 0).*

Nesting For Loops

You can nest a for loop just as you can nest if statements. For example, the following program prints five rows of ten X characters:

```cpp
#include <iostream>
using namespace std;
```

```cpp
int main(void)
{
    for (int x = 1; x <= 5; x++)
    {
        for (int y = 1; y <= 10; y++)
            cout << "X";
        cout << '\n';
    }
    return 0;
}
```

The for loop *for (int x = 1; x <= 5; x++)* is the outer for loop. The for loop *for (int y = 1; y <= 10; y++)* is the inner for loop.

With nested for loops, for each iteration of the outer for loop, the inner for loop goes through all its iterations. By analogy, in a clock, minutes are the outer loop, seconds the inner loop. In an hour, there are 60 iterations of minutes, but for each iteration of a minute, there are 60 iterations of seconds.

In the rows and columns example, for the first iteration of the outer for loop, the inner for loop goes through all ten of its iterations, printing ten X characters and one new line character. Then, for the next iteration of the outer for loop, the inner for loop again goes through all ten of its iterations, again printing ten X characters and one new line character. The same thing happens on the third, fourth, and fifth iterations of the outer for loop, resulting in five rows of ten X characters.

While nested for loops can be used to print rows and columns for tables, they also have other uses. For example, the following program prompts the user for the total number of salespersons as well as the number of sales per salespersons, and has the user input each sale of each salesperson, and then afterward displays the average sale for each salesperson. The number of iterations of the outer for loop will be the number of salespersons. The number of iterations of the inner for loop will be the number of sales per salesperson.

```cpp
#include <iostream>
using namespace std;
int main(void)
{
    int persons, int numSales;
    cout << "Enter number of salespersons: ";
    cin >> persons;
    cout << "Enter number of sales per salesperson: ";
    cin >> numSales;
    for (int x = 1; x <= persons; x++)
    {
        int sale, total = 0;
```

```
        float average;
        for (int y = 1; y <= numSales; y++)
        {
            cout << "Enter sale " << y << " for salesperson "
                 << x <<": ";
            cin >> sale;
            total += sale;
        }
        average = (float) total / numSales;
        cout << "Average sales for salesperson #" << x
             << " is " << average << endl;
    }
    return 0;
}
```

The input and output could be

```
Enter number of salespersons: 2
Enter number of sales per salesperson: 3
Enter sale 1 for salesperson 1: 4
Enter sale 2 for salesperson 1: 5
Enter sale 3 for salesperson 1: 7
Average sales for salesperson #1 is 5.33333
Enter sale 1 for salesperson 2: 8
Enter sale 2 for salesperson 2: 3
Enter sale 3 for salesperson 2: 4
Average sales for salesperson #2 is 5
```

NOTE: *If you place a break or continue keyword in the inner loop, it will affect only that inner loop, and have no effect on the outer loop.*

Summary

You use a loop to repeat the execution of code statements. A loop is a structure that repeats the execution of code until a condition becomes false.

You learned in this chapter how to use one type of loop: the for loop. However, before discussing the for loop, I showed you how to use increment and decrement operators, which are used in for and other types of loops. I then explained the difference between prefix and postfix when using the increment and decrement operators.

You also learned in this chapter how to use the break keyword to prematurely terminate a for loop and the continue keyword to prematurely terminate the current iteration of the loop. You then learned how to use the logical operators as an alternative to the break and continue keywords. You also learned about nesting one for loop inside another.

The for loop generally is used when the loop will execute a fixed number of times. However, sometimes the number of times a loop will execute is unpredictable, depending on user input during runtime. For example, in a data entry application, you may want a loop that, upon entry of invalid data, asks the user whether they want to retry or quit, and if they want to retry, gives the user another opportunity to enter data. The number of times this loop may execute is unpredictable, since it will keep repeating until the user either enters valid data or quits.

The next chapter will show you how to use two other types of loops, the while loop and the do while loop, that work better than a for loop when the number of times a loop will execute is unpredictable.

Quiz

1. What does the increment operator do?

2. What does the decrement operator do?

3. Which occurs first, decrementing or the outputting of the value of *num*, in the statement *cout << --num?*

4. What is an iteration?

5. What is the usual purpose of the first expression in the parentheses following the for keyword?

6. What is the purpose of the second expression in the parentheses following the for keyword?

7. What is the usual purpose of the third expression in the parentheses following the for keyword?

8. Can one or more of the expressions in the parentheses following the for keyword be empty?

9. What is the purpose of the break keyword in a for loop?

10. What is the purpose of the continue keyword in a for loop?

11. If you were going to use nested for loops to print rows and columns, which for loop would print the columns—inner or outer?

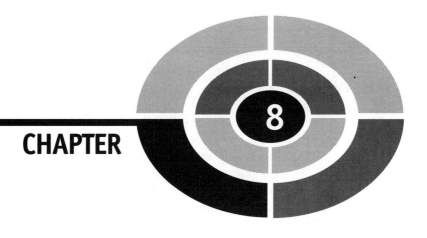

CHAPTER

8

While and Do While Loops

The for loop generally is used when the loop will iterate a fixed number of times. However, sometimes the number of times a loop will iterate is unpredictable, depending on user input during runtime. For example, in a data entry application, you may want a loop that, upon entry of invalid data, asks the user whether they want to retry or quit, and if they want to retry, gives the user another opportunity to enter data. The number of times this loop may iterate is unpredictable, since it will keep repeating until the user either enters valid data or quits.

This chapter will show you how to use the while loop, which is a better choice than a for loop when the number of times a loop will iterate is unpredictable.

While the total number of loop iterations may be unpredictable, there often are situations in which the loop will iterate at least once. An example is a loop that displays a menu with various choices, including exiting the program. In this menu example, the menu always displays at least once; the user cannot choose to exit before being given that choice. In such situations, a do while loop, which this chapter will show you how to use, is a better choice than a while loop.

The While Loop

The while loop is similar to a for loop in that both have the typical characteristics of a loop: the code inside each continues to iterate until a condition becomes false. The difference between them is in the parentheses following the for and while keywords.

The parentheses following the for keyword consists of three expressions, initialization, condition, and update. By contrast, the parentheses following the while keyword consists only of the condition; you have to take care of any initialization and update elsewhere in the code.

This difference is illustrated by the following program that outputs the numbers between 1 and 10. Chapter 7 included the following program that outputs the numbers between 1 and 10 using the for loop.

```cpp
#include <iostream>
using namespace std;
int main(void)
{
    for (int num = 1; num <= 10; num++)
        cout << num << " ";
    return 0;
}
```

The same program using the while loop could be

```cpp
#include <iostream>
using namespace std;
int main(void)
{
    int num = 1;
    while (num <= 10)
    {
        cout << num << " ";
        num++;
    }
    return 0;
}
```

NOTE: The two statements in the body of the while loop could have been combined into one statement, cout << num++. Two statements are used instead to make this example easier to understand by eliminating the precedence issue in the one statement between the stream insertion and increment operators.

With the while loop, the integer variable *num* had to be declared and initialized before the loop since this cannot be done inside the parentheses following the while keyword. Further, *num* was updated inside the code of the loop using the increment operator. This update also can be done inside the parentheses following the while keyword as shown by an example later in this section.

The update of the variable is particularly important with the while loop. Without that update, the loop would be infinite. For example, in the following excerpt from this program, if num is not incremented, the loop would be infinite. The value of num would not change from 1, so the condition *num <= 10* always would remain true.

```
int num = 1;
while (num <= 10)
    cout << num << " ";
```

Forgetting to update the value of the variable you are using in the condition is a common mistake with a while loop. Forgetting the update is less common with a for loop because that update is the usual purpose of the third expression in the paren theses following the for keyword.

Otherwise, the syntax rules discussed in Chapter 7 concerning the for loop apply equally to the while loop. For example, if more than one statement belongs to the while loop, then the statements must be contained within curly braces. That is why in the program that outputs the numbers between 1 and 10 using the while loop, the two statements in the body of the while loop are contained within curly braces.

```
while (num <= 10)
{
    cout << num << " ";
    num++;
}
```

In the program we just analyzed, the update of the value of *num* was done within the body of the loop. The update could also be done within the condition itself:

```
#include <iostream>
using namespace std;
int main(void)
{
    int num = 0;
    while (num++ < 10)
        cout << num << " ";
    return 0;
}
```

Updating the counter within the condition requires two changes from the previous code. First, the value of *num* has to be initialized to 0 instead of to 1 because the increment inside the parentheses during the first iteration of the loop would change that variable's value to 1. Second, the relational operator in the condition is < rather than <= because the value of *num* is being incremented before it is outputted.

Updating the counter within the condition raises the question: Given the condition *num++ < 10,* which comes first, the comparison or the increment? Since the increment is postfix, the answer is the comparison.

The counter also could be updated within the condition using a prefix increment. However, then the condition should be *++num <= 10* to obtain the desired output.

As with the for loop, the statement or statements following the while keyword and parentheses will not execute if the parentheses is followed by a semicolon, as that would be interpreted as an empty statement. Test yourself on this; what would be the output if we placed a semicolon after the while condition as in the following code fragment?

```
while (num <= 10);
    cout << num++ << " ";
```

The only number that would output is 11. The reason is that the loop continues, and the empty statement executes, until the condition fails when *num* is 11, at which time the statement following the loop executes and the value of *num* (11) is outputted.

Comparison of for and while Loops

The practical difference between the for and while loops is not apparent in a program with a predictable number of iterations, such as the program we have been discussing thus far that outputs the numbers between 1 and 10. Rather, a while loop is a superior choice to a for loop in a program where the number of iterations is unpredictable, depending on user input during runtime.

For example, in the following program, the program asks the user to enter a positive number, and in a loop continues that request until the user does so. The number of times this loop may execute is unpredictable. It may never execute if the user enters a positive number the first time, or it may execute many times if it takes the user several tries to enter a positive number.

```
#include <iostream>
using namespace std;
int main(void)
{
    int num;
    cout << "Enter a positive number: ";
    cin >> num;
```

```
    while (num <= 0)
    {
       cout << "Number must be positive; please retry: ";
       cin >> num;
    }
    cout << "The number you entered is " << num << " ";
    return 0;
}
```

Here is some sample input and output:

```
Enter a positive number: 0
Number must be positive; please retry: -1
Number must be positive; please retry: 3
The number you entered is 3
```

This program would be more difficult to write with a for loop. While it could be done, the for loop is designed for situations in which the number of iterations is predictable.

Using the break Keyword

Even though the while loop is a better choice than a for loop for this program, which requires the user to enter a positive number, there are two problems with this program: one minor and one major.

The minor problem is that there is some repetition of code; the user is requested both before and inside the loop to enter a positive number. A do while loop, which is explained in the following section, avoids this repetition, but repeats other code (there are tradeoffs in loops as well as in life).

The major problem is that the user is trapped inside the loop until they enter a positive number. That is not a good programming design. While the user should be required to enter good data if they are going to enter any data at all, they should have the option, when told the data entered was not valid, of quitting the data entry.

The following modification of the program uses the break keyword to provide the user with the option of quitting the data entry:

```
#include <iostream>
using namespace std;
int main(void)
{
    int num;
    char choice;
    cout << "Enter a positive number: ";
    cin >> num;
```

```
    while (num <= 0)
    {
       cout << "Number must be positive; try again (Y/N): ";
       cin >> choice;
       if (choice == 'Y')
       {
          cout << "Enter number: ";
          cin >> num;
       }
       else
          break;
    }
    cout << "The number you entered is " << num << " ";
    return 0;
}
```

Here is some sample input and output when the user eventually enters a positive number:

```
Enter a positive number: 0
Number must be positive; try again (Y/N): Y
Enter number: -1
Number must be positive; try again (Y/N): Y
Enter number: 3
The number you entered is 3
```

Here is some sample input and output when the user does not enter a positive number but instead decides to quit:

```
Enter a positive number: -2
Number must be positive; try again (Y/N): N
The number you entered is -2
```

Flags

The flags modification is an improvement because the user no longer is trapped inside the loop until they enter a positive number, but instead has the option of quitting data entry. However, the second sample input and output, in which the user quits data entry, illustrates a problem. The final cout statement outputs the number entered, even if the number is invalid data.

Ideally, we would only want to output the data if it were valid. If the data were not valid, then we would want to output that fact instead. However, the code thus far does not enable us to differentiate whether the while loop ended because the user entered valid data or because the user decided to quit after entering invalid data.

In Chapter 7, I recommended that you use the break keyword sparingly because it created multiple exit points for the for loop, making your code more difficult to understand and increasing the possibility of logic errors. That advice also applies to the while loop. I recommended then, and recommend now, as an alternative the use of a logical operator. The following program modification adopts that alternative.

```cpp
#include <iostream>
using namespace std;
int main(void)
{
    int num;
    char choice;
    bool quit = false;
    cout << "Enter a positive number: ";
    cin >> num;
    while (num <= 0 && quit == false)
    {
        cout << "Number must be positive; try again (Y/N): ";
        cin >> choice;
        if (choice != 'Y')
        {
            cout << "Enter number: ";
            cin >> num;
        }
        else
            quit = true;
    }
    if (quit == false)
        cout << "The number you entered is " << num << " ";
    else
        cout << "You did not enter a positive number";
    return 0;
}
```

Here is some sample input and output when the user eventually enters a positive number:

```
Enter a positive number: -3
Number must be positive; try again (Y/N): Y
Enter number: 3
The number you entered is 3
```

Here is some sample input and output when the user does not enter a positive number but instead decides to quit. This time the final output is not of the number entered, but rather that the user did not enter a positive number:

```
Enter a positive number: 0
Number must be positive; try again (Y/N): Y
Enter number: -1
Number must be positive; try again (Y/N): N
You did not enter a positive number
```

This program modification, in addition to using the logical && operator, uses a Boolean variable named *quit*. This Boolean variable is used as a *flag*. A flag is a Boolean variable whose value indicates whether a condition exists.

In this program, the while loop continues to loop as long as the data entered is invalid *and* the user wants to keep going. Accordingly, the while keyword is followed by two conditions, joined by the logical && operator.

NOTE: A common programming mistake in a while condition using a logical operator is to use && when you should use || or vice versa. While the logical && operator may seem the obvious choice in this example, the correct choice in other situations may be less intuitive. For example, if you want to loop while a number is not between 1 and 10, would the loop be while (num < 1 && num > 10) or while (num < 0 || num > 10)? The answer is the latter; the condition always would be false using the && operator since a number cannot be both less than 1 and greater than 10. If you wanted to use the && operator, the condition instead would be while (num >= 1 && num <= 10).

The first condition is if *num* <= 0. If this expression is false, the data is valid, so the issue of whether the user wants to quit does not arise. Accordingly, the second condition, whether *quit* is true, is not even evaluated. As discussed in Chapter 7, with a logical && operator, the right expression is evaluated only if the left expression is true. Therefore, the while loop ends with the value of *quit* being false, its initialized value, and code execution continues with the if / else statement following the while loop.

However, if *num* <= 0 is true, then the data is invalid, and the second condition, whether *quit* is true, is evaluated.

The value of *quit* may be true under either of two possibilities. The first possibility is that this is the user's first attempt to enter data and the data was invalid. In this case, the user has not yet been asked whether they want to quit. It is assumed they don't, so they have the opportunity to answer whether they want to retry. Therefore, the *quit* variable is initialized to the value of false when it is declared.

The second possibility is that this is the user's second or later attempt to enter data and the data was invalid. In this case, the user has already been asked whether they want to quit, so the value of quit is based on the user's answer.

If the value of *quit* is false, the while loop continues. However, if the user wants to quit, then the right expression *quit == false* will be false because the value of *quit* is true. Therefore, the while loop ends with the value of *quit* being true, and code execution continues with the if / else statement following the while loop.

At some point (hopefully) the while loop will end, either because the user has entered a valid number or has not and decided to quit trying. Code execution then continues with the if / else statement following the while loop.

The value of *quit* being false necessarily indicates that the user entered valid data, because if they were still trying to do so, the loop would not have ended. Conversely, the value of *quit* being true necessarily indicates that the user entered invalid data.

Accordingly, we use the value of *quit* in the if / else statement after the while loop to differentiate whether the while loop ended because the user entered valid data or instead decided to quit after entering invalid data.

Thus, inside the while loop, *quit* is a flag whose value indicates whether the user wants to try again, and after the while loop ends, *quit* is a flag whose value indicates whether the user entered valid data.

While (true)

In Chapter 7, we discussed the use of the for loop with the omission of the condition that is the second expression, such as *for (; ;)*. There, an infinite loop was avoided by using the break keyword inside the loop. While I did not recommend this use of the for loop, I mentioned it because you may encounter it as programmers do use the for loop this way.

Similarly, programmers sometimes make the condition of the while loop always true, such as while (true) or while (1), and break out of the while loop with, you guessed it, the break keyword. Here is an example that is a modification of the program we have been using that asks the user to enter a positive number.

```cpp
#include <iostream>
using namespace std;
int main(void)
{
    int num;
    char choice;
    bool quit = false;
    while (true)
    {
        cout << "Enter a positive number: ";
        cin >> num;
        if (num > 0)
```

```
      break;
      else
      {
      cout << "Number must be positive; try again (Y/N): ";
      cin >> choice;
      if (choice != 'Y')
      {
      quit = true;
      break;
      }
      }
   }
   if (quit == false)
      cout << "The number you entered is " << num << " ";
   else
      cout << "You did not enter a positive number";
   return 0;
}
```

The one advantage of this modification is that it renders unnecessary having to prompt the user both before and inside the loop to enter a positive number. However, the use of the *while (true)* syntax has the disadvantage of making your code less readable because the condition that stops the loop cannot be discerned from the parentheses following the while keyword. The do while loop (explained later in this chapter) avoids this disadvantage and would be a preferable choice.

The continue Keyword

You can use the continue keyword in a while loop just as you can in a for loop. As discussed in Chapter 7, the continue keyword, like the break keyword, is used within the code of a loop, commonly within an if / else structure. If the continue statement is reached, the current iteration of the loop ends, and the next iteration of the loop begins.

Chapter 7 demonstrated the use of the continue keyword in a program in which the user is charged $3 an item, but not charged for a "baker's dozen," so every 13th item is free—that is, the user is only charged the price for a dozen items, even though they receive 13. The following is a modification of that program using a while loop.

```
#include <iostream>
using namespace std;
int main(void)
```

```
{
   int num, counter = 0, total = 0;
   cout << "How many items do you want to buy: ";
   cin >> num;
   while (counter++ < num)
   {
      if (counter % 13 == 0)
         continue;
      total += 3;
   }
   cout << "Total for " << num << " items is $" << total;
   return 0;
}
```

NOTE: *The % (modulus) operator is used if the remainder is 0, 13, or a multiple of 13 items.*

While this use of the continue keyword certainly works, as I cautioned in Chapter 7, you should use it (as well as the break keyword) sparingly. Normally, each iteration of a for loop has one end point. However, when you use a continue statement, each iteration has multiple end points. This makes your code more difficult to understand, and can result in logic errors.

I suggested in Chapter 7, in an example using the for loop, that you could use the logical ! (Not) operator as an alternative to using the continue keyword. Here is how you could do so using the while loop.

```
#include <iostream>
using namespace std;
int main(void)
{
   int num, counter = 0, total = 0;
   cout << "How many items do you want to buy: ";
   cin >> num;
   bool keepgoing = true;
   while (counter++ < num)
   {
      if (! (counter % 13 == 0 ))
         total += 3;
   }
   cout << "Total for " << num << " items is $" << total;
   return 0;
}
```

NOTE: *You also could use the relational != (not equal) operator, changing the if statement to if (counter % 13 != 0).*

Nesting While Loops

In Chapter 7, I showed you how you can nest one for loop inside another. Similarly, you can nest one while loop inside another. You also can nest a while loop inside of a for loop, or a for loop inside of a while loop.

Chapter 7 demonstrated nested for loops with a program that prints 5 rows of 10 X characters. The following is a modification of that program using nested while loops.

```
#include <iostream>
using namespace std;
int main(void)
{
    int x = 0;
    while (x++ < 5)
    {
        int y = 0;
        while (y++ < 5)
            cout << "X";
        cout << '\n';
    }
    return 0;
}
```

The variable *y,* used as a counter in the inner while loop, needs to be reinitialized in the outer while loop. The variable *y* could be declared outside the loops, but it needs to be assigned (or reassigned) the value of zero inside the outer loop since the inner loop goes through all of its iterations for each iteration of the outer loop.

Since each loop has a predictable number of iterations, using nested for loops is somewhat simpler than using nested while loops. However, both work.

The Do While Loop

The do while loop is similar to the while loop. The primary difference is that with a do while loop the condition is tested at the bottom of the loop, unlike a while loop where the condition is tested at the top. This means that a do while loop will always execute at least once, whereas a while loop may never execute at all if its condition is false at the outset.

Syntax

The syntax of a do while loop is

```
do {
    statement(s);
} while (condition);
```

The do keyword starts the loop. The statement or statements belonging to the loop are enclosed in curly braces. After the close curly brace, the while keyword appears, followed by the condition in parentheses, terminated by a semicolon.

A Do While Loop Example

The following program is a modification of the one earlier in this chapter that used a while loop to continue to prompt the user to enter a positive number until the user either did so or quit, and then either outputted the positive number or a message that the user did not enter a positive number. This modification uses a do while loop instead of a while loop.

```cpp
#include <iostream>
using namespace std;
int main(void)
{
    int num;
    char choice;
    bool quit = false;
    do {
        cout << "Enter a positive number: ";
        cin >> num;
        if (num <= 0)
        {
        cout << "Number must be positive; try again (Y/N): ";
        cin >> choice;
        if (choice != 'Y')
        quit = true;
        }
    } while (num <= 0 && quit == false);
    if (quit == false)
        cout << "The number you entered is " << num << " ";
    else
        cout << "You did not enter a positive number";
    return 0;
}
```

The following are sample inputs and outputs. The first one has the user success-fully enter a positive number the first time.

```
Enter a positive number: 4
The number you entered is 4
```

The next sample input and output has the user enter a positive number after two unsuccessful tries.

```
Enter a positive number: 0
Number must be positive; try again (Y/N): Y
Enter a positive number: -1
Number must be positive; try again (Y/N): Y
Enter a positive number: 4
The number you entered is 4
```

The final sample input and output has the user quit after two unsuccessful tries.

```
Enter a positive number: 0
Number must be positive; try again (Y/N): Y
Enter a positive number: -1
Number must be positive; try again (Y/N): N
You did not enter a positive number
```

Comparison of the Do While and While Loop

The preceding program, which used the do while loop, did not need to prompt the user both before and inside the loop to enter a number as did the corresponding program that used the while loop. However, this program using the do while loop repeats the *num <= 0* condition inside the loop, whereas the corresponding program that used the while loop did not need to do that.

As a general rule, I prefer a do while loop over a while loop in those situations in which the loop must execute at least once before a condition may be tested, simply because under these circumstances it seems illogical to test the condition prematurely on the first iteration of the loop. As you may recall, in the program variation that used the while loop, the value of *quit* could be true in the loop condition under either of two possibilities, one being it was the user's first attempt to enter data so the user has not yet been asked whether they want to quit, and the other being it was the user's second or later attempt to enter data and the user answered that they wanted to quit. By con-trast, using the do while loop eliminates the first possibility.

The preceding program, in which the user had to enter a number, whether that number is positive or not, is an example of the situation in which the loop must exe-cute at least once before a condition may be tested. Another common example of this situation is when a menu is displayed. Assume the program displays a menu such as the following:

```
Menu
====
1. Add an entry
2. Edit an entry
3. Delete an entry
4. Exit
```

If the user chooses options 1, 2, or 3, the program performs the indicated operation (add, edit, or delete) and then again displays the menu for the user's next choice. If the user chooses option 4, the program ends.

In this menu example, the menu always displays at least once; the user cannot choose to exit before being given that choice. Accordingly, a do while loop normally is preferable to a while loop when choosing a loop to display a menu.

Scope

With a do while loop, it is important that a variable used in the condition following the while keyword not be declared inside the loop.

In the program that demonstrated the do while loop, the variables num and *quit* were declared before the loop:

```
int num;
char choice;
bool quit = false;
do {
    // statements
} while (num <= 0 && quit == false);
```

These variables could not be declared inside the do while loop, as in the following code excerpt, because the code would not compile. The parentheses following the while keyword is highlighted, and the compiler error is that *num* and *quit* are undeclared identifiers.

```
char choice;
do {
    int num;
    bool quit = false;
    // more statements
} while (num <= 0 && quit == false);
```

The reason why this alternative will not compile concerns variable *scope*.

As you know from Chapter 3, a variable must be declared before it can be referred to in code. Once a variable is declared, it may be referred to wherever in the code it has scope.

Thus far, variables have been declared in main, just after the open curly brace which begins the body of the main function. This gives these variables scope until the close curly brace, which ends the body of the main function. Since thus far our programs have had only one function, main, as a practical matter, the variables, once declared, could be referred to throughout the entire program.

In this example, however, the variables *num* and *quit* are declared after the open curly brace that begins the body of the do while loop. That means their scope is limited to the area between that open curly brace and the close curly brace that ends the body of the do while loop. This area between an open and close curly brace also is referred to as a *block*.

The while keyword and the parentheses that follow it are outside the body of the do while loop, or put another way, after the close curly brace that ends the body of the do while loop. Since the variables *num* and *quit* were declared within the body of the do while loop, they do not have scope outside the body of the loop where the while parentheses are located. Therefore, these variables are regarded as undeclared when referred to within those parentheses.

This issue arises far more often with the do while loop than with the for or while loops. With for or while loops, the condition precedes the body of the loop, so any variables used in the condition necessarily would be declared before the loop or, in the case of the for loop, within the parentheses following the for keyword. By contrast, since the condition of a do while loop comes after the body of the loop, it is an easy mistake to declare the variables used in the condition before it, in the body of the loop.

This is our first discussion of the variable scope issue. However, it is by no means our last. This issue is not limited to the do while loop. It arises frequently when we start adding other functions to our programs, as we will do in upcoming chapters.

Summary

Chapter 7 introduced the first of several loops: the for loop. The for loop works well in situations where the loop will iterate a fixed number of times.

Often, however, the number of times a loop will iterate is unpredictable since the number of iterations depends on user input during runtime. One example discussed in this chapter is a data entry application in which the loop, upon entry of invalid data, asks the user whether they want to retry or quit, and if they want to retry, gives the user another opportunity to enter data. The number of times this loop may iterate is unpredictable, since it will keep repeating until the user either enters valid data or quits.

This chapter showed you how to use the while loop, which works better than a for loop when the number of times a loop will execute is unpredictable. While the parentheses following the for keyword consists of three expressions, initialization, condition, and update, the parentheses following the while keyword consists only of the condition; you have to take care of initialization and update elsewhere in the code.

There also are situations in which, while the number of times this loop may execute is unpredictable, the loop will execute at least once. An example discussed in this chapter is a loop that displays a menu with various choices, including exiting the program. In this menu example, the menu always displays at least once; the user cannot choose to exit before being given that choice. In such situations, a do while loop is a better choice than a while loop. This chapter showed you how to use a do while loop, and introduced the issue of variable scope.

So far, all of our programs have had only one function, main. While all programs must have a main function, a C++ program may have additional functions. As programs get more sophisticated, it is helpful not to put all the code in main, but instead to allocate the code among different functions. The next chapter will show you how to add and use additional functions.

Quiz

1. Which of the three loops—for, while, or do while—executes at least once?

2. Which of the three loops—for, while, or do while—is the best choice when the number of iterations is predictable?

3. Is the parenthetical expression following the while keyword for initialization, condition or update?

4. May the parenthetical expression following the while keyword be true, such as *while (true)*?

5. Can the parenthetical expression following the while keyword combine two expressions?

6. What is the purpose of the break keyword in a while loop?

7. What is the purpose of the continue keyword in a while loop?

8. What is a flag?

9. If you were going to use nested while loops to print rows and columns, which for loop would print the rows, inner or outer?

10. Does a variable declared inside the body of a do while loop have scope in the parenthetical expression following the while keyword?

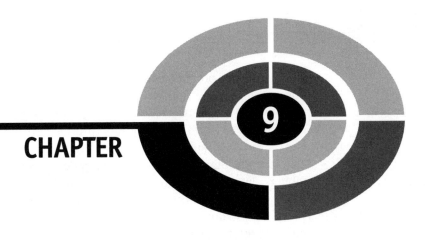

CHAPTER 9

Functions

A function is a group of statements that together perform a task. So far, our programs have had one function, *main*. Additionally, at times we have used functions defined in a standard library, such as the *pow* function in the *cmath* library, used to raise a number to a certain power.

No program needs more than a *main* function. However, as you write more complex and sophisticated programs, you may find your *main* function becoming extremely long.

Neither the compiler nor the runtime cares if your *main* function is short or long. However, you should care. A *main* function that continues for pages is difficult to understand or fix if errors arise.

By analogy, this book is several hundred pages long. It would be harder to understand if each chapter was not divided into sections. This book would be still harder to understand if it consisted of only one, very long chapter. By dividing this book's content into chapters, and each chapter into sections, this book is easier to understand.

Similarly, you can divide up your code into separate functions. How you divide up your code among different functions is up to you, but logically the division usually is so each function performs a specific task.

For example, in a program that performs arithmetic calculations, one function obtains user input, another function performs the calculation, and a third function performs output of the result. This is analogous to how a book is divided up into chapters and sections. Each chapter explores a different subject. One chapter focuses on variables, another (this one) on functions.

There are advantages to dividing your code into separate functions in addition to making your code easier to understand. For example, if a function performs a specific task, such as sending output to a printer, which is performed several times in a program, you only need to write once in a function the code necessary to send output to the printer, and then call that function each time you need to perform that task. Otherwise, the code necessary to send output to the printer would have to be repeated each time that task was to be performed.

Hopefully, I have persuaded you that organizing your code into separate functions can be useful. I will now show you how to do it.

Defining and Calling a Function

Implementing any function in addition to *main* involves two steps:

1. Defining the function
2. Calling the function

The explanation of these steps uses terminology we have not discussed before, so that terminology is reviewed first.

Terminology of a Function

Let's look at a simple program with one function, *main:*

```
#include <iostream>
using namespace std;
int main ()
{
   cout << "Hello world!";
   return 0;
}
```

The first line, int main (), is the *function header*. Unlike a statement, the function header is not followed by a semicolon.

The function header consists of a *return type,* a *function name,* and an *argument list.* The data type int preceding main is the return type, main is the function name, and the parentheses, empty in this example but not always, contains the argument list.

A function header always is followed by an open curly brace, which begins the *function body.* The function body ends with a close curly brace. There may be other open and curly braces between the open curly brace that begins the function body and the close curly brace that ends it, such as to enclose multiple statements that belong to an if statement or a loop.

The function body consists of one or more statements. In this example, the function body consists of two statements. The last statement, *return 0,* is a *return statement.* The function body must contain a return statement unless the return type is void, in which case the return statement is optional.

The function header and body together are referred to as the *function definition.* A function cannot execute until it is first defined. Once defined, a function executes when it is *called.*

Normally, a function is called through code. The *main* function is the exception. The *main* function is called automatically when your program begins to run.

The next sections will explain how to define your own function and then call it.

Defining a Function

Let's take our "Hello World" example and divide the code into two functions, *main* and a *printMessage* function that outputs "Hello world!" The comments (beginning with //) indicate the beginning and end of the definition of the *printMessage* function and where that function is called.

```
#include <iostream>
using namespace std;

// begins definition of printMessage function
void printMessage (void)
{
    cout << "Hello world!";
}
// ends definition of printMessage function
int main ()
{
    printMessage(); // calls printMessage function
    return 0;
}
```

The *printMessage* function is defined first. The *void* keyword preceding the function name *printMessage* means that this function does not return a value. The *void* keyword in parentheses following the function name means this function has no arguments. The parentheses also could be left empty, such as after *main;* empty parentheses following the function name in a function header is the same as placing the *void* keyword within the parentheses. Which syntax you choose is a matter of taste; one is no better or worse than the other.

The body of the *printMessage* function has one statement, which outputs "Hello world!" The function body does not need to contain an explicit return statement because, since the return type is void, the return statement is implied. However, you may include an explicit return statement. If you did, then the *printMessage* function would read

```cpp
void printMessage (void)
{
    cout << "Hello world!";
    return;
}
```

Calling a Function

Unless the *printMessage* function is called, it is the programming equivalent of the tree that falls in the forest without anyone seeing or hearing it; it is there in the program, but it doesn't do anything. The *printMessage* function is called in *main* with the line:

```cpp
printMessage();
```

In this example, *printMessage* is the *called function,* since it is the function being called from *main.* The empty parentheses indicate that no arguments are being passed to this function. I will show you later in this chapter how to pass arguments, as well as how to use return values.

The order of execution is as follows:

1. Execution always starts with the main function.

2. The first statement in main, *printMessage(),* is executed.

3. Execution next shifts to the *printMessage* function, and begins with the first statement in that function, which outputs "Hello world!"

4. After the *printMessage* function completes executing, execution returns to the *main* function with the next unexecuted statement, *return 0,* which completes the *main* function.

Figure 9-1 shows the order of execution graphically.

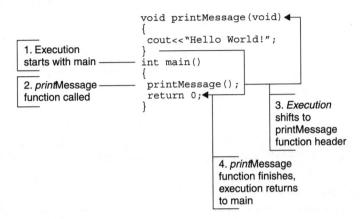

Figure 9-1   Order of execution of the Hello World Program

Prototyping

Since execution always starts with main, it seems more logical to place the main function first, ahead of the *printMessage* function, such as in the following example:

```
#include <iostream>
using namespace std;

int main ()
{
    printMessage();
    return 0;
}
void printMessage (void)
{
    cout << "Hello world!";
}
```

However, this code will not compile. The call in *main* to *printMessage()* will be highlighted, with the compiler error message being "undeclared identifier."

The reason for this compiler error is that when the compiler, going from top to bottom in your code, encounters a function call, it must already know of the function's name, return type, and arguments. This was not a problem when the *printMessage* function was defined above the main function. However, when the *printMessage* function was defined below the main function, when the compiler encounters the call in *main* to *printMessage()*, it does not yet know of the *printMessage* function's name, return type, and arguments.

One solution to this problem is to define all functions above *main*. However, this may make your code difficult to read. A program's execution always starts with *main*, regardless of the order in which functions are defined. In a program with many functions, the *main* function often acts as a "switchboard," calling one function after another. Therefore, viewing the *main* function can provide an excellent overview of the order of events. Burying the *main* function beneath numerous other functions requires someone reviewing your code to hunt for *main* to obtain that overview. Additionally, in complex programs in which one function calls another function which calls still another function, the order in which to define these functions to avoid a compiler error can be confusing.

The solution of preference is to *prototype* each function, except *main,* which does not have to be prototyped since it is required by every program. The following program shows how to prototype the *printMessage* function in the Hello World program:

```cpp
#include <iostream>
using namespace std;
void printMessage(void);   // this is the prototype!

int main ()
{
   printMessage();
   return 0;
}
void printMessage (void)
{
   cout << "Hello world!";
}
```

The prototype is above all function definitions. This ensures that the compiler, compiling the code from top to bottom, will encounter the prototype before any function.

The prototype is similar to a function header. The primary difference is that it has a semicolon at the end because it is a statement. By contrast, a function header must not be followed by a semicolon.

NOTE: *There are other differences between the prototype and the function header when, unlike here, the parentheses following the function name includes one or more arguments. Those differences will be discussed in the section "Sending Information to a Function" later in this chapter.*

Variable Scope and Lifetime

Thus far, all variables have been defined at the top of the *main* function. In programs where the only function is *main,* those variables can be accessed throughout the entire program since *main* is the entire program. However, once we start dividing up the code into separate functions, issues arise concerning variable *scope* and *lifetime*.

The issue of variable scope was introduced in Chapter 8 in connection with the do while loop. The issue of variable lifetime is new.

Local Variables

You can call the same function multiple times. The following program attempts to call the *printMessage* function in a loop until the user decides to stop, and each time outputs the number of times the *printMessage* function has been called. The goal is that the first time the *printMessage* function is called, the output will be "This function called 1 times" (pardon the bad grammar), the second time the *printMessage* function is called, the output will be "This function called 2 times" and so on.

```cpp
#include <iostream>
using namespace std;
void printMessage(void);

int main ()
{
    int times = 0;
    char choice;
    do {
        cout << "Enter Q to quit, any other character to continue: ";
        cin >> choice;
        if (choice == 'Q')
            cout << "Input stopped";
        else
            printMessage();
        } while (choice != 'Q');
    return 0;
}
void printMessage (void)
{
    times++;
    cout << "This function called " << times << " times\n";
}
```

This code will not compile. The reference to the string variable *times* in the *printMessage* function will be highlighted, the error message being that this variable is an "undeclared identifier."

The reason for the compiler error is that the scope of the variable *times* is limited to the *main* function in which it was declared. The issue of variable scope was discussed in Chapter 8 in connection with the do while loop. You cannot refer to a variable outside the scope in which it was declared. A variable's scope is within the curly braces in which it was declared. Therefore, the scope of the variable *times* is limited to the *main* function. Stated another way, the variable *times* is a *local variable,* in this case local to the *main* function. An attempt to access a local variable outside of the function in which it was declared results in a compiler error.

This compiler error can be fixed by moving the declaration of times into the *printMessage* function as in the following program:

```cpp
#include <iostream>
using namespace std;
void printMessage(void);

int main ()
{
    char choice;
    do {
        cout << "Enter Q to quit, any other character to continue: ";
        cin >> choice;
        if (choice == 'Q')
            cout << "Input stopped";
        else
            printMessage();
        } while (choice != 'Q');
    return 0;
}
void printMessage (void)
{
    int times = 0;
    times++;
    cout << "This function called " << times << " times\n";
}
```

Here is some sample input and output:

```
Enter Q to quit, any other character to continue: X
This function called 1 times
Enter Q to quit, any other character to continue: Y
This function called 1 times
```

```
Enter Q to quit, any other character to continue: Z
This function called 1 times
Enter Q to quit, any other character to continue: Q
Input stopped
```

While this program compiles, the output is not exactly what we wanted. The variable *times* in the *printMessage* function does not "remember" the previous times that function was called.

Variables, like people, have a lifetime. A person's lifetime begins at birth. A variable's lifetime begins when it is declared. A person's lifetime ends with death. A variable's lifetime ends when it goes out of scope.

The variable *times* is local to the *printMessage* function since it was declared in that function. Being a local variable, each time the *printMessage* function is called, the variable *times* is created, and each time the *printMessage* function ends, the variable *times* is destroyed. Accordingly, the variable *times* the second time the *printMessage* function is called is not a continuation of the variable *times* that was created the first time the *printMessage* function was called. Rather, the variable *times* starts all over again each time the *printMessage* function is called.

There are two alternative methods to having the value of a variable persist between function calls. One is to make the variable global rather than local. The other is to keep the variable local but make it static. These alternatives are covered next.

Global Variables

A variable may be *global* instead of local. The term global means that the variable has scope throughout the program. Since the variable has scope throughout the program, its lifetime does not end until the program ends.

To make a variable global, it must be declared above all function definitions, generally with function prototypes. The following program makes only one change from the previous one. The declaration of the variable *times* is moved from inside *main* to above *main,* making *times* a global variable.

```
#include <iostream>
using namespace std;
void printMessage(void);
int times;

int main ()
{
    times = 0;
    char choice;
    do {
```

```
        cout << "Enter Q to quit, any other character to continue: ";
        cin >> choice;
        if (choice == 'Q')
           cout << "Input stopped";
        else
           printMessage();
        } while (choice != 'Q');
    return 0;
}
void printMessage (void)
{
    times++;
    cout << "This function called " << times << " times\n";
}
```

Here is some sample input and output:

```
Enter Q to quit, any other character to continue: X
This function called 1 times
Enter Q to quit, any other character to continue: Y
This function called 2 times
Enter Q to quit, any other character to continue: Z
This function called 3 times
Enter Q to quit, any other character to continue: Q
Input stopped
```

This is the output we wanted!

Perhaps because of the ease of using global variables to solve the issue of the scope and lifetime of the times variable, beginning programmers often make all variables global so they can access these variables anywhere and anytime in their program. This is not a good idea.

While the good news is that a global variable can be accessed throughout your program, this also is the bad news. The fact that a global variable can be accessed and changed anywhere in your program makes it more difficult to determine why, for example, a global variable has an invalid value than if the variable's scope was far more limited. This is simply because the more limited a variable's scope, the less places there are in the code that might affect its value.

Therefore, global variables can make it more difficult to fix problems with your programs. For this reason, some programmers, and programming teachers, go to the extreme and pronounce that "all global variables are evil." I'm not sure I would go that far, but I would recommend that you not use global variables unless you have a very good reason to do so, since there usually are better alternatives. One alternative, a static local variable, is examined next.

Static Local Variables

Up until now a variable's lifetime was dictated by its scope. Since a local variable's scope was limited to the function in which it was declared, the local variable's lifetime ended when that function ended. Since a global variable had scope throughout a program, the global variable's lifetime did not end until the entire program ended.

A static local variable is different. A static local variable has the scope of a local variable but the lifetime of a global variable. This may seem counter-intuitive, so to illustrate let's modify the *printMessage* function we have been working with.

A static local variable is declared exactly like a local variable, within a function rather than above all functions as with a global variable. The difference between the declaration of a static local variable and a nonstatic, or automatic, local variable is that a static local variable is declared with the *static* keyword, and usually also with a starting value. Thus, in the following program, instead of the declaration

```
int times;
```

the declaration is

```
static int times = 0;
```

Here is the program in its entirety:

```
#include <iostream>
using namespace std;
void printMessage(void);

int main ()
{
   char choice;
   do {
      cout << "Enter Q to quit, any other character to continue: ";
      cin >> choice;
      if (choice == 'Q')
         cout << "Input stopped";
      else
         printMessage();
      } while (choice != 'Q');
   return 0;
}
void printMessage (void)
{
   static int times = 0;
```

```
    times++;
    cout << "This function called " << times << " times\n";
}
```

Here is some sample input and output:

```
Enter Q to quit, any other character to continue: X
This function called 1 times
Enter Q to quit, any other character to continue: Y
This function called 2 times
Enter Q to quit, any other character to continue: Z
This function called 3 times
Enter Q to quit, any other character to continue: Q
Input stopped
```

This output also is correct. Let's now analyze how the program works.

The first time the *printMessage* function is called, the variable *times* is declared, and initialized to zero, by the statement:

```
static int times = 0;
```

The variable *times* then is incremented and outputted, resulting in the output:

```
This function called 1 times
```

So far, this is the same as when *times* was an automatic local variable rather than a static local variable. The difference is that when the *printMessage* function ends, *times,* being a static local variable, is *not* destroyed. That variable and its value remain in memory.

The next (second) time the *printMessage* function is called, the statement declaring and initializing variable *times* is *not* executed because that variable, being static, still exists from the first time the *printMessage* function was called. Further, the value of the *times* variable at the end of the first call of the *printMessage* function, 1, remains in memory. That value then is incremented to 2, and outputted, so the output to the second call of the *printMessage* function is

```
This function called 2 times
```

Accordingly, we were able to persist the value of the *times* variable between function calls by making that variable either global or static local. The difference was that as a static local variable the scope of *times* still was limited to the *printMessage* function, as opposed to having scope throughout the program if it were a global variable. This more limited scope would make it easier to fix your program if the value of the *times* variable were incorrect somewhere in your code.

Sending Information to a Function

The *printMessage* function in the Hello World program outputs "Hello world!" It does not need any further information to do its job.

Let's make the *printMessage* function more useful so that it does not always output "Hello world" but instead outputs whatever message we ask it to. Of course, the *printMessage* function is not a mind reader; we need to tell it the message we want it to output.

Let's try to write a program in which the user enters in *main* the string to be outputted, that user input is stored in a string variable *str*, and then the *printMessage* function attempts to output the value of that *str* variable. One approach is to make the variable *str* global so it can be accessed in both the *main* and *printMessage* functions:

```
#include <iostream>
#include <string>
using namespace std;
void printMessage();
string str;

int main ()
{
    cout << "Enter a string: ";
    cin >> str;
    printMessage( );
    return 0;
}
void printMessage ( )
{
    cout << "You inputted " << str;
}
```

Note: *With a string variable, a statement cin >> str does not compile unless you include the <string> standard library. Additionally, the cin object and the stream insertion operator (>>) will only accept the input of a string variable up to the first embedded white space. Therefore, if the input were "Jeff Kent," the output still would be only "Jeff." In Chapter 10, we will cover the getline function, which will work with string input that has embedded spaces.*

Here is some sample input and output:

```
Enter a string: Jeff
You inputted Jeff
```

While this works, as discussed in the previous section, global variables can make it more difficult to fix problems with your programs. There is a better alternative here, involving passing arguments.

As discussed earlier in this chapter, the parentheses following the function name in the function header contain the function's arguments. Arguments are information that is provided to a function so that it may perform its task.

As also discussed earlier, some functions don't need further information to do their job, such as the *printMessage* function in the Hello World program, which simply outputs "Hello world!" It does not need any further information to do its job.

However, when we want to modify the *printMessage* function so that it does not always output "Hello world!" but instead outputs whatever message we ask it to, we need to tell it the message we want it to output. We can do so by passing the function an argument that specifies the message.

This chapter will discuss two ways of passing arguments, by value and by reference. A third way, passing arguments by address, will be covered after we discuss pointers in Chapter 11.

Passing Arguments by Value

The following is a modification of the program that uses the *printMessage* function to output a message. This time, the content of the message to be output is passed to the *printMessage* function as an argument:

```cpp
#include <iostream>
#include <string>
using namespace std;
void printMessage(string);

int main ()
{
    string str;
    cout << "Enter a string: ";
    cin >> str;
    printMessage(str);
    return 0;
}
void printMessage (string s)
{
```

```
   cout << "You inputted " << s;
}
```

Here is some sample input and output:

```
Enter a string: Jeff
You inputted Jeff
```

The Function Prototype and Header

Both the function prototype and the function header have one argument, of the string data type. However, the function prototype's argument just has the argument's data type (string), whereas the function header's argument has both a data type and an argument name (string s).

The function prototype may include an argument name as well as data type, as in:

```
void printMessage(string someArg);
```

However, that argument is called a *dummy argument* because it serves no purpose.

By contrast, the function header's argument must include an argument name as well as a data type. The purpose of that argument name in the function header's argument is explained next.

Using the Function Argument

The following code calls the *printMessage* function:

```
   printMessage(str);
```

The string variable *str,* whose value previously was assigned by user input, is passed as an argument to the *printMessage* function. The value of *str* then is passed to the string variable *s,* which is the argument name in the function header of the *printMessage* function:

```
void printMessage (string s)
```

The string variable *s* then is used in the body of the *printMessage* function to output the message:

```
   cout << "You inputted " << s;
```

Figure 9-2 shows how the value of the argument of the function call is passed to the argument in the function header and then used in the body of the called function.

The function header must include an argument name as well as a data type so the value which is being passed by the function call, stored in *str* in *main,* may be stored in a variable that can be used in the *printMessage* function. Otherwise, the value passed would have no place to be stored for use in the *printMessage* function.

```
...
int main()
{
 ...
 printMessage(str);
 return0;
}

void printMessage (string s)
{
 count<<"You inputted"<<s;
}
```

Value of *str*
copied into *s*

Figure 9-2   The passing of the function argument

The argument name in the function header can be the same as the name of the variable passed in the function argument:

```
printMessage(str);
void printMessage (string str)
```

Even if so, the *str* in *main* is a separate variable from the *str* in *printMessage*. Nevertheless, I recommend, to avoid confusion, using different names in the program.

Using Multiple Function Arguments

The program we just discussed used one function argument. However, a function may have two or even more function arguments.

The following modification of the *printMessage* function uses two arguments, one for the first name and one for the last name:

```
#include <iostream>
#include <string>
using namespace std;
void printMessage(string, string);

int main ()
{
   string name1, name2;
   cout << "Enter first name: ";
   cin >> name1;
   cout << "Enter last name: ";
   cin >> name2;
   printMessage(name1, name2);
   return 0;
}
void printMessage (string firstName, string lastName)
{
```

```
    cout << "Your name is " << firstName << " " << lastName
<< endl;
}
```

Here is some sample input and output:

```
Enter first name: Jeff
Enter last name: Kent
Your name is Jeff Kent
```

The order of arguments in the function call must correspond to the order of the arguments in the function header. The function call and the function header here are

```
printMessage(first, last);
void printMessage (string firstName, string lastName)
```

The first variable in the function call is *name1*. Therefore, the value of *name1* in main is copied into the first variable in the *printMessage* function header, *firstName*. Similarly, since the second variable in the function call is *name2*, the value of *name2* in *main* is copied into the second variable in the *printMessage* function header, *lastName*.

If the arguments in the function call were reversed, as in:

```
printMessage(last, first);
```

then the sample input and output instead would be

```
Enter first name: Jeff
Enter last name: Kent
Your name is Kent Jeff
```

In this example, not paying careful attention to the correspondence between the order of arguments in the function call and the order of the arguments in the function header resulted in my name being outputted backwards. However, the consequences of a lack of correspondence between the order of arguments in the function call and the order of the arguments in the function header is more drastic when the multiple function arguments have different data types.

In the following program, the first argument, the person's name, is a string, whereas the second argument, the person's age, is a different data type, an integer.

```
#include <iostream>
#include <string>
using namespace std;
void printMessage(string, int);

int main ()
{
    string name;
```

```
    int age;
    cout << "Enter name: ";
    cin >> name;
    cout << "Enter age: ";
    cin >> age;
    printMessage(name, age);
    return 0;
}
void printMessage (string theName, int theAge)
{
    cout << "Your name is " << theName
        << " and your age is " << theAge << endl;
}
```

Here is some sample input and output (fortunately the program has no way to verify my age):

```
Enter first name: Jeff Kent
Enter age: 21
Your name is Jeff Kent and your age is 21
```

The function call and the function header here are

```
printMessage(name, age);
void printMessage (string theName, int theName)
```

The first argument of the *printMessage* function expects a string, so it is critical that the first argument in the function call is a string. Similarly, the second argument of the *printMessage* function expects an integer, so it is critical that the second argument in the function call is an integer. If the arguments in the function call were reversed, as in:

```
printMessage(age, name);
```

then the consequence would not be illogical output as in the prior example, but instead a compiler error "cannot convert parameter 1 from 'int' to 'string'." This is because the compiler was expecting from the function prototype that the first argument (or parameter) would be a string, not an int.

Passing Arguments by Reference

Passing arguments by value is fine when you don't want to change their value in the called function. The *printMessage* function did not change the value of its arguments; it simply outputted them.

However, sometimes the intent of a function is to change the value of the argument passed to it. Consider the following example, in which the *doubleIt* function is
supposed to double the value of the argument passed to it:

```cpp
#include <iostream>
using namespace std;
void doubleIt(int);

int main ()
{
    int num;
    cout << "Enter number: ";
    cin >> num;
    doubleIt(num);
    cout << "The number doubled in main is " << num << endl;
    return 0;
}
void doubleIt (int x)
{
    cout << "The number to be doubled is " << x << endl;
    x *= 2;
    cout << "The number doubled in doubleIt is "
    << x << endl;
}
```

Here is some sample input and output:

```
Enter number: 3
The number to be doubled is 3
The number doubled in doubleIt is 6
The number doubled in main is 3
```

As the sample input and output reflects, the value of *num* was not changed by the
doubling of its counterpart argument in the *doubleIt* function.

The reason the value of *num* was not changed in *main* is that a copy of it was
passed to *doubleIt*. The change was made to the copy, but the original, the variable
num in *main,* was not affected by the doubling of the copy. The logic is the same as if
I gave you a copy of this page, which you then proceeded to rip up. The original I
kept would be unaffected.

In order for the called function to change the value in *main* of a variable passed to
it, the variable must be passed by *reference.* The variable in the called function is
called a *reference variable.* The reference variable is not a copy of the variable in
main. Instead, the reference variable is an alias for the variable in main. You may
recall from television that an alias is another name a person may use, such as James

Bond's alias of 007. However, whether you refer to him as James Bond or 007, you are still referring to the same person.

In order to pass a variable by reference, the data type in the argument, both in the function header and in the prototype, is followed by an ampersand. Yes, this is the same ampersand that is used as the address operator. Here, however, the ampersand is used in a different context.

The following program passes the variable to be doubled by reference:

```
#include <iostream>
using namespace std;
void doubleIt(int&);

int main ()
{
    int num;
    cout << "Enter number: ";
    cin >> num;
    doubleIt(num);
    cout << "The number doubled in main is " << num << endl;
    return 0;
}
void doubleIt (int& x)
{
    cout << "The number to be doubled is " << x << endl;
    x *= 2;
    cout << "The number doubled in doubleIt is " << x << endl;
}
```

Here is some sample input and output:

```
Enter number: 3
The number to be doubled is 3
The number doubled in doubleIt is 6
The number doubled in main is 6
```

There were only two changes. The prototype and function header for *doubleIt* when the argument is passed by value is

```
void doubleIt(int);
void doubleIt (int x)
```

By contrast, the prototype and function header for *doubleIt* when the argument is passed by reference each includes the ampersand following the data types:

```
void doubleIt(int&);
void doubleIt (int& x)
```

However, the function call is the same whether the variable is passed by value or by reference; there is no ampersand in either case. Whether the program passes an argument in a function call by value or by reference is dictated by the function's prototype.

You can pass multiple values by reference as well as by value. Indeed, you can pass some values by reference and others by value. You pass by reference those values you need to change, and you pass by value those values you are not changing.

NOTE: *There is another difference between passing by value and passing by reference. You can pass by value expressions and constants (constants are covered in Chapter 10) as well as variables. However, you can only pass variables by reference.*

For example, in the following program the function *addNumbers* has three arguments. The first two arguments are the numbers to be added, and are passed by value. The third argument will be the sum of the two numbers and will be passed by reference, since its value is being changed in the called function:

```
#include <iostream>
using namespace std;
void addNumbers(int, int, int&);

int main ()
{
    int firstNum, secondNum, sum = 0;
    cout << "Enter first number: ";
    cin >> firstNum;
    cout << "Enter second number: ";
    cin >> secondNum;
    addNumbers (firstNum, secondNum, sum);
    cout << firstNum << " + " << secondNum << " = " << sum;
    return 0;
}
void addNumbers (int x, int y, int& z)
{
    z = x + y;
}
```

Here is some sample input and output:

```
Enter first number: 3
Enter first number: 6
3 + 6 = 9
```

Returning a Value from a Function

Arguments are used to pass values to a called function. A return value can be used to pass a value from a called function back to the function that called it.

For example, in the previous program the function *addNumbers* had three arguments, the first two being the numbers to be added, the third being their sum. The following program modifies the previous one by eliminating the third argument, but adding a return value to the function:

```cpp
#include <iostream>
using namespace std;
int addNumbers(int, int);

int main ()
{
   int firstNum, secondNum, sum = 0;
   cout << "Enter first number: ";
   cin >> firstNum;
   cout << "Enter second number: ";
   cin >> secondNum;
   sum = addNumbers (firstNum, secondNum);
   cout << firstNum << " + " << secondNum << " = " << sum;
   return 0;
}
int addNumbers (int x, int y)
{
   return x + y;
}
```

The sample input and output may be the same as in the previous program:

```
Enter first number: 3
Enter first number: 6
3 + 6 = 9
```

The return value is added by indicating its data type, here an int, in front of the function name in both the function prototype and header:

```cpp
int addNumbers(int, int);
int addNumbers (int x, int y)
```

The function call is on the right side of the assignment operator. To the left of the assignment operator is a variable of the same data type as the return value of the function. The concept is that the return value from the function call is assigned to the variable *sum* on the left side of the assignment operator.

```
sum = addNumbers (firstNum, secondNum);
```

The body of the called function has the return keyword followed by a value of the data type compatible with the function prototype and header, here int. The function's return value is the value that follows the return keyword, here the sum of the two arguments:

```
return x + y;
```

That sum of x + y then is assigned to the variable sum in *main*.
Figure 9-3 shows the order of execution graphically.

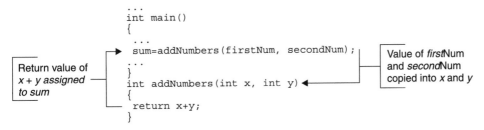

Figure 9-3   The order of execution of the return value of a function

It is common that a function returning a value is called on the right side of an assignment operator with a variable on the left side of the assignment operator to capture the return value. However, this is not required. In the program, the variable *sum* was not necessary. Instead of the lines

```
sum = addNumbers (firstNum, secondNum);
cout << firstNum << " + " << secondNum << " = " << sum;
```

the return value could have been displayed as:

```
cout << firstNum << " + " << secondNum <<   " = "
    << addNumbers (firstNum, secondNum);
```

The only difference is that once this cout statement completes, the return value of the function cannot be used in later statements since it was not stored in a variable. In this program, that is not a problem because the return value is not used again. However, if you are going to use a return value more than once, it's generally a good idea to store that return value in a variable. This is typically done by calling the function on the right side of an assignment operator with a variable on the left side of the assignment operator to capture the return value.

While multiple values can be passed to a function as arguments, at this point, multiple values cannot be returned from functions using the data types we have covered so far. This will change when we cover arrays in the next chapter, and structures and classes in later chapters.

Summary

A function is a group of statements that together perform a task. While no program needs more than a *main* function, as you write more complex and sophisticated programs, your code will be easier to write, understand, and fix if you divide the code up among different functions, each function performing a specific task.

You implement a function in addition to *main* by first defining it and then calling it. A function definition consists of a function header and a function body. The function header consists of a return type, a function name, and an argument list. The function header always is followed by an open curly brace, which begins the *function body*. The function body ends with a close curly brace and contains one or more statements, generally ending with a return statement. Additionally, unless the function is defined above where it is called, it must be prototyped.

In programs where the only function is *main,* all variables defined at the top of that function necessarily can be accessed throughout the entire program. However, once we start dividing up the code into separate functions, issues arise concerning variable scope and lifetime. A variable's scope determines where it can be referred to in the code. A variable's lifetime determines when it is destroyed. A local variable's scope and lifetime is limited to the function in which it was declared. By contrast, a global variable's scope and lifetime are throughout the entire program. Finally, a static local variable's scope is limited to the function in which it was declared like a local variable, but its lifetime lasts throughout the entire program like a global variable.

You can pass information to a function by using arguments, and pass arguments by value or by reference. You can also pass a variable argument by value when you don't intend any change to that variable in the called function to affect that variable's value in the calling function. Conversely, you pass a variable argument by reference when you intend a change to that variable in the called function to affect that variable's value in the calling function. The order and data type of the arguments in the function prototype must correspond to the order and data type of the arguments in the function header. Similarly, the order and data type of the arguments in the function call must correspond to the order and data type of the arguments in the function header.

While arguments are used to pass values to a called function, a return value can be used to pass a value from a called function back to the function that called it. However, while multiple values can be passed to a function as arguments, multiple values cannot be returned from functions.

So far, the variables we've used have only been able to hold one value at a time. In the next chapter, we'll discuss a type of variable that can hold multiple values simultaneously.

Quiz

1. What is the difference between variable scope and lifetime?
2. Must a function other than main be prototyped?
3. Is a function required to have at least one argument?
4. Can a function have more than one argument?
5. What is the effect on a variable in *main* if it is passed by value to another function which changes the argument corresponding to that variable?
6. What is the effect on a variable in main if it is passed by reference to another function which changes the argument corresponding to that variable?
7. Must a function have a return value?
8. Can a function have more than one return value?
9. May a function have neither a return value nor any arguments?
10. May a function have both a return value and arguments?

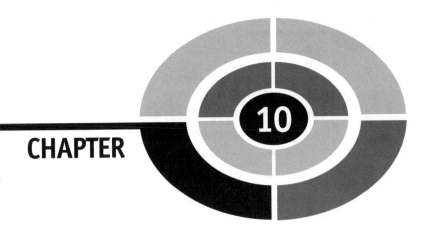

Arrays

The variables we have worked with so far can hold only one value at a time. For example, if you declare an integer variable named *testScore* to represent a student's test score, that variable can hold only one test score.

The fact that the variable *testScore* can hold only one test score is not a problem so long as that student only takes one test. However, if the same student takes another test, or another student takes the same test, where do you store the second test score? If you store the second score in *testScore,* then you lose the ability to retrieve the first score from the variable *testScore,* since that variable can hold only one test score at a time.

Therefore, if you wanted to keep track of, for example, 100 test scores, your code might look like this:

```
int testScore1;
int testScore2;
int testScore3;
int testScore4;
int testScore5;
int testScore6;
int testScore7;
int testScore8;
int testScore9;
int testScore10;
```

```
// declare testScore11 through testScore99
int testScore100;
```

Yikes! That's a lot of code to write. Wouldn't it be easier just to declare 1 variable that can hold 100 values, like this:

```
int testScore[100];
```

The good news is you can do exactly that, using an array! An array enables you to use a single variable to store many values. The values are stored at consecutive indexes, starting with zero and then incrementing by one for each additional element of the array.

Using 1 array variable to store 100 values has many advantages over having to declare 100 separate variables that can hold only 1 value each. In addition to being a lot less code to write, it is far easier to keep track of 1 variable than 100. Furthermore, and more important, as I will show you in this chapter, you can use a loop to access each consecutive element in an array, whereas this is not possible with three separate variables.

Declaring an Array

An array is a variable. Therefore, like the other variables we have covered so far, an array must be declared before it can be used.

The syntax for declaring an array is almost identical to the syntax for declaring integers, characters, or other variables. For example, you would declare an integer variable *testScore* as follows:

```
int testScore;
```

By contrast, you would declare an array of three test scores this way:

```
int testScore[3];
```

This declaration contains an array of integers. You instead could declare an array of floats, characters, or strings in the following manner:

```
float GPA [5];
char grades[7];
string names[6];
```

While an array may be one of several data types, all the values in a particular array must be of the same data type. You cannot have an array in which some elements are floats, others are strings, still others are integers, and so on.

The declaration of both a single variable and an array of variables begins with the data type followed by a variable name and ending with a semicolon. The only difference between declaring a variable that holds a single value and an array is that, when declaring an array, the variable name is followed by a number within square brackets. That number is the array's *size declarator.*

NOTE: *There is one exception to the necessity of having a size declarator. As discussed later in this chapter in the section on "Initialization," the square brackets may be empty if you initialize the array when you declare it.*

The purpose of the size declarator is to tell the computer how much memory to reserve. The size declarator, combined with the data type of the array, determines how much memory to reserve.

As you may recall from Chapter 3, the declaration of a variable reserves memory for the number of bytes required by the data type of that variable, that number of bytes depending on the particular operating system and compiler. For example, if an integer variable required 4 bytes on your operating system and compiler, then declaring the integer variable *testScore* would reserve 4 bytes. If instead you declared an array of three integer variables, then the amount of memory reserved by that declaration would be 12 bytes, 4×3.

TIP: *You should give careful consideration to the number of elements in an array before you declare the array since you can't resize an array in the middle of a program in the event the array is too small or unnecessarily large. Sometimes, the number of elements is obvious; an array of the days in a week will have seven elements. However, other times the number of elements is not intuitive. In those circumstances, you should err on the side of declaring too many rather than too few elements. The reason is that the consequence of declaring too many elements, wasted memory, is less severe than the consequence of declaring too few elements, the inability to store values in the array.*

Constants

Each of the size declarators used in the previous section was a *literal.* A literal is a value that is written exactly as it is meant to be interpreted. For example, the number 3 is a literal. Its value cannot be anything other than 3. You can't change the number 3 to have some different value. Accordingly, the number 3 may be used in the following program as the size declarator:

```
#include <iostream>
using namespace std;
int main ()
{
```

```
    int testScore[3];
    return 0;
}
```

The size declarator may not be a variable. The following program attempts, unsuccessfully, to use a variable *numTests* in declaring the size of an array:

```
#include <iostream>
using namespace std;
int main ()
{
    int numTests;
    cout << "Enter the number of test scores:";
    cin >> numTests;
    int testScore[numTests];
    return 0;
}
```

The result is a compiler error. The compiler will flag the declaration of the array (*int testScore[numTests]*) and complain that a constant expression was expected.

NOTE: *It is possible to declare the size of an array with a variable if you use a different array declaration technique, dynamic memory allocation, which is covered in Chapter 11.*

The term *constant* is new. A constant is a name that represents the same value throughout a program. That value may be any one you specify. This is different than mathematical constants such as PI, which correspond to a given value.

A constant is the converse of a variable, while a variable is a name that may represent different values during the execution of a program. However, the value of a constant cannot change during the execution of a program.

NOTE: *While neither a literal nor a constant changes its value during the execution of a program, they are not the same. While a constant is a name that represents a value, a literal is not a name, but instead the value itself.*

You may use a constant instead of a literal as a size declarator. The size declarator in the following program uses a constant for the value 3 rather than the literal 3.

```
#include <iostream>
using namespace std;
int main ()
{
    const int numTests = 3;
```

```
   int testScore[numTests];
   return 0;
}
```

Going back to the definition of a constant, a name that represents the same value throughout a program, the name is *numTests,* and it represents the value 3.

The syntax for declaring a constant is similar to, but not the same as, a syntax for declaring a variable. Each requires a data type (here *int*) and a variable name (here *numTests*) and ends in a semicolon. However, there are two differences.

First, the declaration of a constant must begin with the *const* keyword. This tells the compiler that you are declaring a constant instead of a variable.

Second, the declaration terminates by assigning the constant a value. You also *may* assign a variable a value when you are declaring it; you learned in Chapter 3 this is called initialization. However, assigning a variable a value when you declare it is optional. On the other hand, assigning a constant a value when you are declaring it is mandatory; the declaration of the constant will not compile if you don't, the compiler error being that a constant object must be initialized. The reason is, since you cannot assign a value of a constant *after* you declare it, the only time you can assign a value to a constant is *when* you declare it.

NOTE: *The declaration of a constant does reserve memory just as does the declaration of a variable. The difference is that with a constant the value stored at the memory address cannot change during the life of the program.*

The following program illustrates that you cannot assign a value of a constant *after* you declare it:

```
#include <iostream>
using namespace std;
int main ()
{
   const int numTests = 3;
   cout << "Enter the number of test scores:";
   cin >> numTests;
   int testScore[numTests];
   return 0;
}
```

The result is a compiler error. The compiler will flag the attempt to assign a value to the constant (*cin >> numTests*) and complain that the stream extraction operator >> cannot have a right-hand operand that is a constant. This is simply another way of saying you can't assign a value to a constant after you declare it.

The following program modifies the previous one by assigning the user input to a variable (so far so good) and then attempting to assign that variable to the constant (not good):

```cpp
#include <iostream>
using namespace std;
int main ()
{
    const int numTests = 3;
    int num;
    cout << "Enter the number of test scores:";
    cin >> num;
    numTests = num;
    int testScore[numTests];
    return 0;
}
```

Once again, the result is a compiler error. The compiler will flag the attempt to assign a value to the constant (*numTests = num*); the error message will be different than in the previous example, that "l-value specifies const object." The 1 in "l-value" is a small L, not the number one, and refers to the value to the *left* of the assignment operator. This again is another way of saying you can't assign a value to a constant after you declare it.

While you can use a constant instead of a literal array to declare the size of an array, the question remains: why would you go to the trouble of doing so? The reason is that in your code you may need to often refer to the size of the array, not only when declaring it, but also, as shown later in this chapter, when assigning values to, and displaying them from, the array. However, the needs of the program may require you to modify the code to change the size of the array, usually to make it larger. For example, if as a teacher I change my policy from giving three tests to giving five tests, I need to change the size of the *testScore* array from three to five. If I use the literal number 3, I have to find that number each time it is referred to in the program and change it to 5. Not only is this time-consuming, but the potential exists that I could miss a reference I needed to change. By contrast, if I use a constant, such as *const int numTests = 3,* then all I need to do is change the 3 to 5 in that one place, and I'm done.

You may be thinking, "Wait a second, you just told me earlier in this chapter that you can't resize an array." Yes, you cannot resize an array while the program is running. However, you can change the size of the array in the code, and then recompile the program.

Constants have many uses in addition to signifying the size of an array, and those uses will be covered in this and further chapters of this book.

Array Index

The entire array has only one name. However, you need to be able to refer to individual elements of the array. You can refer to the individual elements of the array by their position within the array. This position is referred to as an *index* or *subscript*. I will use the term index in this book, but both terms are used, and are equally correct.

The first index in an array is always 0. There are no exceptions. The last index in an array is always 1 less than the number of elements in the array; again, with no exceptions.

The fact that the first index in an array is 0 instead of 1 is explained by the concept of an *offset*. An offset refers to a value added to a base address to produce a second address.

Figure 10-1 may be helpful in illustrating how offsets work with arrays. This figure shows graphically the result of declaring a three-element integer array such as *int testScore[3]*. The base address of an array is the address where the array begins. In Figure 10-1, the base address of the *testScore* array is 101.

int testScore [3];

Index	0	1	2
Offset*	0*4=0	1*4=4	2*4=8
Address	101	105	109

* Assumes integer data type is 4 bytes

Figure 10-1   Indices of a three-element integer array

The address of the first element of the array in Figure 10-1, 101, is the same as the base address of the array itself. Therefore, the value that would be added to the base address of the array to obtain the address of the first element of the array is 0, which is the index of the first element of the array.

The address of the second element of the array is the base address of the array, 101, plus 1 times the size of the data type of the array, 4, which is $101 + (1 \times 4)$, or 105. Similarly, the address of the third element of the array is the base address of the array, 101, plus 2 times the size of the data type of the array, 4, which is $101 + (2 \times 4)$, or 109.

Thus, the address of any element of the array is the base address of the array plus the offset, and in turn the offset is determined by the index of the array multiplied by the size of the array's data type.

Note: *We will revisit addresses and offsets in the next chapter on pointers.*

Since the first index in an array must always be 0, the last index in an array must always be 1 less than the number of elements in the array. If you were counting three numbers, starting at 1, the last element would be number 3. However, if you are starting at 0 instead of 1, then the last number would be 2, not 3.

CAUTION: A common beginning programming mistake is to assume the index of the last element of the array is equal to the number of elements in the array. As you will learn later in this chapter, this can result in (depending on the compiler) run-time errors or unpredictable results, neither of which is good.

At this point, we have not assigned a value to any of the elements of the array. The value of each element likely will be some strange number such as –858993460. As discussed in Chapter 3, the program does its best to interpret whatever value is at a given memory address, perhaps left over from some other program, but the resulting output often makes little sense.

NOTE: If the array variable is declared globally rather than locally, then each element is initialized to a default value, 0 for numeric data types and the null character for a character array. However, I already have given you my lecture against global variables.

You can assign values to an array after you declare it, and later in this chapter I will show you how. However, it is also possible to assign values to an array at the same time that you declare it, as I will show you in the very next section.

Initialization

As first discussed in Chapter 3, initialization is when you assign a value to a variable in the same statement in which you declare that variable. By contrast, assignment is when you assign a value to a variable in a statement after the one in which you declare that variable.

We will discuss assigning values to an array later in this chapter in the section "Assigning and Displaying Array Values." This section covers initialization of an array.

You have two alternative methods of initializing an array. The first alternative is *explicit array sizing,* in which the square brackets contain a numerical constant that explicitly specifies the size of the array. The second alternative is *implicit array*

sizing, in which the square brackets are empty and the size of the array is indicated implicitly by the number of elements on the right side of the assignment operator.

Explicit Array Sizing

The following are examples of explicit array sizing:

```
int testScore[3] = { 74, 87, 91 };
float milesPerGallon[4] = { 44.4, 22.3, 11.6, 33.3};
char grades[5] = {'A', 'B', 'C', 'D', 'F' };
string days[7] = {"Sunday", "Monday", "Tuesday", "Wednesday",
    "Thursday", "Friday", "Saturday"};
```

The syntax of initialization, with both explicit and implicit array sizing, is that the array declaration, such as *int testScore[3],* is followed by an assignment operator and then, enclosed in curly braces, the values to be assigned to each array element, in order, are separated by commas. For example, in the following statement, the value of the first element of the array (*testScore[0]*) would be 74, the value of the second element of the array 87, and the value of the third element of the array 91.

```
int testScore[3] = { 74, 87, 91 };
```

The number of elements on the right-hand side of the assignment operator cannot be greater than the number within the square brackets. Thus, the following statement will not compile, the error message being "too many initializers."

```
float milesPerGallon[4] = { 44.4, 22.3, 11.6, 33.3, 7.4}; // won't compile
```

You do not have to assign values to each element of the array; the number of elements on the right-hand side of the assignment operator may be less than the number within the square brackets:

```
float milesPerGallon[4] = { 44.4, 22.3, 11.6};
```

If you do not initialize all of the elements of an array, the uninitialized elements have a default value that depends on the data type of the array. For example, the default value is 0 for an integer array, 0.0 for a float array, and the null character, '\0', for a character array.

NOTE: *The null character is discussed later in this chapter in the section "Initializing a Character Array."*

Additionally, if you leave an element uninitialized, all elements that follow it must be uninitialized. You can't, for example, alternate initializing and not initializing array elements. For example, the following statement won't compile:

```
float milesPerGallon[4] = { 44.4, , 11.6, 33.3}; // won't compile
```

Implicit Array Sizing

The following are examples of implicit array sizing:

```
int testScore[ ] = { 74, 87, 91 };
float milesPerGallon[ ] = { 44.4, 22.3, 11.6, 33.3};
char grades[ ] = {'A', 'B', 'C', 'D', 'F' };
string days[7] = {"Sunday", "Monday", "Tuesday", "Wednesday",
    "Thursday", "Friday", "Saturday"};
```

The first array, *testScore,* allocates memory for three integers. Since the square brackets are blank, the compiler allocates memory based on the number of elements to the right side of the assignment statement.

Similarly, the second array, *milesPerGallon,* allocates memory for four floats, the third array, *grades,* allocates memory for five characters, and the fourth array, *days,* allocates memory for seven strings.

The compiler only allocates memory based on the number of elements to the right side of the assignment statement if the square brackets are empty. Otherwise, memory is allocated based on the number in the square brackets. Thus, in the following example, the declaration of the array *testScore* would allocate memory for five integers even though only three integers are in the initialization statement because memory allocation is determined by the number within the square brackets. As discussed in the previous section, the fourth and fifth elements of the array would be initialized to a default value, 0.

```
int testScore[5] = { 74, 87, 91 };
```

However, you must tell the compiler one way or the other how much memory to allocate. Therefore, when declaring an array, you cannot have both empty square brackets and no initialization, as in the following example:

```
int testScore[ ];
```

The compiler error message will be that the array is of unknown size. This of course is a problem since the computer has no way of knowing how much memory to allocate for the array.

Initializing a Character Array

As the previous section showed, you can initialize a character array using the same syntax as you would to initialize an array of another data type such as an integer or a float. However, as you will see in this chapter, there are some important differences between character arrays and arrays of numeric data types. This section will show you the first difference.

The following two initializations of a character array to my first name are different in syntax but identical in effect:

```
char name[ ] = {'J', 'e', 'f', 'f', '/0' };
char name = "Jeff";
```

The latter syntax usually is preferred by programmers simply because it is easier to type.

The character '\0' is the escape sequence for a null character. The 0 in '\0' is a zero, not a big letter o. The zero corresponds to the ASCII value of the null character.

Chapter 2 introduced escape sequences, starting with '\n', the newline character, which causes the cursor to go to the next line for further printing. The '\n' in a string is not displayed literally by cout because the backslash signals cout that '\n' is an escape sequence.

The null character has a different purpose, which is to signal cout when to end the output of a character array. For example, the following program outputs, as expected, "Jeff":

```
#include <iostream>
using namespace std;
int main ()
{
    char name[ ] = {'J', 'e', 'f', 'f', '/0' };
    cout << name;
    return 0;
}
```

The result would be the same if the alternate syntax of *char name = "Jeff"* was used to initialize the character array.

By contrast, the following program outputs "Jeff‖‖+ ?."

```
#include <iostream>
using namespace std;
int main ()
{
    char name[ ] = {'J', 'e', 'f', 'f'};
    cout << name;
    return 0;
}
```

The strange characters after "Jeff" (which may differ when you run the program) sometimes are referred to as "garbage characters." However, that really is not a fair or accurate description. What really is happening is that cout keeps outputting the values at each succeeding address after the end of the array until it reaches a value that it interprets as a null character. As discussed earlier in this chapter, the program does its best to interpret whatever value is at a given memory address, perhaps left over from some other program, but the resulting output often makes little sense. In general, "garbage characters" are ASCII representations of integers stored in a memory address.

All this does not mean that the last element of a character array always should be a null character. When each element of a character array is separate from the other, such as a separate grade for each test, there is no need to use a null character. However, if the character array elements are related, such as a character array representing a person's name, then usually the last element should be a null character. The syntax of *char name* = *"Jeff"* accomplishes that, automatically inserting a null character as the fifth element of the array.

Finally, the alternate syntax of *char name* = *"Jeff"* is quite similar to how you initialize a string data type:

```
char name[] = "Jeff";
string name = "Jeff";
```

Indeed, a character array that ends with a null character often is referred to colloquially as a string. However, a character array that ends with a null character is not thereby converted to a string data type; it is still a character array. Indeed, there is no guarantee that a compiler's implementation of the string data type will result in the last character of a true string being a null character.

Thus, while character arrays and strings have many similarities, they are not the same. There are important differences. One is you cannot safely assume that a string ends with a null character. Other differences will be discussed later in this chapter in the sections on the cin Object's *get* and *getline* member functions.

Constant Arrays

You can create arrays that are constants. For example, the following array contains the number of days in each month (for February, we assume a non–leap year).

```
const int daysInMonth [] = { 31, 28, 31, 30, 31, 30,
    31, 31, 30, 31, 30, 31 };
```

Using a constant array here is a good choice since the number of days in each month will not change.

You must use initialization when creating a constant array, just as you must use initialization when creating a constant variable. Since you cannot change the values later, you must specify the values when you create the constant.

When to Use Initialization

C++ gives you the option of just declaring an array, with the values of the array elements unassigned, and initializing an array, assigning values to some or all of the array elements.

Initialization usually is the better choice when you know in advance some or all of the array element values, but it is not limited to that scenario. Initialization sometimes is used to provide each array element with an initial default value. For example, we might initialize each element of the *testScore* array to –1 as a signal that no test score has yet been assigned. The number –1 is a better choice for this purpose than 0 since a student could get a zero on a test, but not a –1.

However, initializing to a default value can be cumbersome when there are many array elements. Additionally, when you don't know in advance the array values, such as for test scores, you may decide against initializing for a default value. Further, even if you do use initialization, you may later want to change the values of some or all of the array elements. Accordingly, you need to know how to assign values to an array. You also will want to display array values. The next section shows you how.

Assigning and Displaying Array Values

The following program shows how to assign values to an array, one element at a time. The assignment starts with the first index, 0, and ends with the last index, 2, which is one less than the number of elements, 3. The program then outputs the array values, one at a time.

```cpp
#include <iostream>
using namespace std;
int main ()
{
   int testScore[3];
   cout << "Enter test score #1: ";
   cin >> testScore[0];
   cout << "Enter test score #2: ";
   cin >> testScore[1];
   cout << "Enter test score #3: ";
   cin >> testScore[2];
   cout << "Test score #1: " << testScore[0] << endl;
   cout << "Test score #2: " << testScore[1] << endl;
   cout << "Test score #3: " << testScore[2] << endl;
   return 0;
}
```

Some sample input and output could be:

```
Enter test score #1: 77
Enter test score #2: 91
Enter test score #3: 84
Test score #1: 77
Test score #2: 91
Test score #3: 84
```

However, this one-element-at-a-time approach has no advantage over the following program, which does not use an array at all, but just three separate variables:

```cpp
#include <iostream>
using namespace std;
int main ()
{
   int testScore1, testScore2, testScore3;
   cout << "Enter test score #1: ";
   cin >> testScore1;
   cout << "Enter test score #2: ";
   cin >> testScore2;
   cout << "Enter test score #3: ";
   cin >> testScore3;
   cout << "Test score #1: " << testScore1 << endl;
   cout << "Test score #2: " << testScore2 << endl;
   cout << "Test score #3: " << testScore3 << endl;
   return 0;
}
```

The advantage of an array over using separate variables is the ability to use a loop. This is shown by the following program:

```cpp
#include <iostream>
using namespace std;
int main ()
{
   int testScore[3];
   for (int i = 0; i < 3; i++)
   {
      cout << "Enter test score #" << i + 1 << ": ";
      cin >> testScore[i];
   }
   for (i = 0; i < 3; i++)
   {
      cout << "Test score #" << i + 1 << ": "
           << testScore[i] << endl;
```

```
    }
    return 0;
}
```

Better yet, you can use a constant instead of an integer literal for the number of array elements:

```
#include <iostream>
using namespace std;
const int MAX = 3;
int main ()
{
    int testScore[MAX];
    for (int i = 0; i < MAX; i++)
    {
        cout << "Enter test score #" << i + 1 << ": ";
        cin >> testScore[i];
    }
    for (i = 0; i < MAX; i++)
    {
        cout << "Test score #" << i + 1 << ": "
             << testScore[i] << endl;
    }
    return 0;
}
```

This example illustrates an advantage of using constants rather than literals for the size declarator. Assume I wrote this program to keep track of a student's test grades at a time when my policy is to give three tests during a semester. However, later I change my policy to giving five tests during a semester. Since I used a constant as a size declarator, I only need to make one code change, which is to initialize the constant *MAX* to 5 instead of 3. In contrast, had I instead used the numeric literal 3 as the size declarator, I have to find that number each time it is referred to in the program, once in the array declaration, and once each in the two for loops. This means only three changes, but in a more complex program the number could be much higher. Not only is this time-consuming, but the potential exists that I could miss a reference to 3 which I needed to change to 5.

In this example, the constant *MAX* is global. However, making the constant *MAX* global is not contrary to my recommendation in Chapter 9 against making variables global. The primary reason for my recommendation against global variables is that a global variable may be changed from anywhere in the program, making it more difficult to trace—for example, why such a variable has an incorrect value. By contrast, the value of a constant cannot be changed at all. Consequently, the reason for the recommendation that a variable should not be global simply does not apply to a constant. Therefore, global constants, as opposed to global variables, are relatively common.

However, whether you use a constant or an integer literal for the number of array elements, you must take care not to go beyond the bounds of the array. The following program demonstrates a common programming mistake.

```cpp
#include <iostream>
using namespace std;
const int MAX = 3;
int main ()
{
    int testScore[MAX];
    for (int i = 0; i <= MAX; i++)
    {
        cout << "Enter test score #" << i + 1 << ":";
        cin >> testScore[i];
    }
    for (i = 0; i <= 3; i++)
    {
        cout << "Test score #" << i + 1 << ": "
            << testScore[i] << endl;
    }
    return 0;
}
```

This program is the same as the previous program, expect that the relational operator in the condition of each for loop has been changed from < to <=. The result is an attempt to access index 3 of the array. The problem, of course, is that there is no such index in a three-element array; the last index is 2. The result depends on the particular compiler and operating system, varying from weird output to run-time errors to the computer locking up, but the result is never good.

Using the cin and cout Objects with Arrays

You can assign values to a character array using the same technique as you used in the previous section to assign values to an integer array:

```cpp
#include <iostream>
using namespace std;
const int MAX = 3;
int main ()
{
    char grades[MAX];
```

```
    for (int i = 0; i < MAX; i++)
    {
        cout << "Enter grade for test #" << i + 1 << ":";
        cin >> grades[i];
    }
    return 0;
}
```

This technique is a logical choice when each element of the array is separate from the other, such as a separate grade for each test. However, sometimes the character array elements are related, such as a character array representing a person's name.

As discussed previously in this chapter in connection with initialization, there are important differences between character arrays and arrays of numeric data types. Another difference is the ability to use the cin object and the stream extraction op erator >> to assign a value to all elements of a character array, and the cout object and the stream insertion operator << to display the values of all elements of a character array. This is demonstrated by the following program:

```
#include <iostream>
using namespace std;
int main ()
{
    char name[ 80] = {'J', 'e', 'f', 'f', '/0' };
    cout << "Enter your name: ";
    cin >> name;
    cout << "Your name is " << name;
    return 0;
}
```

Some sample input and output could be

```
Enter your name: Jeff
Your name is Jeff
```

This approach has the advantage of not requiring two loops for input and display, respectively. The assignment takes place in one step with the cin object and the stream extraction >> operator. Similarly, the display takes place in one step with the cout object and the stream insertion << operator.

Using the cout Object with Numeric Arrays

You can use the cout object and the stream insertion << operator with a numeric array rather than a character array without experiencing a compiler or run-time error, but you will likely not get the result you expect. The following program modifies a previous one by, instead of using a second loop to display test scores, attempting to display the test scores in one step with the cout object and the stream insertion << operator.

```
#include <iostream>
using namespace std;
const int MAX = 3;
int main ()
{
    int testScore[MAX];
    for (int i = 0; i < MAX; i++)
    {
        cout << "Enter test score #" << i + 1 << ": ";
        cin >> testScore[i];
    }
    cout << "The test scores are: " << testScore;
    return 0;
}
```

Some sample input and output could be

```
Enter test score #1: 76
Enter test score #2: 84
Enter test score #3: 91
The test scores are: 0012FECC
```

What happened is that the value of the name of the array is the base address of the array. Therefore, the output of *cout << testScore* is the base address of the *testScore* array, which happens to be the hexadecimal address 0012FECC.

This explains why you obtain an address rather that array values when you use the stream insertion operator << with a numeric array. However, it does not explain why you obtain array values rather than an address when you use the stream insertion operator << with a character array. After all, the name of a character array, like the name of a numeric array, is a constant whose value is the base address of the array.

The answer simply is that the C++ programming language treats the stream extraction operator >> differently with a character array than with a numeric array. When so used, the character array name is not interpreted as a constant whose value is the base address of the array, but rather the starting point for display. This is just another example of the differences between character arrays and numeric arrays.

Using the cin Object with Numeric Arrays … Not!

While you can use the cout object and the stream insertion operator << with numeric arrays as well as character arrays (albeit with different results), you can use the cin object and the stream extraction operator >> only with a character array. You cannot

use the cin object and the stream extraction operator >> with numeric arrays. This is demonstrated by the following program:

```cpp
#include <iostream>
using namespace std;
const int MAX = 3;
int main ()
{
    int testScore[MAX];
    cin >> testScore;
    return 0;
}
```

The result is a compiler error. The compiler will highlight the statement *cin >> testScore* and complain that the stream extraction operator >> cannot have a right-hand operand that is an integer array.

This compiler error may sound familiar. Previously in this chapter, an attempt to use the stream extraction operator to assign a value to the constant, such as *cin >> numTests* when *numTests* was an integer constant, resulted in a compiler error, the message being that the stream extraction operator >> cannot have a right-hand operand that is a constant.

This is essentially the same problem. As you will learn more about in Chapter 11, the name of the integer array, *testScore,* is a constant whose value is the base address of the array.

While this explains why you can't use the stream extraction operator >> with an integer array, you may now be wondering why you can use the stream extraction operator >> with a character array since the name of a character array, like the name of an integer array, is a constant whose value is the base address of the array. The answer is essentially the same as the one to the similar question in the preceding section regarding the stream insertion operator <<. The C++ programming language supports use of the stream extraction operator >> with a character array. When so used, the character array name is not interpreted as a constant whose value is the base address of the array. This is just another example of how the C++ programming language treats character arrays differently than arrays of other data types.

The cin Object's *getline* Function

The following program from the previous section worked fine when the input had no embedded spaces, such as "Jeff."

```cpp
#include <iostream>
using namespace std;
int main ()
```

```
{
    char name[ 80] = {'J', 'e', 'f', 'f', '/0' };
    cout << "Enter your name: ";
    cin >> name;
    cout << "Your name is " << name;
    return 0;
}
```

However, examine the following sample input and output:

```
Enter your name: Jeff Kent
Your name is Jeff
```

We examined this same issue in Chapter 3 with the following program, which used a string variable instead of a character array:

```
#include <iostream>
using namespace std;
#include <string>
int main(void)
{
    string name;
    cout << "Enter your name: ";
    cin >> name;
    cout << "Your name is " << name;
    return 0;
}
```

The explanation in Chapter 3 of why the value of name is outputted only as "Jeff", omitting "Kent", is that the cin object interprets the space between "Jeff" and "Kent" as indicating that the user has finished inputting the value of the name variable. The solution is to use the *getline* function of the cin object.

NOTE: The cin object also has a get function that would solve this issue. The only difference between the two is that the get function reads the user's input up to, but not including, the newline character (the ENTER *key that terminates input, whereas the getline function reads the user's input up to and including the newline character. This difference makes the getline function easier to use than the get function when working with character arrays. The get function usually is used with single characters, not character arrays.*

The *getline* function of the cin object is *overloaded*. By overloaded I do not mean overworked. Rather, the term overloaded when used in connection with the function means the function may be called more than one way, each way differing by the number, data type, or order of arguments.

The following program uses the *getline* function to read the user's input and assign that input to the character array:

```cpp
#include <iostream>
using namespace std;
int main ()
{
    char name[80] = {'J', 'e', 'f', 'f', '/0' };
    cout << "Enter your name: ";
    cin.getline(name, 80);
    cout << "Your name is " << name;
    return 0;
}
```

Now, as shown by the following sample input and output, you can input a string such as "Jeff Kent" that includes an embedded space:

```
Enter your name: Jeff Kent
Your name is Jeff
```

The first argument is the name of the character array into which the input will be stored. The second argument is one more than the number of characters that will be read from standard input, here the keyboard. Since the second argument is 80, the number of characters that will be read from standard input is 79, the 80th character saved for the null character. Since the declared size of the character array in this example is 80, and one element is needed for the null character, that leaves 79 characters for user input.

Another variant of the overloaded *getline* function has three arguments, such as in the following example:

```cpp
cin.get(name, 80, '\n');
```

The third argument is the character that should terminate the reading in of input if it is encountered before the number of characters specified in the second argument. Here the third argument is the newline character, created when the user presses the ENTER key. Since the pressing of the ENTER key will end input anyway, the third argument of '\n' often is superfluous. However, you could use another character as the third argument if it fits the needs of your program.

You cannot use the *get* or *getline* functions of the cin object with strings. Instead, you use the standalone *getline* function. By standalone, I mean the *getline* function is not called with a preceding cin and a dot (*cin.getline*) as in the case of character arrays.

The following code fragment shows how to use the *getline* function with a string:

```cpp
String name;
getline(cin, name);
```

The first argument is the *cin* object. The second argument is the string into which the input will be stored. Since you do not have to specify the size of a string, there is no argument limiting the number of characters for input.

Passing Arrays as Function Arguments

Previously in this chapter, we used the following program to demonstrate how loops are effective in assigning and displaying array values:

```cpp
#include <iostream>
using namespace std;
const int MAX = 3;
int main ()
{
    int testScore[MAX];
    for (int i = 0; i < MAX; i++)
    {
        cout << "Enter test score #" << i + 1 << ": ";
        cin >> testScore[i];
    }
    for (i = 0; i < MAX; i++)
    {
        cout << "Test score #" << i + 1 << ": "
            << testScore[i] << endl;
    }
    return 0;
}
```

Now we are going to make this program more modular by writing one function to assign values to the array, and another function to display values from the array, rather than doing all that work in the *main* function.

```cpp
#include <iostream>
using namespace std;
void assignValues(int[], int);
void displayValues(int[], int);
const int MAX = 3;

int main ()
{
    int testScore[MAX];
    assignValues(testScore, MAX);
```

```
    displayValues(testScore, MAX);
    return 0;
}

void assignValues(int tests[], int num)
{
    for (int i = 0; i < num; i++)
    {
        cout << "Enter test score #" << i + 1 << ": ";
        cin >> tests[i];
    }
}

void displayValues(int scores[], int elems)
{
  for (int i = 0; i < elems; i++)
    {
        cout << "Test score #" << i + 1 << ": "
            << scores[i] << endl;
    }
}
```

The *assignValues* function is used to assign values to the array. The *displayValues* function is used to display values from the array.

Each function has two arguments. The first argument is the array. The second argument is the number of elements in the array. Each function loops through the array, its first argument, using as an index limit the number of elements in the array, the second argument.

Since the first argument is not just an integer, but an array of integers, the argument is specified with brackets, [], signifying that what is being passed is an array.

NOTE: *You do not, and should not, put a number in the square brackets in the argument list of either the prototype or the function header.*

There is one remaining question. The *assignValues* function changes the values in the array in *main* that was passed as its argument. As discussed in Chapter 9, for that to happen, the argument should be passed by reference rather than value. However, the array is not passed by reference.

Actually, Chapter 9 mentioned a third way of passing arguments: by address. Passing by address works the same way as passing by reference in that the called function can change in the calling function the value of a variable passed to it. As discussed previously in this chapter, the value of the name of an array is the base address of the

array. Thus, in a function call such as *assignValues(testScore, MAX),* in which the first argument is the array name, the first argument is being passed by address. There will be much more on passing by address in Chapter 11.

Summary

The variables we have worked with before this chapter could hold only one value at a time. In this chapter, you learned about an array, which permits you to use a single variable to store many values. The values are stored at consecutive indexes, starting with zero and then incrementing by one for each additional element of the array.

The data type of an array may be integer, float, or character. However, a particular array cannot contain integers, floats, and characters. All the elements of an array must be of the same data type.

You need to declare an array before you can use it. The syntax for declaring an array is almost identical to the syntax for declaring integer, character, or other variables. The only difference between declaring a single scalar variable and an array of scalar variables is that, when declaring an array, the variable name is followed by a number within square brackets. That number is the array's *size declarator.*

The size declarator must be a *literal* or a *constant.* A *literal* is a value that is written exactly as it is meant to be interpreted. A *constant* is a name that represents the same value throughout a program. You learned in this chapter how to declare and use a constant.

You also can create an array through initialization. Initialization is when you assign a value to a variable in the same statement in which you declare that variable, as contrasted to assignment, which is when you assign a value to a variable in a statement after the one in which you declare that variable.

You have two alternative methods of initializing an array. The first alternative is *explicit array sizing,* in which the square brackets contain a numerical constant that explicitly specifies the size of the array. The second alternative is *implicit array sizing,* in which the square brackets are empty and the size of the array is indicated implicitly by the number of elements on the right side of the assignment operator.

You learned in this chapter how to assign values to an array using a loop. You also learned how to use the cin object's *get* and *getline* functions to assign values to a character array.

Finally, you learned how to pass an array as a function argument. When you do so, the argument is being passed by address.

Quiz

1. Can a particular array contain integers, floats, and characters?

2. What is the number of the starting index of an array?

3. What is the number of the ending index of an array?

4. What is the difference between initialization and assignment?

5. What are the two alternative methods of initializing an array?

6. What is the purpose of the null character?

7. What is the value of the name of an array?

8. Should the last element of a character array always be a null character?

9. What is the difference between the *get* and *getline* functions of the cin object?

10. When you pass an array name as a function argument, are you passing it by value, reference, or address?

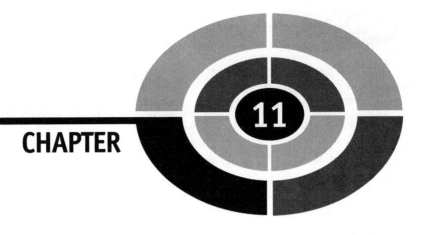

CHAPTER 11

What's the Address? Pointers

My parents told me when I was a child that it was not polite to point. However, each semester I teach my computer programming students how to point. No, I am not trying to promote rude behavior. Rather, I am teaching my students about pointers, which "point" to another variable or constant.

You yourself may have acted as a pointer in the past. Have you ever been asked where someone lives? If that house was nearby, you may have pointed it out.

The pointer performs a similar function. A pointer points to another variable or constant. Of course, the pointer does not point with an arm and fingers as you would. Rather, the pointer's value is the address of the variable or constant to which it points. Indeed, you may have done something similar. If you were asked where someone lives and that house was not close enough to physically point out, you instead may have provided an address by which the house could be located.

Pointers have had a reputation among programming students for being difficult to learn. I think that reputation is overblown; pointers are not difficult if you take the time to understand what they do. In any event, difficult or not, it is important to learn about pointers. Some C++ tasks are performed more easily with pointers, and other C++ tasks, such as dynamic memory allocation, cannot be performed without them.

So, on that note, let's now learn how to create and work with pointers.

Declaring a Pointer

Like any variable or constant, you must declare a pointer before you can work with it. The syntax of declaring a pointer is almost the same as declaring a variable which stores a value rather than an address. However, the meaning of the pointer's data type is quite different than the meaning of the data type of a variable which stores a value rather than an address.

Syntax of a Pointer Declaration

The syntax of declaring a pointer is almost the same as the syntax of declaring the variables we have worked with in previous chapters. The following statement declares an integer pointer variable:

```
int* iPtr;
```

The asterisk you use to declare a pointer is the same asterisk that you use for multiplication. However, in this statement the asterisk is being used in a declaration, so in this context it is being used to designate a variable as a pointer. Later in this chapter, we will use the asterisk for a third purpose, as an indirection operator.

NOTE: *It is common in C++ for a symbol to have different meanings depending on the context. For example, an ampersand (&) in an argument list means you are passing an argument by reference, whereas an ampersand in front of a variable name is the address operator.*

The integer pointer variable also can be declared with the asterisk preceding the variable name instead of following the data type:

```
int *iPtr;
```

Either alternative syntax is equally correct because the compiler generally ignores white spaces between an operator and a variable name, constant name, or number. Indeed, the following pointer declaration also works:

```
int*ptr;
```

My preference is the first example, in which the asterisk follows the data type and is separated by a white space from the variable name, since (in my opinion) it best signifies that the variable is a pointer. However, all three syntax variations are correct. In any of these variations, the only difference between declaring a pointer variable and a variable which stores a value rather than an address is the asterisk between the data type and the pointer name.

The Meaning of Pointer Data Types

While the syntax of declaring a pointer is almost the same as declaring the variables and constants which store a value rather than an address, the meaning of the data type in the declaration of a pointer is different than in the declaration of those other variables and constants.

With the variables we have worked with previously, the data type in the variable declaration describes the type of data that can be stored in that variable. Thus, the value of an integer variable or constant is an integer, the value of a character variable or constant is a character, and so forth.

However, with a pointer, the data type in the declaration means something different, namely the data type of another variable (or constant) whose memory address is the value of the pointer. In other words, the value of an integer pointer must be the address of an integer variable or constant, the value of a float pointer must be the address of a float variable or constant, and so forth.

The actual data type of the value of all pointers, whether integer, float, character, or otherwise, is the same, a long hexadecimal number that represents a memory address. The only difference between pointers of different data types is the data type of the variable or constant that the pointer points to. This is demonstrated by the following program, which uses the *sizeof* operator to show that the sizes of pointers of different data types are the same (a long data type uses 4 bytes on my operating system and compiler) even though the different data types (int, float, char) are not all the same size:

```
#include <iostream>
using namespace std;

int main ()
{
```

```
    int* iPtr;
    float* fPtr;
    char *cPtr;
    cout << "The size of iPtr is " << sizeof(iPtr) << endl;
    cout << "The size of fPtr is " << sizeof(fPtr) << endl;
    cout << "The size of cPtr is " << sizeof(cPtr) << endl;
    return 0;
}
```

The output is therefore:

```
The size of iPtr is 4
The size of fPtr is 4
The size of cPtr is 4
```

Otherwise, a pointer is similar to the variables or constants we have studied previously. A pointer itself may be a variable or a constant, and like other variables or constants, it is also stored at a memory address. What distinguishes a pointer is that its value is the memory address of another variable or constant.

Assigning a Value to a Pointer

This section will explain how you assign a value to a pointer. Though, before I explain how, perhaps I should explain why.

Why You Should Not Try to Use an Unassigned Pointer

Back in elementary school we were taught a verse: "I shot an arrow into the air, where it lands, I don't care." Looking back, I wonder why young children were taught this verse. It may rhyme, but its message is really not appropriate for little ones. However, when you declare a pointer but then use it without first assigning it a value, you are, alas, doing the programming equivalent of that verse.

The following program declares a pointer and then attempts to output its value without first assigning it a value:

```
#include <iostream>
using namespace std;

int main ()
{
    int* iPtr;
```

```
    cout << "The value of iPtr is " << iPtr << endl;
    return 0;
}
```

The result, depending on your compiler and operating system, may be a compiler error, a runtime error, or a computer that locks up. Regardless, attempting to use a declared pointer without first assigning it a value is not a good idea.

As you may recall from previous chapters, when you declare a variable and then attempt to output its value without first assigning it a value, the result is a so-called "garbage value" that makes little sense. The reason for this result is that the computer attempts to interpret whatever value is left over from previous programs at the address of the variable.

When the variable is a pointer, that leftover value is interpreted as another memory address, which the pointer then tries to access when you attempt to use it. There are a number of memory address ranges that you are not permitted to access programmatically, such as those reserved for use by the operating system. If the leftover value is interpreted as one of those prohibited addresses, the result is an error.

Null Pointers

If it is too early in your code to know which address to assign to the pointer, then you first assign the pointer NULL, which is a constant with a value of zero defined in several standard libraries, including *iostream*. The following program does so:

```
#include <iostream>
using namespace std;

int main ()
{
    int* iPtr;
    iPtr = NULL;
    cout << "The value of iPtr is " << iPtr << endl;
    return 0;
}
```

NOTE: *You also could use initialization instead of declaration followed by assignment, thus combining the first two statements in main to int* iPtr = NULL.*

The resulting output is

```
The address of x using iPtr is 00000000
```

A pointer that is assigned NULL is called a *null pointer*.

On most operating systems, programs are not permitted to access memory at address 0 because that memory is reserved by the operating system. You may now be thinking: "Wait a minute! He just told me how bad it was to risk having pointers point to memory addresses reserved by the operating system. Now he's having us do that on purpose." However, the memory address 0 has special significance; it signals that the pointer is not intended to point to an accessible memory location. Thus, if it is too early in your code to know which address to assign to a pointer, you should first assign the pointer to NULL, which then makes it safe to access the value of a pointer before it is assigned a "real" value such as the address of another variable or constant.

Assigning a Pointer the Address of a Variable or Constant

Let's now assign a pointer a "real" value, the address of another variable or constant. To do so, you need to access the address of the variable or constant before you can assign that address to the pointer. You use the address operator, covered in Chapter 3, to accomplish this task.

The following program shows how to use the address operator to assign the address of a variable to a pointer. This program also demonstrates that the value of a pointer is the same as the address to which the pointer points.

```
#include <iostream>
using namespace std;

int main ()
{
    int num = 5;
    int* iPtr = &num;
    cout << "The address of x using &num is " << &num << endl;
    cout << "The address of x using iPtr is " << iPtr << endl;
    return 0;
}
```

The output on my computer (the following addresses likely will be different on yours) is

```
The address of x using &num is 0012FED4
The address of x using iPtr is 0012FED4
```

Figure 11-1 shows graphically how the pointer points to the integer variable.

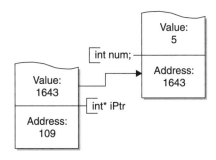

Figure 11-1 Pointer pointing to an integer variable

Indirection Operator and Dereferencing

The primary use of a pointer is to access and, if appropriate, change the value of the variable that the pointer is pointing to. In the following program, the value of the integer variable *num* is changed twice.

```cpp
#include <iostream>
using namespace std;

int main ()
{
   int num = 5;
   int* iPtr = &num;
   cout << "The value of num is " << num << endl;
   num = 10;
   cout << "The value of num after num = 10 is "
      << num << endl;
   *iPtr = 15;
   cout << "The value of num after *iPtr = 15 is "
      << num << endl;
   return 0;
}
```

The resulting output is

```
The value of num is 5
The value of num after num = 10 is 10
The value of num after *iPtr = 15 is 15
```

The first change should be familiar, by the direct assignment of a value to *num,* such as *num = 10.* However, the second change is accomplished a new way, using the indirection operator:

```
*iPtr = 15;
```

The indirection operator is an asterisk, the same asterisk that you used to declare the pointer or to perform multiplication. However, in this statement the asterisk is not being used in a declaration or to perform multiplication, so in this context it is being used as an indirection operator.

NOTE: As mentioned earlier in this chapter, this is another example of a symbol having different meanings in the C++ programming language depending on the context in which it was used.

The placement of the indirection operator before a pointer is said to dereference the pointer. Indeed, some texts refer to the indirection operator as the dereferencing operator. The value of a dereferenced pointer is not an address, but rather the value at that address—that is, the value of the variable that the pointer points to.

For example, in the preceding program, *iPtr*'s value is the address of *num.* However, the value of *iPtr* dereferenced is the value of *num.* Thus, the following two statements have the same effect, both changing the value of *num:*

```
num = 25;
*iPtr = 25;
```

Similarly, a dereferenced pointer can be used in arithmetic expressions the same as the variable to which it points. Thus, the following two statements have the same effect:

```
num *= 2;
*iPtr *= 2;
```

In these examples, changing a variable's value using the indirection operator rather than through a straightforward assignment seems like an unnecessary complication. However, there are instances covered later in this chapter, such as looping through an array using a pointer, or using dynamic memory allocation, in which using the indirection operator is helpful or even necessary.

The Pointer as a Variable or a Constant

A pointer may be a variable or a constant. Let's examine both possibilities.

Pointer as a Variable

The preceding program had the pointer pointing to one integer variable. However, a pointer variable, being a variable, can point to different variables at different times in the program. In the following program, the value of the pointer is changed to point to two different integer variables.

```
#include <iostream>
using namespace std;

int main ()
{
    int num1 = 5, num2 = 14;
    int* iPtr = &num1;
    cout << "The value of num1 is " << num1 << endl;
    *iPtr *= 2;
    cout << "The value of num1 after *iPtr *= 2 is "
        << *iPtr << endl;
    iPtr = &num2;
    cout << "The value of num2 is " << num2 << endl;
    *iPtr /= 2;
    cout << "The value of num after *iPtr /= 2 is "
        << *iPtr << endl;
    return 0;
}
```

The resulting output is therefore:

```
The value of num1 is 5
The value of num1 after *iPtr *= 2 is 10
The value of num2 is 14
The value of num after *iPtr /= 2 is 7
```

The Array Name as a Constant Pointer

While the pointer may be a variable, it also may be a constant. Indeed, in the previous chapter we actually discussed a constant pointer: the name of an array.

As you may recall from Chapter 10, the value of the name of an array is the base address of the array, which also is the address of the first element of an array. Thus, in the following program, both *testScore* and *&testScore[0]* have the same value.

```
#include <iostream>
using namespace std;
const int MAX = 3;
```

```
int main ()
{
    int testScore[MAX] = {4, 7, 1};
    cout << "The address of the array using testScore is "
        << testScore << endl;
    cout << "The address of the first element of the array "
        "using &testScore[0] is " << &testScore[0] << endl;
    cout << "The value of the first element of the array "
        "using *testScore is " << *testScore << endl;
    cout << "The value of the first element of the array "
        "using testScore[0] is " << testScore[0] << endl;
    return 0;
}
```

The resulting output is

```
The address of the array using testScore is 0012FECC
The address of the first element of the array using &testScore[0] is 0012FECC
The value of the first element of the array using *testScore is 4
The value of the first element of the array using testScore[0] is 4
```

Similarly, if you dereference the name of an array, its value is the same as the value of the first element of the array. Therefore, in the preceding program, both *testScore* and *testScore[0]* have the same value.

However, you cannot change the value of the name of the array. For example, a statement such as *testScore++* would result in a compiler error, the error message being "++ needs l-value." As you may recall from Chapter 10, the term l-value refers to the value to the *left* of the assignment operator. This error message is another way of saying you can't increment a constant because that would be changing the value of a constant after you declare it.

Pointer Arithmetic

The value of a pointer, even though it is an address, is a numeric value. Therefore, you can perform arithmetic operations on a pointer just as you can a numeric value.

Using a Variable Pointer to Point to an Array

Pointer arithmetic is done often with arrays. However, since you cannot change the value of the name of an array, it being a constant pointer, you first should declare a variable pointer and then assign it to the address of an array.

So, we begin with an established point of reference, let's start with the following program, which outputs the address and value at each element of an array using the name of the array:

```cpp
#include <iostream>
using namespace std;
const int MAX = 3;

int main ()
{
   int testScore[MAX] = {4, 7, 1};
   for (int i = 0; i < MAX; i++)
   {
      cout << "The address of index " << i
         << " of the array is "<< &testScore[i] << endl;
      cout << "The value at index " << i
         << " of the array is "<< testScore[i] << endl;
   }
   return 0;
}
```

The resulting output is

```
The address of index 0 of the array is 0012FECC
The value at index 0 of the array is 4
The address of index 1 of the array is 0012FED0
The value at index 1 of the array is 7
The address of index 2 of the array is 0012FED4
The value at index 2 of the array is 1
```

This program used the name of the array, *testScore,* to access, by index, each element of the array. The name of the array is a constant pointer. The following program modifies the previous program by using a variable pointer, *iPtr,* to access by index each element of the array.

```cpp
#include <iostream>
using namespace std;
const int MAX = 3;

int main ()
{
   int testScore[MAX] = {4, 7, 1};
   int* iPtr = testScore;
   for (int i = 0; i < MAX; i++)
   {
```

```
        cout << "The address of index " << i
           << " of the array is "<< & iPtr[i] << endl;
        cout << "The value at index " << i
           << " of the array is "<< iPtr[i] << endl;
    }
    return 0;
}
```

The following statement in this program sets the variable pointer *iPtr* to point to the same address as the array name *testScore:*

```
int* iPtr = testScore;
```

The array name is not preceded with the address operator (&) because the array name already is an address, namely, the base address of the array. Therefore, after this assignment, *iPtr* and *testScore* both point to the beginning of the array. Accordingly, as shown in Figure 11-2, *iPtr[2]* and *testScore[2]* have the same value.

Incrementing a Pointer

An important reason for declaring a variable pointer so it points to the same address as the array name is so the variable pointer can be incremented, unlike the array name which cannot be incremented because it is a constant pointer. The fol-

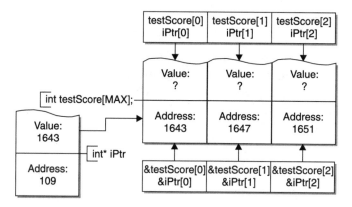

Figure 11-2   Variable and constant pointers used to access array elements

lowing program increments the variable pointer to access each succeeding element of the array:

```cpp
#include <iostream>
using namespace std;
const int MAX = 3;

int main ()
{
    int testScore[MAX] = {4, 7, 1};
    int* iPtr = testScore;
    for (int i = 0; i < MAX; i++, iPtr++)
    {
        cout << "The address of index " << i
            << " of the array is "<< iPtr << endl;
        cout << "The value at index " << i
            << " of the array is "<< *iPtr << endl;
    }
    return 0;
}
```

Incrementing an integer variable increases its value by 1. However, incrementing a pointer variable increases its value by the number of bytes of its data type. This is an example of pointer arithmetic. When you run this program, the first address outputted is 0012FECC, the second 0012FED0, and the third 0012FED4. These hexadecimal addresses are 4 bytes apart because, on the compiler and operating system used by me to run this program, the integer data type takes 4 bytes.

For this reason, as shown in Figure 11-3, *iPtr + 1* is not the base address plus 1, but instead is the base address + 4. The same is true of *testScore + 1*. Consequently, the value at the second element of the array can be expressed one of four ways:

- testScore[1];
- *(testScore + 1);
- iPtr[1];
- *(iPtr + 1);

Comparing Addresses

Addresses can be compared like any other value. The following program modifies the previous one by incrementing the variable pointer so long as the address to which

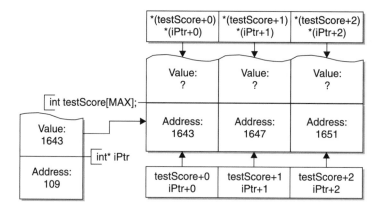

Figure 11-3   Effect of incrementing or adding 1 to an address

it points is either less than or equal to the address of the last element of the array, which is *&testScore[MAX - 1]:*

```cpp
#include <iostream>
using namespace std;
const int MAX = 3;

int main ()
{
   int testScore[MAX] = {4, 7, 1};
   int* iPtr = testScore;
   int i = 0;
   while (iPtr <= &testScore[MAX - 1])
   {
      cout << "The address of index " << i
         << " of the array is "<< iPtr << endl;
      cout << "The value at index " << i
         << " of the array is "<< *iPtr << endl;
      iPtr++;
      i++;
   }
   return 0;
}
```

As Figures 11-2 and 11-3 depict, the comparison to *&testScore[MAX - 1]* instead could have been made to *testScore + MAX – 1.*

Decrementing a Pointer

The same considerations apply to decrementing a pointer, which decreases its value by the number of bytes of its data type. Decrementing a pointer can be used to step "backwards" through an array.

```cpp
#include <iostream>
using namespace std;
const int MAX = 3;

int main ()
{
   int testScore[MAX] = {4, 7, 1};
   int* iPtr = &testScore[MAX - 1];
   int i = MAX - 1;
   while (iPtr >= &testScore[0])
   {
      cout << "The address of index " << i
         << " of the array is "<< iPtr << endl;
      cout << "The value at index " << i
         << " of the array is "<< *iPtr << endl;
      iPtr--;
      i--;
   }
   return 0;
}
```

The output is therefore

```
The address of index 2 of the array is 0012FED4
The value at index 2 of the array is 1
The address of index 1 of the array is 0012FED0
The value at index 1 of the array is 7
The address of index 0 of the array is 0012FECC
The value at index 0 of the array is 4
```

The key statement is

```cpp
int* iPtr = &testScore[MAX - 1];
```

This statement has the variable pointer point to the last address in the array. That address then is decremented in the loop so that the pointer variable points to the preceding address in the array. The loop continues so long as the address pointed to by the pointer variable is not before the base address of the array.

As discussed previously, the pointer variable also could have been initialized as follows:

```
int* iPtr = testScore + MAX - 1;
```

Pointers as Function Arguments

Pointers may be passed as function arguments. Pointer notation usually is used to note that an argument is a pointer. However, if the pointer argument is the name of an array, subscript notation alternatively may be used.

Passing an Array Using Pointer Notation

In Chapter 10, we employed the following program that used one function to assign values to the array and another function to display values from the array, rather than doing all that work in the *main* function.

```cpp
#include <iostream>
using namespace std;
void assignValues(int[], int);
void displayValues(int[], int);
const int MAX = 3;

int main ()
{
   int testScore[MAX];
   assignValues(testScore, MAX);
   displayValues(testScore, MAX);
   return 0;
}

void assignValues(int tests[], int num)
{
   for (int i = 0; i < num; i++)
   {
      cout << "Enter test score #" << i + 1 << ": ";
      cin >> tests[i];
   }
}

void displayValues(int scores[], int elems)
```

```
{
 for (int i = 0; i < elems; i++)
   {
      cout << "Test score #" << i + 1 << ": "
         << scores[i] << endl;
   }
}
```

As discussed in Chapter 10, the two functions, *assignValues* and *displayValues,* passed their first argument, the array, by address. An argument passed by address can be changed in the calling function (here *main*) by the called function (here *assignValues*) just as if the argument had been passed by reference. Thus, the *assignValues* function changed the value of the *testScore* array in *main* by assigning values to the elements of that array.

The function prototypes and headers of the *assignValues* and *displayValues* functions used a subscript [] to indicate that an array is being passed. However, you can also use pointer notation—for instance, asterisk * instead of a subscript []—as the following example demonstrates:

```
#include <iostream>
using namespace std;
void assignValues(int*, int);
void displayValues(int*, int);
const int MAX = 3;

int main ()
{
   int testScore[MAX];
   assignValues(testScore, MAX);
   displayValues(testScore, MAX);
   return 0;
}

void assignValues(int* tests, int num)
{
   for (int i = 0; i < num; i++)
   {
      cout << "Enter test score #" << i + 1 << ": ";
      cin >> tests[i];
   }
}

void displayValues(int* scores, int elems)
{
```

```
for (int i = 0; i < elems; i++)
  {
     cout << "Test score #" << i + 1 << ": "
        << scores[i] << endl;
  }
}
```

The following comparison of the prototypes of the *assignValues* function using subscript and pointer notation, respectively, shows that the only difference is whether a subscript [] or an asterisk * is used to denote that the argument is an array:

```
void assignValues(int[], int);
void assignValues(int*, int);
```

Similarly, the following comparison of the function headers of the *assignValues* function using subscript and pointer notation, respectively, shows that the only difference is whether a subscript [] or an asterisk * is used to denote that the argument is an array. This time, however, the asterisk precedes the variable name, whereas the subscript follows the variable name.

```
void assignValues(int tests[], int num)
void assignValues(int* tests, int num)
```

Whether you use subscript or pointer notation to pass an array really is a matter of preference. There is no programming advantage one way or the other. However, the next section discusses a situation in which subscript notation is not an option, so pointer notation is the only choice.

Passing a Single Variable Using Pointer Notation

Passing an array name by address is relatively simple because the value of the array name is an address. However, you may often want to pass a single variable by address. By single variable I don't mean a variable that is unmarried, but instead, for example, an int as opposed to an int array.

With a single variable, subscript notation is not an option. Subscripts make sense only with an array. Rather, you need to use pointer notation to pass a single variable by address.

Passing an argument by reference or by address both enable the passed argument to be changed in the calling function by the called function—only the syntax is different. For comparison, let's start with the following program from Chapter 9 that passes the variable to be doubled by reference:

```
#include <iostream>
using namespace std;
void doubleIt(int&);
```

```
int main ()
{
    int num;
    cout << "Enter number: ";
    cin >> num;
    doubleIt(num);
    cout << "The number doubled in main is " << num << endl;
    return 0;
}
void doubleIt (int& x)
{
    cout << "The number to be doubled is " << x << endl;
    x *= 2;
    cout << "The number doubled in doubleIt is " << x << endl;
}
```

Here is some sample input and output:

```
Enter number: 3
The number to be doubled is 3
The number doubled in doubleIt is 6
The number doubled in main is 6
```

Let's now modify this program so it passes the variable to be doubled by address instead of by reference:

```
#include <iostream>
using namespace std;
void doubleIt(int*);

int main ()
{
    int num;
    cout << "Enter number: ";
    cin >> num;
    doubleIt(&num);
    cout << "The number doubled in main is " << num << endl;
    return 0;
}
void doubleIt (int* x)
{
    cout << "The number to be doubled is " << *x << endl;
    *x *= 2;
    cout << "The number doubled in doubleIt is " << *x << endl;
}
```

There are four syntax differences between these two programs.

1. In the function prototype, you use an ampersand (&) for passing by reference but an asterisk (*) for passing by address:

```
void doubleIt(int&);    // by reference
void doubleIt(int*);    // by address
```

2. Similarly, in the function header, you use an ampersand (&) for passing by reference but an asterisk (*) for passing by address:

```
void doubleIt (int& x)    // by reference
void doubleIt (int* x)    // by address
```

3. When you call the function, you don't need the address operator (&) for passing by reference, but you do need one for passing by address since you are supposed to be passing by the address of *x.*:

```
doubleIt(num);     // by reference
doubleIt(&num);    // by address
```

4. In the body of the called function, you don't need to dereference the argument when you pass it by reference, but you do need to when you pass by address since *x,* being passed by address, is not a value but is instead a pointer:

```
// by reference - no dereference
{
   cout << "The number to be doubled is " << x << endl;
   x *= 2;
   cout << "The number doubled in doubleIt is " << x << endl;
}
// by address - need to dereference
{
   cout << "The number to be doubled is " << *x << endl;
   *x *= 2;
   cout << "The number doubled in doubleIt is " << *x << endl;
}
```

You may legitimately be wondering why, with a single variable argument, I would want to pass it by address when the syntax for passing it by reference seems easier. The pat answer I give my students is that there are certain sadistic computer science teachers (I'm not mentioning any names here) who insist their students pass by address to make them suffer. All kidding aside though, there are actually certain library functions that do use pass by address. Additionally, when using dynamic memory allocation and returning pointers from functions (to be covered in the following sections), passing by address may be the only option.

Dynamic Memory Allocation

As discussed in Chapter 10, when declaring an array, the size declarator must be either a literal or a constant, and may not be a variable. The following program from Chapter 10 attempts, unsuccessfully, to use a variable *numTests* in declaring the size of an array:

```
#include <iostream>
using namespace std;
int main ()
{
    int numTests;
    cout << "Enter the number of test scores:";
    cin >> numTests;
    int testScore[numTests];
    return 0;
}
```

The result is a compiler error. The compiler will flag the declaration of the array (*int testScore[numTests]*) and complain that a constant expression was expected. The reason a constant (or literal) expression is required is that in this program we are allocating memory for the array at compile time. The compiler needs to know exactly how much memory to allocate. However, if a variable is the size declarator, the compiler does not know how much memory to allocate because a variable's value may change. Indeed, in the preceding example, the value of the variable used as the size declarator is not even known until runtime.

Having said this though, it is often desirable to have the user determine at runtime the size of the array so it is neither too small nor too large, but just right. To accomplish this, you need to declare the array using dynamic memory allocation. The following program modifies the previous one to use dynamic memory allocation:

```
#include <iostream>
using namespace std;
int main ()
{
    int numTests;
    cout << "Enter the number of test scores:";
    cin >> numTests;
    int * iPtr = new int[numTests];
    for (int i = 0; i < numTests; i++)
    {
        cout << "Enter test score #" << i + 1 << " : ";
        cin >> iPtr[i];
    }
```

```
    for (i = 0; i < numTests; i++)
        cout << "Test score #" << i + 1 << " is "
            << iPtr[i] << endl;
    delete [] iPtr;
    return 0;
}
```

Some sample input and output follows:

```
Enter the number of test scores: 3
Enter test score #1: 66
Enter test score #2: 88
Enter test score #3: 77
Test score #1 is 66
Test score #2 is 88
Test score #3 is 77
```

Dynamic memory allocation works, even though using a variable as a size declarator does not, because with dynamic memory allocation, memory is not being allocated at compile time. Instead, memory is being allocated at runtime, and from a different place (the "heap") rather than where it is allocated at compile time (the "stack").

NOTE: *The terms heap and stack also have meaning in data structures. Here, however, these terms are used to identify different areas of memory: the stack for memory allocated at compile time; the heap for memory allocated at runtime.*

While you could dynamically allocate a single variable, normally dynamic memory allocation is used with arrays (as in this example), or with objects such as structures or classes, which are discussed in Chapter 14.

You need to use a pointer to dynamically allocate memory. The pointer must be of the same data type as the array that is to be allocated dynamically. An assignment statement is used, as in the following statement from the program:

```
int * iPtr = new int[numTests];
```

The pointer is on the left side of the assignment operator. Immediately to the right of the assignment statement is the *new* operator, whose purpose is to dynamically allocate memory. The array that is to be allocated dynamically immediately follows the new operator, described by data type and a size declarator in a subscript [], but with no array name. The size declarator may be a variable instead of a literal or constant.

Since the array has no name, it and its elements are referred to through the pointer that created it, such as *iPtr[i]* in the for loops used to assign values to and output the values of the array elements. Therefore, the scope of the dynamically created array is the same as the scope of the pointer used to declare it.

The significance of dynamic memory allocation is not scope, but lifetime. Like a global variable or a static local variable, the lifetime of a dynamically created variable is as long as that of the program's execution. However, if before the end of the program the pointer that points to a dynamically created variable goes out of scope, you no longer have any way of accessing the dynamically created memory. Therefore, the dynamically created variable still takes up memory, but is inaccessible. This is called a memory leak.

Having programs that dynamically allocate memory but never release it is akin to a library where patrons check out books but never return them. Sooner or later the library will run out of books, and the computer will run out of memory.

A memory leak is not a particular concern in the preceding program since the pointer that points to the dynamically allocated memory does not go out of scope until immediately before the program ends. However, if you dynamically allocate memory inside a function using a local pointer (as in a program in the next section), then when the function terminates, the pointer will be destroyed but the memory will remain, orphaned since there is no longer a way of accessing it for the remainder of the program.

You release dynamically allocated memory with the *delete* operator. Just as the new operator is used to create dynamically allocated memory, the delete operator is used to return dynamically allocated memory to the operating system. The syntax is the delete operator followed by the pointer that points to the dynamically created memory. Additionally, if the dynamically created memory is an array as opposed to a single variable, then empty subscripts [] are placed between the delete operator and the pointer, as in the following statement from the program:

```
delete [] iPtr;
```

While the delete operator operates on a pointer, the delete operator does not delete the pointer. Instead, the delete operator deletes the memory at the address pointed to by the pointer.

NOTE: You should only use the delete operator with a pointer that points to dynamically created memory. Using the delete operator with a pointer that points to memory created on the stack rather than from the heap can lead to unpredictable results.

Finally, since the pointer is the only way to which you can refer to the dynamically allocated variable, you should not change the value of the pointer to point to a different address unless you first assign a different pointer to the dynamically allocated memory. Otherwise, you no longer have a way of accessing the dynamically created memory. The result would be a memory leak.

Returning Pointers from Functions

In Chapter 10, you learned several ways to initialize a character array. The following program shows you an additional way:

```
#include <iostream>
using namespace std;
char * setName();

int main (void)
{
   char* str = "Jeff Kent";
   cout << str;
   return 0;
}
```

With some sample input and output:

```
Enter your name: Jeff Kent
Your name is Jeff Kent
```

The key statement is

```
   char* str = "Jeff Kent";
```

This statement is almost the same as:

```
   char str[] = "Jeff Kent";
```

In both statements, *str* is a character pointer, and implicit array sizing is used. The difference is that *str* in the first statement (*char* * *str*) is a variable pointer whereas *str* in the second statement (*char str[]*) is a constant pointer.

Returning a Pointer to a Local Variable (Not a Good Idea)

Now, following the advice in Chapter 9 to make your program more modular, you try to write a separate function, *setName,* to obtain the user input. The *setName* function creates a character array, assigns user input to that array using the *getline* function of the cin object, and then returns a pointer to that character array. The address which is returned by the setName function then is assigned to the character pointer *str* in *main.* The following program implements this concept:

```
#include <iostream>
using namespace std;
```

```
char * setName();

int main (void)
{
char* str = setName();
cout << str;
return 0;
}

char* setName (void)
{
char name[80];
cout << "Enter your name: ";
cin.getline (name, 80);
return name;
}
```

The following is some sample input and output:

```
Enter your name: Jeff Kent
..................D ............    ........8   ........
```

While the outputted name is interesting, it certainly would be difficult to write, and in any event, it is not what I inputted. What went wrong is that the pointer returned by the *setName* function points to a local character array whose lifetime ended when that function finished executing and returned control to *main*.

Accordingly, the indicated solution is to extend the lifetime of that character array to the life of the program execution itself. Of course, one way to accomplish this is by making the character array a global variable, but as you should recall from Chapter 9, there are other and better alternatives.

Returning a Pointer to a Static Local Variable

One superior alternative is to make the character array in *setName* static, as in the following program:

```
#include <iostream>
using namespace std;
char * setName();

int main (void)
{
char* str = setName();
cout << str;
```

```
   return 0;
}

char* setName (void)
{
   static char name[80];
   cout << "Enter your name: ";
   cin.getline (name, 80);
   return name;
}
```

The output from the following sample input now looks much better:

```
Enter your name: Jeff Kent
Jeff Kent
```

This works because while the scope of a static local value is limited to the function in which it is declared, its lifetime is not similarly limited, but instead lasts as long as the execution of the program. Therefore, the pointer returned by the *setName* function points to a local character array whose lifetime, since it was declared with the static keyword, persisted after the *setName* function finished executing and returned control to *main*.

Returning a Pointer to a Dynamically Created Variable

Another alternative, which you learned in this chapter, is dynamic memory allocation:

```
#include <iostream>
using namespace std;
char * setName();

int main (void)
{
char* str;
str = setName();
cout << str;
delete [] str;
return 0;
}

char* setName (void)
{
char* name;
```

```
name = new char[80];
cout << "Enter your name: ";
cin.getline (name, 80);
return name;
}
```

This works because the pointer returned by the *setName* function points to a character array whose lifetime, since it was declared using dynamic memory allocation, persisted after the *setName* function finished executing and returned control to *main*.

As discussed in the previous section, if you dynamically allocate memory inside a function using a local pointer, then when the function terminates, the pointer will be destroyed but the memory will remain, orphaned since there is no longer a way of accessing it for the remainder of the program. This problem is avoided in this program since the local pointer's address is returned by the *setName* function and is assigned in main to another pointer variable, *str*. The pointer variable *str* then is used at the end of *main* with the delete operator to deallocate the character array which was dynamically allocated in the *setName* function.

This is an example where different pointers point to the same memory address. However, in the case of dynamically created memory, once you use one of those pointers with the delete operator, don't make the common mistake of using another of the pointers with the delete operator. You should only use the delete operator with a pointer that points to dynamically created memory. If that dynamically allocated memory already has been deallocated using the delete operator, using the delete operator the second time will lead to unpredictable results.

Summary

A pointer is a variable or constant whose value is the address of another variable or constant. Some C++ tasks are performed more easily with pointers, while other C++ tasks, such as dynamic memory allocation, cannot be performed without pointers.

Like any variable or constant, you must declare a pointer before you can work with it. The only difference between declaring a pointer and a variable or constant which stores a value instead of an address is that the pointer declaration includes an asterisk between the data type and the pointer name. However, the data type in the declaration of a pointer is not the data type of its value, as is the case with a variable or constant which stores a value instead of an address. The actual data type of the value of all pointers, whether integer, float, character, or otherwise, is the same, a long hexadecimal number that represents a memory address. Rather, the data type in the declaration of a pointer refers to the data type of another variable (or constant) whose memory address is the value of the pointer. In other words, the value of an integer pointer variable must be the address of an integer variable or constant, the value of a float pointer variable must be the address of a float variable or constant, and so forth.

You should always explicitly assign a pointer a value before you use it; otherwise, you risk a runtime error or worse. When you are ready to assign a pointer the address of another variable or constant, you use the address operator with the target variable or constant. However, if it is too early in your code to know which address to assign to the pointer, you first assign the pointer NULL, which is a constant defined in several standard libraries, including *iostream*. The value of NULL, the memory address 0, signals that the pointer is not intended to point to an accessible memory location.

The indirection operator is used on a pointer to obtain the value of the variable or constant to which the pointer points. This operation is said to dereference the pointer.

A pointer may be a variable or a constant. The name of an array is a constant pointer, pointing to the base address of the array. A pointer variable, being a variable, may point to different variables or constants at different times in the program.

A pointer variable may be incremented. Incrementing a pointer variable is common when looping through consecutive indices of an array. Incrementing a pointer variable does not necessarily increase its value by 1. Instead, incrementing a pointer variable increases its value by the number of bytes of its data type.

Pointers may be passed as function arguments. This is called passing by address. Pointer notation usually is used to note that an argument is a pointer. The difference in syntax between passing by reference and passing by address is that, in the function prototype and header, you use an ampersand (&) for passing by reference, but an asterisk (*) for passing by address. Additionally, if the pointer argument is the name of a single variable as opposed to an array, there are two further differences in syntax between passing by reference and passing by address. First, when you call the function, you don't need the address operator (&) for passing by reference, but you do for passing by address. Second, in the body of the called function, you don't need to dereference the argument when you pass it by reference, but you do when you pass by address.

You can use a variable as a size declarator for an array if you use dynamic memory allocation because memory is allocated at runtime from a different place—the heap—than where memory is allocated for variables declared at compile time on the stack. You need to use a pointer with the new operator to dynamically allocate memory, and the pointer must be of the same data type as the array which is to be allocated dynamically.

The lifetime of a dynamically allocated variable may be as long as that of the program's execution. However, if before the end of the program the pointer that points to a dynamically created variable goes out of scope, you no longer have any way of accessing the dynamically created memory. Therefore, the dynamically created variable still takes up memory, but is inaccessible. This is called a memory leak. To avoid memory leaks, you use the delete operator on the pointer that points to the dynamically allocated memory. This deallocates the dynamically allocated memory.

The return value of a function may be a pointer. If so, the pointer should point to either a static local variable or a dynamically created variable, not a local variable.

Quiz

1. What is a pointer?
2. Name a C++ task that requires a pointer to be performed.
3. What is the difference between declaring an integer variable and declaring an integer pointer variable?
4. What is the meaning of the data type in the declaration of a pointer?
5. What is the meaning and purpose of NULL?
6. What operator do you use to assign a pointer the address of another variable or constant?
7. What is the purpose of the indirection operator?
8. May a pointer point to different memory addresses at different times in the program?
9. May more than one pointer point to the same memory address?
10. What is the effect of incrementing a pointer variable?
11. What are the purposes of the new and delete operators?

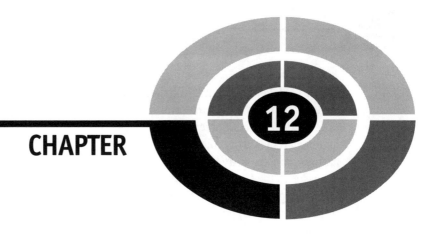

Character, C-String, and C++ String Class Functions

The word "character" has many meanings. One complimentary definition is used to denote a person with good character. A less complimentary meaning, which I heard more than once from my parents and teachers, was that I was a character.

The word character has a third meaning in programming, though—as a data type. As you learned in Chapter 2, each printable (letter, digit, punctuation) or whitespace (ENTER, TAB, SPACEBAR) key on the keyboard has a corresponding ANSI, ASCII, or Unicode value. Thus, you can assign any single user input to a character variable without fear of a data type mismatch.

Of course, often a user's input may consist of more than one character. As you learned in Chapter 10, individual characters may be organized together as a character array. Usually, a character array is ended by a null character, so its value can be outputted by the cout object and the stream insertion operator (<<). Such a null-terminated character array often is referred to as a "C-string." The "C" in "C-string" refers to this character array being used in the C programming language, which was the predecessor to the C++ programming language.

C-strings often are used for data entry. For example, if the user is supposed to enter a four-digit number, but instead enters "Jeff," an attempt to assign that input directly to an integer variable will result in either a run-time error or the integer variable having a so-called "garbage" value such as –858993460. However, if the user input is first assigned to a five-element character array (the fifth element for the null character), no run-time error would occur since any input can be represented as a character, and each character in the character array can be verified as a digit. If proper input is verified, then you can use standard library functions, as I will show you in this chapter, to convert the character array representation of an integer, long, or float value into an actual integer, long, or float value.

The C++ programming language introduced the string data type, also referred to as the C++ string class. The C++ string class often is used instead of a C-string. The functions used by C-strings and the C++ string class, respectively, will be compared and contrasted in this chapter.

Reading a Character

You may legitimately be wondering why I am devoting an entire section of this chapter to reading a character. After all, reading a character usually is relatively simple. You just use the cin object and the stream insertion operator (>>) as in the following code fragment:

```
char grade;
cout << "Enter a grade: ";
cin >> grade;
```

However, in programming, as in life, matters rarely are as simple as they first appear to be, and this is no exception. The seemingly minor detail of the ENTER key being pressed to end input gives rise to several interesting, and fortunately quite solvable, problems.

The "Press Any Key to Continue" Problem

The preceding code fragment had the user enter a character which was then assigned to a character variable. However, the purpose of a user inputting a character is not always to assign that input to a variable.

For example, programs often prompt the user to press any key to continue. Indeed, a standard technical support joke concerns a user who complains that their keyboard does not have an "any" key. Of course, any key means any key on the keyboard, including the ENTER key.

While this joke may be entertaining, implementing the "press any key to continue" functionality to include the ENTER key is more complicated than is first apparent.

Let's examine the following program:

```
#include <iostream>
using namespace std;

int main(void)
{
   char ch;
   do {
      cout << "Press Q or q to quit, any other key to continue: ";
      cin >> ch;
      if (ch != 'Q' && ch != 'q')
         cout << "You want to continue?\n";
      else
         cout << "You quit";
   } while (ch != 'Q' && ch != 'q');
return 0;
}
```

The program works fine if you press Q or q to quit. The program also works fine if you press any other printable character to continue, such as a letter other than Q or q, a digit, or a punctuation mark.

However, what if you press the ENTER key to continue? The answer is: nothing happens; cin is still waiting for you to enter something. You have to enter a printable character to continue. The reason is that the stream extraction operator (>>) ignores all leading whitespace characters, such as the newline character caused by pressing the ENTER key.

The *cin.get* Function

In Chapter 10, we discussed the *getline* function of the cin object. The *getline* function is called a *member function*. A member function is a function that is not called by itself, as is, for example, the *pow* function we used in Chapter 4 to raise a number to a certain power. Instead, a member function is called from an object. Here, *getline* is a member function of cin. It is called from cin, and separated by a dot, as in *cin.getline(name, 80)*.

Here we will use another member function of cin, *get*. The get member function was briefly explained in Chapter 10. There, the *get* function, like the *getline* function, could be called with two or three arguments, the first argument being a character array.

In addition to the two and three argument versions, the *get* member function also may be called with no arguments or with one argument. Unlike the two and three argument versions, the zero and one argument versions of the *get* member function are used to read a single character rather than a character array. The one-argument version will be discussed in this section. The no-argument version will be discussed in the next section, titled "The *cin.ignore* Function."

The data type of the one argument is a character, and the value of this argument changes to whichever keyboard key the user pressed. This is true even if the keyboard key is the ENTER key. Thus, the get member function, unlike the cin object with the stream insertion operator (<<), may be used to assign to a character variable the newline character resulting from pressing the ENTER key.

We will make one change to the previous program. We will change the statement *cin >> ch* to *cin.get(ch)*, so the program now reads as follows:

```cpp
#include <iostream>
using namespace std;

int main(void)
{
    char ch;
    do {
        cout << "Press Q or q to quit, any other key to continue: ";
        cin.get(ch);
        if (ch != 'Q' && ch != 'q')
            cout << "You want to continue?\n";
        else
            cout << "You quit";
    } while (ch != 'Q' && ch != 'q');
    return 0;
}
```

Now, as the following input and output show, the program works if you press the ENTER key to continue:

```
Press Q or q to quit, any other key to continue:
You want to continue?
Press Q or q to quit, any other key to continue: q
You quit
```

However, as shown by the following input, if you press a printable character to continue, you are not able to input at the next prompt, which is seemingly skipped:

```
Press Q or q to quit, any other key to continue: x
You want to continue?
Press Q or q to quit, any other key to continue: You want to continue?
Press Q or q to quit, any other key to continue:
```

As this output reflects, by curing the problem of a whitespace character not being recognized, we have introduced a new problem when a printable character is inputted.

A description of why this new problem occurred first requires a brief explanation of the term *input buffer*. The input buffer is an area of memory that stores input, such as from the keyboard, until that input is assigned, such as by cin and the stream extraction operator (>>) or by the *get* or *getline* member functions of the cin object.

When the loop begins, the input buffer is empty. Accordingly, execution of the loop halts at the statement *cin.get(ch)* until you enter some input.

As shown in Figure 12-1, if you press the ENTER key, the only character in the input buffer is the newline character. That character, being the first (and only) one in the input buffer, is removed from the input buffer to be assigned to the variable *ch*. Thus, at the next iteration of the loop, the input buffer again is empty.

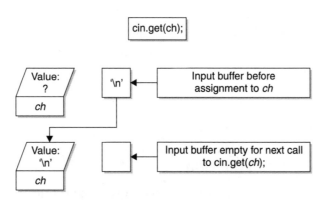

Figure 12-1   The input buffer when only the ENTER key is pressed

By contrast, if you type the letter *x* and then press the ENTER key to end input, then, as depicted in Figure 12-2, the input buffer contains not one but two characters, *x* and the ENTER key, shown by the newline character.

The *get* member function of the cin object removes the first character, *x*, from the input buffer and assigns that value to the variable *ch*. As shown in Figure 12-2, the newline character still remains in the input buffer.

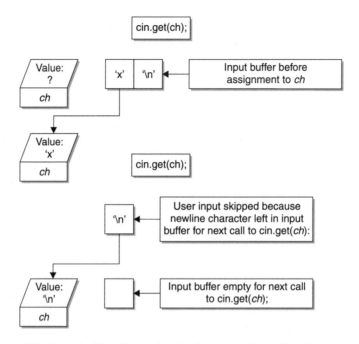

Figure 12-2   The input buffer after typing the letter x and pressing the ENTER key

Since the newline character remains in the input buffer, at the next iteration of the loop, you do not have the opportunity to enter input. Instead, the *get* member function, which reads whitespace as well as printable characters, removes the newline character from the input buffer and assigns that newline character to the variable *ch*. Now the input buffer is empty, so at the next loop iteration you will have the opportunity to enter input.

The *cin.ignore* Function

The solution is to clear the newline character out of the input buffer before calling the *getline* function. You do this by using the *ignore* member function of the cin object.

The *ignore* member function, like the *get* and *getline* member functions, also is overloaded. It can be called with no arguments, one argument, or two arguments.

Calling the *ignore* function with no arguments will cause the next character in the input buffer to be read, and then discarded—that is, it won't be assigned to anything. This is exactly what we want. We don't need to assign the newline character left over in the input buffer into some variable. Rather, we just need to get rid of it.

Note: *The one- and two-argument versions of the* ignore *member function are used with character arrays instead of with an individual character. In the one argument version of the ignore member function, the one argument is the maximum number of characters to be removed from the input buffer. For example, the statement* cin.ignore(80) *removes up to the next 80 characters from the input buffer. In the two-argument version, the second argument is a character which, if encountered before the number of characters specified in the first argument, causes the removal from the input buffer to stop. Thus, the statement* cin.ignore(80, '\n') *skips the next 80 characters or until a newline is encountered, whichever comes first.*

You also could use the *get* member function with no arguments to the same effect as the *ignore* member function with no arguments. The following two statements do the same thing:

```
cin.ignore();
cin.get();
```

This section will use the no-argument version of the *ignore* member function, but you could substitute the no argument version of the *get* member function to the same effect.

Accordingly, the following program modifies the previous one by following the call of the *get* member function with a call to the *ignore* member function:

```
#include <iostream>
using namespace std;

int main(void)
{
   char ch;
   do {
      cout << "Press Q or q to quit, any other key to continue: ";
      cin.get(ch);
      cin.ignore();
      if (ch != 'Q' && ch != 'q')
         cout << "You want to continue?\n";
      else
         cout << "You quit";
   } while (ch != 'Q' && ch != 'q');
return 0;
}
```

Now, as the following input and output show, the program works if you press a print-able character to continue:

```
Press Q or q to quit, any other key to continue: x
You want to continue?
Press Q or q to quit, any other key to continue: q
You quit
```

The reason this works is that the no-argument *ignore* member function removes the next character from the input buffer. As Figure 12-3 shows, this removes the left-over newline character from the input buffer.

However, as the following input and output show, if you press the ENTER key to continue, you have to do so twice since the first attempt seems to be skipped:

```
Press Q or q to quit, any other key to continue:

You want to continue?
Press Q or q to quit, any other key to continue: q
You quit
```

This is getting frustrating! We can get either printable or whitespace input to work properly, but not both at the same time.

It is normal to experience frustration in programming. It is how you react to the frustration that is important. Persistence pays in programming, both figuratively and literally. Almost always there is a solution, and there is one here. First, though, you should understand the problem you are trying to solve.

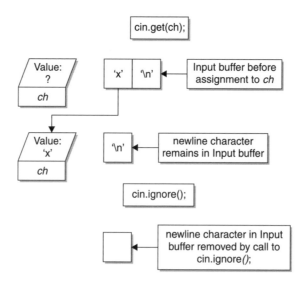

Figure 12-3   The input buffer after *cin.ignore()*

The reason you have to press the ENTER key twice after we added the call to the no-argument *ignore* member function is that the no argument *ignore* member function removes the next character from the input buffer. However, as shown in Figure 12-4, there is nothing in the input buffer when the no-argument *ignore* member function is called. Accordingly, the ENTER key needs to be pressed a second time to put something in the input buffer for the no-argument *ignore* member function to remove.

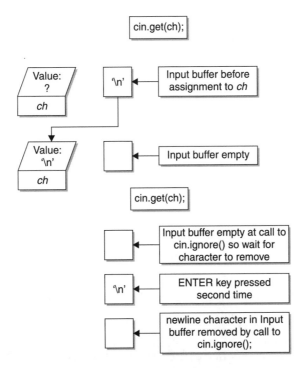

Figure 12-4   Why pressing the ENTER key twice is required

As the previous programs and sample inputs and outputs show, we need to call the *ignore* member function after the *get* member function if, and only if, a newline character remains in the input buffer. Therefore, the suggested solution is to use an if statement to call the *ignore* member function only if the character inputted by the user was not a newline character. If it was, then the input buffer would be empty after the newline character was assigned to the variable *ch,* so the *ignore* member function should not be called. However, if a printable character was entered, then the newline character would remain in the input buffer after the printable character is assigned to the variable *ch,* so the *ignore* function should be called. The following code fragment illustrates this:

```
if (ch != '\n')
        cin.ignore();
```

The following program implements this solution, modifying the previous one by calling the ignore member function only if the input was not a newline character:

```
#include <iostream>
using namespace std;

int main(void)
{
   char ch;
   do {
      cout << "Press Q or q to quit, any other key to continue: ";
      cin.get(ch);
      if (ch != '\n')
         cin.ignore();
      if (ch != 'Q' && ch != 'q')
         cout << "You want to continue?\n";
      else
         cout << "You quit";
   } while (ch != 'Q' && ch != 'q');
return 0;
}
```

Now the program works properly regardless of whether a printable character or the ENTER key is used to continue.

NOTE: *The condition for both the if and while statements is* ch != 'Q' && ch != 'q'. *A common rookie mistake is to use the || operator when the && should be used, and vice versa. Were the || operator used, as in* ch != 'Q' && ch != 'q', *the condition would always be true. A variable can have only one value at a time, so the value of ch will never equal Q or q, since it cannot equal both at the same time. Of course, the expression could be recast using the || operator as* !(ch == 'Q' && ch == 'q').

Combining Use of *cin, cin.get,* and *cin.getline*

The problem of a newline character remaining in the input buffer is not limited to the situation in which the ENTER key is pressed in response to a prompt to press any key to continue. This problem also arises when cin and the *get* or *getline* member functions are used together in one program, since the ENTER key also is used to end input.

The following program is an example of cin and the *getline* member function used together in one program:

```
#include <iostream>
using namespace std;

int main(void)
{
    char name[80];
    int courseNum;
    cout << "Enter course number: ";
    cin >> courseNum;
    cout << "Enter your name: ";
    cin.getline(name, 80);
    cout << "Course number is: " << courseNum << endl;
    cout << "Your name is: " << name << endl;
    return 0;
}
```

Here is some sample input and output:

```
Enter course number: 802
Enter your name: Course number is: 802
Your name is:
```

You did not have the opportunity to enter a name. The reason is similar to the situation in the last section in which the user did not have a chance to enter input.

As Figure 12-5 shows, when you typed 802 and then pressed the ENTER key to end input, the input buffer contained not only the number 802 but also the newline character resulting from pressing the ENTER key. The cin with the stream extraction operator (>>) removed from the input buffer and then assigned to the variable *courseNum,* everything up to, *but not including,* the newline character, which remained in the input buffer.

Since the newline character remains in the input buffer, you do not have the opportunity to enter input at the next statement: the call of the *getline* member function. Instead, as Figure 12-5 depicts, the *getline* member function, which reads whitespace as well as printable characters, removes the newline character from the input buffer and assigns that newline character to the character array *name.* While the character array name has been assigned a value, it is not a printable character, so it appears in the output that *name* has no value.

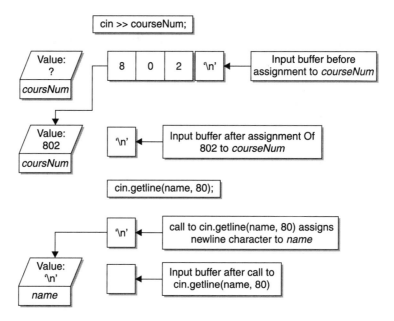

Figure 12-5   The input buffer after *cin >> courseNum* followed by
               cin.getline(name,80)

The solution, as pointed out in the previous section, is to follow use of the cin object and
the stream extraction operator (>>) with the no-argument version of the *ignore* (or *get*)
member function. However, unlike the previous section, there is no need for an if statement, since a cin statement with the stream extraction operator (>>) *always* leaves a
newline character in the input buffer. The following modification of the previous program
implements this solution by adding a call to the no-argument version of the *ignore* member
function after use of the cin object with the stream extraction operator (>>):

```
#include <iostream>
using namespace std;

int main(void)
{
    char name[80];
    int courseNum;
    cout << "Enter course number: ";
    cin >> courseNum;
    cin.ignore();
    cout << "Enter your name: ";
    cin.getline(name, 80);
```

```
    cout << "Course number is: " << courseNum << endl;
    cout << "Your name is: " << name << endl;
return 0;
}
```

As the following sample input and output show, the program now works properly:

```
Enter course number: 802
Enter your name: Jeff Kent
Course number is: 802
Your name is: Jeff Kent
```

Rules to Live By

Here are three simple rules that will avoid the problem caused by a newline character left in the input buffer (assuming, of course, you do not have a programming reason to keep the newline character in the input buffer).

Rule #1: Always follow cin and the stream extraction operator (>>) with the *ignore* member function.

Explanation: The cin object with the stream extraction operator (>>) always leaves a newline character in the input buffer. Clear it out with the *ignore* member function. For example:

```
    char ch;
    cin >> ch;
    cin.ignore();
```

Rule #2: Don't follow the *getline* member function with the no-argument *ignore* member function.

Explanation: The *getline* member function removes the newline character that terminated input from the input buffer. Therefore, it should not be followed with the *ignore* member function.

Rule #3: After using the *get* member function with one argument, such as *cin.get(ch),* check to see if you have a newline character in the input buffer. If you do, clear it with the *ignore* member function. If you don't, don't.

Explanation: The *get* member function with one argument being a single character will leave a newline character in the input buffer if you type a character and then press ENTER. It won't if you just press ENTER. Therefore, you need to check to see if you need to clear the buffer. For example:

```
    char ch;
    cin.get(ch);
    if (ch != '\n')
        cin.ignore();
```

Useful Character Functions

The C++ standard library *cctype* contains a number of functions that are useful when working with characters. Two of these functions convert the case of a letter, either from lower to upper or vice versa. The other functions are used to test the value of a character.

Case Conversion Functions

The *toupper* and *tolower* functions each have one argument, a character. If the character represents a letter, A through Z or a through z, the *toupper* function returns the upper case of that letter. Conversely, the *tolower* function returns the lower case of that letter. If the argument is not a letter, both functions simply return the same character that is the argument.

The *toupper* and *tolower* functions can be useful. For example, the following program from a previous section of this chapter requires that you check, both in an if condition and a while condition, for an uppercase Q and a lowercase q to determine if the user elected to quit:

```
#include <iostream>
using namespace std;

int main(void)
{
    char ch;
    do {
        cout << "Press Q or q to quit, any other key to continue: ";
        cin.get(ch);
        if (ch != '\n')
            cin.ignore();
        if (ch != 'Q' && ch != 'q')
            cout << "You want to continue?\n";
        else
            cout << "You quit";
    } while (ch != 'Q' && ch != 'q');
return 0;
}
```

The use of the *toupper* function eliminates the need to check for the lowercase q:

```
#include <iostream>
#include <cctype>
```

```
using namespace std;

int main(void)
{
   char ch;
   do {
      cout << "Press Q or q to quit, any other key to continue: ";
      cin.get(ch);
      ch = toupper(ch);
      if (ch != '\n')
         cin.ignore();
      if (ch != 'Q')
         cout << "You want to continue?\n";
      else
         cout << "You quit";
   } while (ch != 'Q');
return 0;
}
```

Pressing the lowercase q still will cause the program to recognize that the user quit even though the if condition and the while condition only compare to an uppercase Q:

```
Press Q or q to quit, any other key to continue: q
You quit
```

The first modification was to include the *cctype* standard library in addition to the *iostream* standard library. This is because the *toupper* and *tolower* functions are not defined in the *iostream* standard library but instead in the *cctype* standard library.

The other modification is to call the *toupper* function:

```
   ch = toupper(ch);
```

The call of the *toupper* function passes as an argument the character variable into which the user's input was stored. The return value of the function is assigned to the same character value.

It is important to use the return value. The *toupper* function does not *change* the value of its argument from lower- to uppercase. Rather, it *returns* the uppercase version of the argument if the argument is a letter.

NOTE: This program also could have employed the tolower *function instead of the* toupper *function and then compared it to a lower case q.*

Functions that Check the Value of a Character

A number of functions in the *cctype* standard library permit you to determine the value of a character—that is, whether it is a letter, digit, or whitespace. These functions each take one argument, a character, and return a Boolean value, true or false. Table 12-1 summarizes these functions.

Function	Description
isalpha	Returns true if the argument is a letter of the alphabet; false if otherwise.
isalnum	Returns true if the argument is a letter of the alphabet or a digit; false if otherwise.
isdigit	Returns true if the argument is a digit; false if otherwise.
islower	Returns true if the argument is a lower case letter of the alphabet, false otherwise.
isprint	Returns true if the argument is a printable character (including a space created by pressing the SPACEBAR); false if otherwise.
ispunct	Returns true if the argument is a punctuation character (printable character other than a letter, digit or space); false if otherwise.
isupper	Returns true if the argument is an uppercase letter of the alphabet; false if otherwise.
isspace	Returns true if the argument is a whitespace character (tab, newline, or space); false if otherwise.

Table 12-1   Functions that Check the Value of Characters

You can use these functions to validate user input. For example, the following code fragment illustrates use of a function to validate a three letter password which, to be valid, must consist of an uppercase letter followed by a digit followed by a lowercase letter, such as "Z3s."

```cpp
bool isValidPassWord(char* pw)
{
   if (!isupper(pw[0])
      return false;
   if (!isdigit(pw[1])
      return false;
   if (!islower(pw[2])
      return false;
   return true;
}
```

Useful C-String and C++ String Functions

The *cstring* standard library provides a number of functions that are useful when working with null terminated character arrays, or C-strings. The *string* standard library provides a number of functions that are useful when working with the C++ string class. This section will discuss together the functions you use with a C-string and the C++ string class, respectively, to perform several common tasks.

Determining the Length of a String

You use the *strlen* function to determine the length of a C-string. The *strlen* function takes one argument, which may be a character array, a pointer to a character array, or a literal string. This function returns an integer representing the number of characters, not including the null character. The following code fragment illustrates the use of the *strlen* function:

```
int len;
len = strlen("Jeff") // len is 4
char* stinkydog = "Dante";
len = strlen(stinkydog);    // len is 5
char name[80] = "Devvie";
len = strlen(name);   // len is 6
char crazydog[80] = "Micaela";
len = strlen(crazydog);   // len is 7
```

The *strlen* function is particularly useful in determining the length of a character array. For example, the following code fragment illustrates use of the *strlen* and *isdigit* functions to validate a social security number which, to be valid, must be exactly 11 characters long and consist of three digits, a dash, two digits, a dash, and four digits:

```
bool isValidSSN(char* strInput)
{
    if (!strlen(strInput) == 11)
        return false;
    for (int x = 0; x < 11; x++)
    {
        if (x == 3 || x == 6)
        {
            if (strInput[x] != '-')
                return false;
        }
```

```
    else
    {
        if (!isdigit(strInput[x])
            return false;
    }
  }
  return true;
}
```

The C++ string class member functions that are comparable to the effect of *strlen* are *length* and *size*. Neither has any arguments, and both return an integer representing the length of the string. The following code fragment illustrates the use of the *length* and *size* member functions:

```
string s = "Jeff Kent";
cout << s.length();   // outputs 9
cout << s.size();     // also outputs 9
```

Assigning a Value to a String

You cannot assign the value of one C-string to another with an assignment operator, such as in the following code fragment:

```
char* target = "Jeff Kent";
char source[80] = "Micaela";
target = source;
```

The value of *source* is the base address of the target array. Thus, the assignment operator assigns the *address* of *source* to *target,* not the *value* of *source* to *target.*

Instead, you use the *strcpy* function to assign the value of one C-string (the source string) to another C-string (the target string). The *strcpy* function takes two arguments. The first argument, the target string, is a pointer to a character array. This argument cannot be a string literal since a value is being assigned to it. The second argument, the source string, may be a character array, a pointer to a character array, or a string literal. The following code fragment illustrates the use of the *strcpy* function:

```
char* target = "Jeff Kent";
char source[80] = "Micaela";
strcpy(target, source);
```

You need to be careful when using the *strcpy* function that the source C-string is not larger than the target C-string. To avoid this problem, you can use the *strncpy* function. This function has a third argument, an integer, representing how many

characters to copy from the source C-string to the target C-string. The following
code fragment illustrates the use of the *strncpy* function:

```
char* target = "Jeff Kent";
char source[80] = "Micaela";
strncpy(target, source, 9);
```

In contrast to C-strings, you may use the assignment operator to assign the value
of one C++ string class variable to another, such as in the following code fragment:

```
string target = "Jeff Kent";
string source = "Micaela";
target = source;
```

Appending to a String

The *strcpy* function overwrites the contents of the target C-string with the contents of the
source C-string. Sometimes you don't want to overwrite the contents of the target C-
string, but instead add, or append, to its contents with the contents of the source C-String.
Under these circumstances, use the *strcat* function, the "cat" being shorthand for "con-
catenate," which is a longer way of saying append.

The *strcat* function, like the *strcpy* function, takes two arguments, the source target, a variable pointer to a character array, and the source C-string, which may be a
character array, a pointer to a character array, or a string literal. The following code
fragment illustrates the use of the *strcat* function:

```
char target[80]   = "Jeff";
char* source= " Kent";
strcat(target, source);
cout << target;    // outputs "Jeff Kent"
```

As with the *strcpy* function, you need to make sure when using the *strcat* function that the source string is large enough to accommodate the addition of the target
C-string.

You can append the value of one C++ string class variable to another with the
combined addition and assignment operator, such as in the following code fragment:

```
string target = "Jeff";
string source = " Kent";
target += source;
cout << target;    // outputs "Jeff Kent"
```

Comparing Two Strings

You cannot use relational operators to compare the value of one C-string to another, such as in the following code fragment:

```cpp
char str1[80] = "Devvie Kent";
char str2[80] = "Devvie Kent";
if (str1 == str2)
   cout << "The two C-strings are equal";
else
   cout << "The two C-strings are not equal";
```

The output will always be: "The two C-strings are not equal." The reason is that the value of each array name is the base address of that array. Thus, the comparison is not of values, but of addresses. Two variables cannot have the same address, so the result of the comparison for equality will be false.

Instead, you use the *strcmp* function to compare the values of two C-strings. The *strcmp* function has two arguments, the two C-strings to be compared. This function returns 0 if the two C-strings are equal in value. This is demonstrated by the following code fragment:

```cpp
char str1[80] = "Devvie Kent";
char str2[80] = "Devvie Kent";
if (strcmp(str1, str2 == 0))
   cout << "The two C-strings are equal";
else
   cout << "The two C-strings are not equal";
```

The call to the *strcmp* function could be changed to:

```cpp
if (!strcmp(str1, str2))
```

This works since 0 is logical false, so with the logical ! operator the result of logical false is changed to logical true.

The *strcmp* function returns a negative value if the first C-string is "less than" the second one, a positive value if the first C-string is "greater than" the second one. In this context of comparing two C-strings, whether one string is less or greater than another involves a comparison of the ASCII value of the two strings, starting with the first character, and continuing to each succeeding character as long as it takes to "break the tie." Table 12-2 illustrates the results of several comparisons:

First String (str1)	Second String (str2)	strCmp(str1, str2)	Reason
Jeff	jeff	negative	j has a higher ASCII value than J
aZZZ	Zaaa	positive	a has a higher ASCII value than Z
chess	check	positive	First three characters are the same, but fourth letter of first C-string, s, has higher ASCII value than fourth character of second C-string, c.
Jeff	Jeffrey	negative	First four characters are the same, but fifth character of second C-string, r, has a higher ASCII value than null character in the fifth position of the first C-string

Table 12-2   Results of String Comparisons

Because three different return values are possible, the *strcmp* function often is used in an if / else if / else structure, as in the following program:

```
#include <iostream>
#include <cstring>
using namespace std;

int main(void)
{
    char str1[80], str2[80];
    cout << "Enter first string: ";
    cin >> str1;
    cout << "Enter second string: ";
    cin >> str2;
```

```
    if (strcmp(str1, str2) == 0)
        cout << "The two C-strings are equal";
    else if (strcmp(str1, str2) > 0)
        cout << "The first C-string is larger";
     else
        cout << "The second C-string is larger";
return 0;
}
```

The following are several sample inputs and outputs:

```
Enter first string: Jeff
Enter second string: Jeff
The two C-strings are equal
===
Enter first string: Jeff
Enter second string: jeff
The second C-string is larger
===
Enter first string: chess
Enter second string: check
The first C-string is larger
===
Enter first string: Jeff
Enter second string: Jeffrey
The second C-string is larger
===
```

By contrast, you can use relational operators to compare two variables of the C++ string class. Whether one string is "less than" or "greater than" another works the same way for the C++ string class as it does for C-strings. The following code fragment is illustrative:

```
    string str1 = "Jeff";
    string str2 = "jeff";
    string str3 = "Jeffrey";
    str1 < str2;    // true
    str3 > str1;    // true
    str2 > str3;    // true
```

Conversion Between a C-String and a Number

The *cstdlib* standard library provides several functions for converting the C-string representation of a number to a numeric data type, as well as the reverse.

The *atoi* function's name is an acronym for "ASCII to integer." This function has one argument, a C-string, and returns the integer that the C-string represents. The following code fragment demonstrates how the *atoi* function works:

```
int num = atoi("7654");
```

The *atoi* function does not check if its argument can be converted to a numeric value. Additionally, the C++ programming language does not define the consequences if the argument cannot be converted to a numeric value. For example, the return value of an expression such as *atoi("12Jeff")* might be 12, the compiler attempting to perform the conversion from a character array to a number until a non-digit is reached. However, the return value instead could be 0, indicating the conversion could not be completed successfully.

The *atoi* function often is used in connection with a program that first has the user input a number into a character array, then checks if the character array represents a number before using the *atoi* function. This is demonstrated by the following program:

```
#include <iostream>
#include <cstring>
using namespace std;

int main(void)
{
    char input[80];
    int num;
    cout << "Enter an integer: ";
    cin >> input;
    for (int x = 0; x < strlen(input); x++)
    {
        if (x == 0)
        {
            if (!isdigit(input[x]) && input[x] != '-')
                return false;
        }
        else
        {
            if (!isdigit(input[x]))
                return false;
        }
    }
    num = atoi(input);
    cout << num;
    return 0;
}
```

The advantage of having the user input a number into a character array instead of an integer is to avoid a run-time error or garbage data if the input is non-numeric. The character array then is checked to see if its value is the representation of a number. Since the number may be negative, the first character may be a dash as well as a digit. If the value of the character array is confirmed to be the representation of a number, then the *atoi* function is used to assign that value to an integer variable.

The *atol* function, standing for "ASCII to Long," and the *atof* function, meaning "ASCII to Float," work the same way as the *atoi* function except that their arguments are C-string representations of a long and float, respectively, and their return values likewise are a long and a float, respectively.

The C++ string class has no member functions that correspond to *atoi, atol,* or *atof*. However, a useful alternative is to first assign the value of a string to a character array using the *c_str* member function, after which *atoi, atol,* or *atof* could be used with the character array:

```
string name = "123";
char str1[80];
strcpy(str1, name.c_str());
int num = atoi(str1);
```

The *data* member function of the C++ string class also could be used to the same effect. The call to the *strcpy* function then would be the following:

```
strcpy(str1, name.data());
```

Finally, the *itoa* function is the converse of the *atoi* function, standing for "Integer to ASCII." The *itoa* function takes three arguments, the integer value to be converted, a pointer to the C-string to which the string representation of that integer will be assigned, and the number that represents the base of the converted value. The following code fragment shows how the *itoa* function may be used to assign to the character array *intArray* the C-string representation of the number 776 in base 10:

```
char intArray[20];
itoa (776, intArray, 10);
```

Summary

The three subjects of this chapter were the character data type, a C-String (a null-terminated character array), and the C++ string class.

We first discussed the issues involved in reading a character when a newline character may be left in the input buffer, and derived the following three rules.

The first rule is to always follow cin and the stream extraction operator (>>) with the no-argument *ignore* member function. The reason is that the cin object with the stream extraction operator >> always leaves a newline character in the input buffer, so calling the no-argument *ignore* member function will dispose of that leftover newline character.

The second rule is not to use the *ignore* member function after using the *getline* member function. The reason is that the *getline* member function removes the newline character that terminated input from the input buffer.

The third rule is that after using the *get* member function with one character argument, such as *cin.get(ch),* check to see if you have a newline character in the input buffer, and if you do, clear it with the ignore member function. If you don't, don't. The reason is that the *get* member function with one argument being a single character will leave a newline character in the input buffer if you type a character and then press ENTER, but it won't if you just press ENTER.

The C++ standard library *cctype* contains a number of functions that are useful with characters. The *toupper* and *tolower* functions each have one argument, a character. If the character represents a letter, A through Z or a through z, the *toupper* function returns the uppercase of that letter. Conversely, the *tolower* function returns the lowercase of that letter. If the argument is not a letter, both functions simply return the same character that is the argument. A number of other functions in the *cctype* standard library, including but not limited to *isalpha* and *isdigit,* permit you to determine the value of a character, such as whether it is a letter, digit, or whitespace.

The *cstring* standard library provides a number of functions that are useful when working with C-strings. Similarly, the *string* standard library provides a number of functions that are useful when working with the C++ string class.

You use the *strlen* function to determine the length of a C-string, the *length* or *size* member functions to return the length of a C++ string class variable. You use the *strcpy* function to assign a value to a C-string, and the assignment operator = to assign a value to a C++ string class variable. You use the *strcat* function to append a value to a C-string, and the combined addition and assignment operator += to append a value to a C++ string class variable. You use the *strcmp* function to compare two C-strings, and the relational operators to compare two C++ string class variables.

The *cstdlib* standard library provides several functions for converting the C-string representation of a number to a numeric data type, as well as the reverse. These are *atoi,* or "ASCII to integer," *atol,* or "ASCII to Long," *atof,* or "ASCII to float," and *itoa,* or "Integer to ASCII."

Quiz

1. Which of the following will ignore a leading newline character in the input buffer, the cin object with the stream extraction operator (>>), the *get* member function, or the *getline* member function?

2. Which of the following will not leave a newline character in the input buffer, the cin object with the stream extraction operator (>>), the *get* member function, or the *getline* member function?

3. Which of the following should you always follow with the no-argument *ignore* member function, the cin object with the stream extraction operator (>>), the *get* member function, or the *getline* member function?

4. Which of the following should you never follow with the no-argument *ignore* member function, the cin object with the stream extraction operator (>>), the *get* member function, or the *getline* member function?

5. Is the argument of the *isdigit* function a character, a C-string, or a C++ string class variable?

6. Is the argument of the *atoi* function a character, a C-string, or a C++ string class variable?

7. May a C++ string class variable use the *atoi* function to convert the string representation of a number to a number?

8. Are the functions in the C++ standard library *cctype* used with characters, C-strings, or C++ string class variables?

9. Are the functions in the C++ standard library *cstdlib* used with characters, C-strings, or C++ string class variables?

10. Can you use an assignment operator to assign the value of one C-string to another?

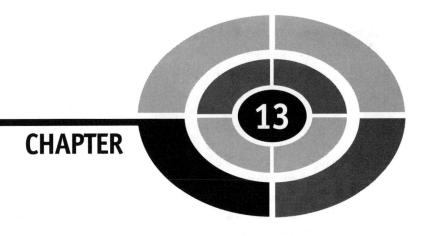

Persistent Data: File Input and Output

As a kid, I had to listen patiently, or not so patiently, to endless (so it seemed at the time) lectures from my parents on how I could be better, or do better. After I became an adult, I realized to my amazement that my parents more often than not were right. Indeed, after I became a parent, I realized to my horror that I was repeating their lectures to my own children, who, of course, today enjoy these "talks" about as much I used to.

One of my parents' favorite lectures was about how important it is to be persistent. Once again, mom and dad showed true insight, because, though persistence is a very valuable trait in any person, it is particularly important in programmers.

Data, as well as programmers, should be persistent. By persistent, I mean the data should survive when the program is finished. Can you imagine if, after typing this chapter, when I exited Microsoft Word, everything I typed was lost?

With the programs we have written so far, this is exactly what would happen. Whatever values we have stored in variables do not persist, or survive, when the program is finished. Instead, the data is lost because the data is stored in RAM (random access memory), which is cleared when the program (or the computer) stops running.

Fortunately, Microsoft Word (and most programs for that matter) has the capability to save data to a file on the computer's hard drive or other storage medium so that data later can be retrieved when needed. That data persists after the termination of the program or even after the computer is turned off.

This chapter will show you how to make your data persistent by saving it to a file. Of course, saving the data accomplishes little unless you can later retrieve it, so this chapter also will show you how to retrieve data from a file.

Text vs. Binary Files

If you work on a computer, you work with files. You may have worked with hundreds if not thousands of files. However, have you ever stopped to think about what a file exactly is?

A file is a collection of data, and is located on persistent storage (discussed in Chapter 2) such as a hard drive, a CD-ROM, or other storage device.

A file is referred to by a name (called, naturally enough, a filename), which often is descriptive of the nature or contents of the file. For example, the Microsoft Word document for this chapter may be named *chapter13*.

A filename usually has an extension, beginning with a period (.). For example, if the file for this chapter is named *chapter13.doc,* the extension is *.doc.*

The purpose of the file extension is to indicate the type of date in the file and the program that normally is used to access the file. Accordingly, by convention, *.doc* is the extension for files normally accessed by Microsoft Word, *.xls* is the extension for files normally accessed by Microsoft Excel, and so forth. One extension you may have used frequently when working with this book is *.cpp,* for C++ source files.

As there are many types of programs, there are many types of files, and many different file extensions. However, fundamentally, there are two types of files: text and binary.

A text file is, as the name suggests, a file that contains text. An example is a file you might create in Notepad or another plain-text editor.

The meaning of binary in a binary file is less intuitive. View a Microsoft Word document in Notepad or another plain-text editor, such as the one I used to type this chapter. You will see, in addition to the text, strange characters such as ã6, ÌL, h5, and dark vertical lines that most definitely do not appear in the text. These are formatting codes used by Microsoft Word to format the text, such as for tables, bulleted and numbered lists, and so forth.

Text files can only store text. By contrast, binary files can store other types of information, such as images, database records, executable programs, and so forth. Consequently, more complex programs, such as Microsoft Word, Excel, or Access, store data in binary files.

Text files are somewhat simpler than binary files to access, read, and write. Consequently, file access usually is introduced using text files, with binary files a more advanced topic. This being an introductory-level book, I will use text files when explaining file access. However, when pertinent during this chapter, I also will refer to binary files.

The fstream Standard Library

We have been using the *iostream* standard library, which supports, among other functionalities, *cin* for reading from standard input (usually the keyboard), and *cout* for outputting to standard output (usually the monitor).

Reading or writing from a file requires another standard library, *fstream*. The fstream standard library is included with the statement:

```
#include <fstream>
```

Both *iostream* and *fstream* have in common the word "stream." This is no accident. Both standard libraries concern streams of bytes. The *iostream* library concerns streams of bytes resulting from the "io" in *iostream,* input and output. The *fstream* standard library concerns streams of bytes resulting from the "f" in *fstream,* a file.

The *fstream* header file defines three new data types:

- *ofstream*   This data type represents the output file stream—the "o" in *ofstream* standing for output. The direction of output is from your program out to a file. The *ofstream* data type is used to create files and to write information to files. It cannot be used to read files.
- *ifstream*   This data type represents the input file stream—the "i" in *ifstream* standing for input. The direction of input is from a file into your program.

The *ifstream* data type is used to read information from files. It cannot be used to create files or to write information to them.

- *fstream*   This data type represents the file stream generally, and has the capabilities of both *ofstream* and *ifstream*. It can create files, write information to files, and read information from files.

The File Access Life Cycle

When your program accesses a file, whether to read it, write to it, or both, it goes through the following steps.

The file first must be opened. This establishes a path of communication between the file and a stream object in your program—*fstream, ofstream,* or *ifstream*—used to access the file.

Your program then reads from, or writes to, the file (or both). This section will discuss writing to a file before reading to it, but in your program the order could be reversed. Additionally, your program may only read from a file, or only write to a file.

Finally, your program closes the file. Maintaining the path of communication between the file and the stream object in your program requires system resources, so closing the file frees those resources when they are no longer needed. Additionally, you may not be able to access the file later in your program if you did not close it after the previous access.

Opening a File

A file must be opened before you can read from it or write to it. As discussed in the introduction to this section, opening a file establishes a path of communication between the file and a stream object in your program. Opening a file for writing is first discussed.

Opening a File for Writing

Either the *ofstream* or *fstream* object may be used to open a file for writing. However, the *ifstream* object cannot be used for this purpose because it only may be used to read from a file.

Both the *ofstream* and *fstream* objects may open a file one of two ways. The first way is using a member function named, as you might expect, *open*. The second alternative is using a constructor, which is explained in the "The *fstream* or *ofstream* Constructor" section later in this chapter.

The *Open* Member Function

Both the *ofstream* and *fstream* objects use an *open* member function, whose first argument is the name and location of the file to be opened. However, whether you include a second argument may depend on whether the *ofstream* or *fstream* object is calling the *open* member function, or whether you want to access the file in a different "mode" than the default.

First Argument—Specifying the File to Be Opened
The file to be opened for writing need not already exist. If it does not, attempting to open it for writing to it automatically will create it with the specified name at the specified location. However, whether or not the file yet exists, you need to specify a file name and location.

Accordingly, whether the *ofstream* or *fstream* object is calling the function, the first argument specifies the name and location of the file to be opened. This information may be provided by using either the *relative path* or *absolute path* of the file. The terms *relative path* and *absolute path* are new, so let's discuss them now.

The relative path is the path relative to the location of your program. For example, the following statements open for writing a file, *students.dat,* that is in the same directory as the program:

```
ofstream outfile;
outfile.open("students.dat");
```

By contrast, the absolute path is the path starting with the drive letter, and including each directory and subdirectory until the file is reached. For example, if the *students.dat* file is in the *Classes* subdirectory of the *College* directory of my C drive, it would be opened for writing, using the absolute path, as follows:

```
ofstream outfile;
outfile.open("c:\\college\classes\\students.dat");
```

Note: *Two backslashes are necessary because one backslash is used to note an escape sequence. Two backslashes is the escape sequence for one backslash.*

Whether you use a relative or absolute path, the argument for the *open* function need not be a string literal. It also may be a string variable, as in the following code fragment:

```
ofstream outfile;
char filename[80];
cout << "Enter name of file: ";
cin >> filename;
outfile.open(filename);
```

Note: *As a general rule, using a relative path is preferable, particularly if the program will be used on different machines. While the location of the data file relative to the program directory may remain the same, there is no guarantee that the particular placement of the program on one computer's directory structure will be the same as another's.*

Second Argument—File Mode

The second argument of the *open* member function defines the *mode* in which the file should be opened. One choice is whether the file should be opened for writing, reading, or both. However, there are other choices, each called a file mode *flag*. Table 13-1 lists the file mode flags:

File Mode Flag	Description
ios::app	Append mode. The file's existing contents are preserved and all output is written to the end of the file.
ios::ate	If the file already exists, the program goes directly to the end of it. Output may be written anywhere in the file. This flag usually is used with binary mode.
ios::binary	Binary mode. Information is written to the file in binary format, rather than in the default text format.
ios::in	Input mode. Information will be read from the file. The file will not be created if it does not exist.
ios::out	Output mode. Information will be written to the file. By default, the existing file contents will be overwritten.
ios::trunc	If the file already exists, its contents will be truncated, another word for deleted or overwritten. This is the default mode of ios::out.

Table 13-1   File Mode Flags

If you use the *ofstream* object to open a file, you do not *need* any file mode flags. Indeed, the examples in the previous section did not use any file mode flags. An *ofstream* object may only be used to open a file for writing, and cannot be used to open a file for reading. Therefore, there is no need to specify the *ios::out* flag; use of that flag is implied by use of the *ofstream* object to open the file.

However, you may want to use one or more file mode flags with the *open* member function of the *ofstream* object if you do not want the default, which is to open the file in text rather than binary mode and overwrite rather than append to the existing file contents. One example of when you might want to append is an error log file, which keeps track of errors that may occur in a program. When a new error occurs, you don't want to erase the history of prior errors, but rather you want to add to that history.

You can combine two or more flags when opening a file. For example, the following statements open a file in binary mode and to append rather than to overwrite. The two file mode flags are combined using the *bitwise or* operator (|):

```
ofstream outfile;
outfile.open("students.dat", ios::binary | ios::app);
```

NOTE: *The bitwise or operator | is not the same as the logical or operator || even though they share the name or and the keystroke |.*

While you don't need to specify any file mode flags if you use the *ofstream* object to open a file, you *should* specify file mode flags if you use the *fstream* object to open a file. Whereas an *ofstream* object may only be used to open a file for writing and not reading, an *fstream* object may be used for both purposes. Therefore, you should specify whether you are using the *open* member function of the *fstream* object to open the file for writing, reading, or both.

The following code fragment uses the *open* member function of the *fstream* object to open the file for writing only:

```
fstream afile;
afile.open("students.dat", ios::out);
```

The *fstream* or *ofstream* Constructor

You also may use the *fstream* or *ofstream* constructor to open a file for writing. A *constructor* is a function that is automatically called when you attempt to create an *instance* of an object.

An object instance is akin to a variable of a primitive data type, such as an int. For example, the following statement could be characterized as creating an instance, named *age,* of an integer:

```
int age;
```

Similarly, the following statement creates an *fstream* instance named *afile:*

```
fstream afile;
```

Object constructors may be overloaded, such that for the same object there may be a constructor with no arguments, a constructor with one argument, a constructor with two arguments, and so forth. For example, the previous statement, *fstream afile,* is called the no-argument constructor of the *fstream* object.

The following statement calls the one-argument constructor of the *ofstream* object, both creating an *ofstream* instance and opening the file *students.dat* for output:

```
ofstream outFile("students.dat", ios:out);
```

The following statement calls the two-argument constructor of the *fstream* object, both creating an *fstream* instance and opening the file *students.dat* for output:

```
fstream aFile("students.dat", ios:out);
```

In essence, declaring an *ofstream* (or *fstream*) variable in one statement and then calling the *open* member function in a second statement is analogous to declaring a primitive variable in one statement and then assigning it a value in a second statement, such as:

```
int age;
age = 39;
```

By contrast, using the one or two argument *ofstream* (or *fstream*) constructor is analogous to initializing a primitive variable, such as:

```
int age = 39;
```

One alternative is not inherently better than the other. Usually, the specific needs of a particular program will dictate which alternative better fits your needs.

Opening a File for Reading

The discussion in the previous section concerning opening a file for writing also applies to opening a file for reading. The primary difference is that the object that calls the *open* member function, or whose constructor you may use, may be, in addition to an *fstream* object, an *ifstream* object instead of an *ofstream* object. Additionally, the file to be opened for reading must already exist. Unlike opening a file for writing, attempting to open a file for reading will not automatically create it if it does not yet exist. This issue is discussed further in the next section.

The following statements use the *open* member function of the *ifstream* object to open a file for reading:

```
ifstream infile;
infile.open("students.dat");
```

You could accomplish the same purpose using the *fstream* object, specifying by a file mode flag that the file is being opened for reading only:

```
fstream afile;
afile.open("students.dat", ios::in);
```

The following statement uses the *ifstream* constructor to open a file for reading:

```
ifstream infile ("students.dat");
```

You could accomplish the same purpose using the *fstream* constructor, specifying in the second argument the file mode flag that the file is being opened for reading only:

```
fstream afile ("students.dat", ios::in);
```

Opening a File for Reading and Writing

You can use the *fstream* object to open a file for reading and for writing. You cannot use either the *ofstream* or *ifstream* object for this purpose, as an *ofstream* object cannot be used to read files, and an *ifstream* object cannot be used to write to files.

The following code fragment uses the *open* member function of the *fstream* object for this purpose:

```
fstream afile;
afile.open("students.dat", ios::in | ios::out);
```

Alternatively, you can use the two-argument *fstream* constructor:

```
fstream afile ("students.dat", ios::in | ios::out);
```

Both alternatives use the *bitwise or* operator (|) discussed in the earlier section "Second Argument—File Mode" to combine the file mode flags for input and output.

NOTE: Combining the ios::in and ios::out flags changes expected defaults. The ios::out flag by itself causes an existing file to be overwritten, and the ios::in flag by itself requires that the file already exist. However, when the ios::in and ios::out files are used together, the file's existing contents are preserved, and the file will be created if it does not already exist.

Checking if the File Was Opened

You should not assume that a file was successfully opened with the *open* member function or the constructor. There are several reasons why the file may not have been successfully opened. If the file was not successfully opened, but your code casually assumes it was and attempts to read from, or write to, the file, errors may occur.

The primary difference between opening a file for reading and for writing is that while you can write to a file that does not exist—the operating system simply creates the file—you cannot read from a file unless it already exists. Therefore, you should check if the file was opened successfully for reading before you attempt to read it.

If the file could not be opened for reading, then the value of the *ifstream* object that called the *open* function is NULL. As you may recall from Chapter 11, NULL is a constant defined in several standard library files whose value is zero.

Alternatively, if the file could not be opened for reading, then the *ifstream* object's *fail* member function returns true, which is the *fail* function's return value if a file operation, in this case attempting to open a file, was not successful.

The following code illustrates the use of both checking if the *ifstream* object used to call the *open* function is NULL and whether the *ifstream* object's *fail* member function returns true:

```
#include <fstream>
#include <iostream>
using namespace std;

int main ()
{
   ifstream infile;
   infile.open("students.dat");
   cout << "(infile) = " << infile << endl;
   cout << "(infile.fail()) = " << infile.fail() << endl;
   return 0;
}
```

If the *students.dat* file does not yet exist, the output would be

```
(infile) = 00000000
(infile.fail()) = 1
```

However, if there was a file named *students.dat* in the same directory as your program, then the output would be

```
(infile) = 0012FE40
(infile.fail()) = 0
```

The value, 0012FE40, is the address of the *ifstream* variable *infile,* and of course could be different if you run this program.

Unlike an *ifstream* object, an *ofstream* object that attempts to open a file that does not yet exist is not NULL, and its *fail* member function would return false, because the operating system will create the file if it does not already exist. However, opening a file for writing is not always successful. For example, before you run the following program, create a file named *students.dat* in the same directory as your program but, through its properties, check read only:

```
#include <fstream>
#include <iostream>
using namespace std;

int main ()
{
   ofstream outfile;
   outfile.open("students.dat");
   cout << "( outfile) = " << outfile << endl;
   cout << "( outfile.fail()) = " << outfile.fail() <<
endl;
   return 0;
}
```

The following output reflects that the *ofstream* object is NULL, and its *fail* function returns true, because you cannot open for writing a file that is read only.

```
(outfile) = 00000000
(outfile.fail()) = 1
```

If you cannot open a file for reading or writing, then you do not want to proceed to execute the code that reads from, or writes to, the file. Instead, you may want to stop execution of the function, as in the following code fragment:

```
ifstream infile;
infile.open("students.dat");
if (infile == NULL)
{
   cout << "Error in opening file for reading";
   return 0;
}
// code to read from file
```

NOTE: *For purposes of brevity and avoiding repetitive code, some of the following code in this chapter omits checking if a file was opened successfully.*

Closing a File

Of course, you are not going to close a file as soon as you open it. You will read or write to the file first. However, closing a file is relatively simple, so I will discuss this issue out of order before discussing the more complex subjects of writing to, and reading from, a file.

You should close a file when you are finished reading or writing to it. While the file object will be closed when the program ends, your program's performance will be improved if you close a file when you are finished with it because each open file requires system resources. Additionally, some operating systems limit the number of open "handles" to files. Finally, you will avoid a "sharing" problem caused by trying in one part of your program to open a file that in another part of the program previously was opened but not closed.

You close a file using, naturally enough, the *close* member function, which takes no arguments. The following example closes a file opened for writing:

```
ofstream outfile;
outfile.open("students.dat");
// do something
outfile.close();
```

The same syntax applies to closing a file for reading.

```
ifstream infile;
infile.open("students.dat");
// do something
infile.close();
```

Writing to a File

You output or write information to a file from your program using the *stream insertion* operator (<<) just as you use that operator to output information to the screen. The only difference is that you use an *ofstream* or *fstream* object instead of the *cout* object.

The following program writes information inputted by the user to a file named *students.dat,* which is created if it does not already exist.

```
#include <fstream>
#include <iostream>
```

```
using namespace std;

int main ()
{
   char data[80];
   ofstream outfile;
   outfile.open("students.dat");
   cout << "Writing to the file" << endl;
   cout << "====================" << endl;
   cout << "Enter class name: ";
   cin.getline(data, 80);
   outfile << data << endl;
   cout << "Enter number of students: ";
   cin >> data;
   cin.ignore();
   outfile << data << endl;
   outfile.close();
   return 0;
}
```

The input and output could be

```
Writing to the file
====================
Enter class name: Programming Demystified
Enter number of students: 32
```

Open the file in a plain-text editor such as Notepad. The contents with the preceding sample input would be as follows:

```
Programming Demystified
32
```

The statement that wrote to the file included the *endl* keyword:

```
   outfile << data << endl;
```

The reason is to write the name of the class ("Programming Demystified") to a different line than the number of students, 32. Otherwise, the file contents would be

```
Programming Demystified32
```

Note: *The call to the ignore member function after cin >> data follows the advice in Chapter 12 to clear the newline character from the input buffer after using the cin object with the stream extraction operator (>>).*

You instead could have used an *fstream* object to write to the file. You would have changed the data type of *outfile* from *ofstream* to *fstream* and then changed the call to the open method to include two arguments:

```
fstream outfile;
outfile.open("students.dat", ios::out);
```

Alternatively, you could have used the *fstream* constructor:

```
fstream outfile ("students.dat", ios::out);
```

If you want to append, you only need to add an *ios:app* flag to the second argument of the constructor or the *open* member function using the *bitwise or* operator (|).

Reading from a File

You input or read information from a file into your program using the *stream extraction* operator (>>) just as you use that operator to input information from the keyboard. The only difference is that you use an *ifstream* (or *fstream*) object instead of the *cin* object.

The following program builds on the previous one. After writing information inputted by the user to a file named *students.dat*, the program reads information from the file and outputs it onto the screen:

```
#include <fstream>
#include <iostream>
using namespace std;

int main ()
{
    char data[80];
    ofstream outfile;
    outfile.open("students.dat");
    cout << "Writing to the file" << endl;
    cout << "===================" << endl;
    cout << "Enter class name: ";
    cin.getline(data, 80);
    outfile << data << endl;
    cout << "Enter number of students: ";
    cin >> data;
    cin.ignore();
    outfile << data << endl;
    outfile.close();
```

```
    ifstream infile;
    cout << "Reading from the file" << endl;
    cout << "=====================" << endl;
    infile.open("students.dat");
    infile >> data;
    cout << data << endl;
    infile >> data;
    cout << data << endl;
    infile.close();
    return 0;
}
```

Sample input and output:

```
Writing to the file
===================
Enter class name: Programming
Enter number of students: 32
Reading from the file
=====================
Programming
32
```

Reading a Line of a File

With the same program, try entering a class name with an embedded space. The following is some sample input and output:

```
Writing to the file
===================
Enter class name: Programming Demystified
Enter number of students: 32
Reading from the file
=====================
Programming
Demystified
```

The following are the contents of the file after the inputted data was written to it:

```
Programming Demystified
32
```

The first read of the file did not read the first line of the file, "Programming Demystified." Instead, the first read of the file only read the word "Programming" and then stopped. Consequently the second line of the program read the remainder of the first line of the file, "Demystified," instead of the number of students.

The *ifstream* object together with the *stream extraction* operator reads the file sequentially, starting with the first byte of the file. The first attempt to read the file starts at the beginning of the file and goes to the first whitespace character (a space, tab, or new line) or the end of the file, whichever comes first. The second attempt starts at the first printable character after that whitespace, and continues to the next whitespace character or the end of the file, whichever comes first.

The first read attempt only read "Programming," not "Programming Demystified," because the read stopped at the whitespace between "Programming" and "Demystified." The second attempt read "Demystified." There were no further read attempts, so the number of students, 32, was never read.

This should seem like déjà vu. We encountered a similar issue in Chapter 10 using the *cin* object with the *stream extraction* operator (>>). As in Chapter 10 with the *cin* object, the solution is to use *getline*.

If you are working with C-strings, then you should use the *getline* member function. The only difference between using the *getline* member function here and in Chapter 10 is that here the *getline* member function is called by an *ifstream* or *fstream* object instead of a *cin* object. Accordingly, we need to replace the two calls to *infile >> data* with the following:

```
infile.getline(data, 80);
```

You also can use *getline* with the C++ string class. The only difference between using the *getline* member function here and in Chapter 10 is that here the first argument of the *getline* member function is an *ifstream* or *fstream* object instead of a *cin* object. Accordingly, we need to replace the two calls to *infile >> data* with the following:

```
getline(infile, data);
```

The following modification of the previous program uses the *getline* function with the C++ string class:

```
#include <fstream>
#include <iostream>
#include <string>
using namespace std;

int main ()
{
    string data;
    ofstream outfile;
    outfile.open("students.dat");
    cout << "Writing to the file" << endl;
    cout << "===================" << endl;
```

```
            cout << "Enter class name: ";
            getline(cin, data);
            outfile << data<< endl;
            cout << "Enter number of students: ";
            cin >> data;
            cin.ignore();
            outfile << data<< endl;
            outfile.close();
            ifstream infile;
            cout << "Reading from the file" << endl;
            cout << "====================" << endl;
            infile.open("students.dat");
            getline(infile, data);
            cout << data << endl;
            getline(infile, data);
            cout << data << endl;
            infile.close();
            return 0;
}
```

As the following sample input and output reflects, the first read now reads the entire first line of the file even when that line contains embedded spaces:

```
Writing to the file
===================
Enter class name: Programming Demystified
Enter number of students: 32
Reading from the file
====================
Programming Demystified
32
```

Looping Through the File

In the previous program, exactly two read attempts were made because we knew there were two lines of data in the file, no more, no less. However, often we may not know the number of pieces of data to be read. All we want is to read the file until we have reached the end of it.

The *ifstream* object has an *eof* function, *eof* being an abbreviation for end of file. This function, which takes no arguments, returns true if the end of the file has been reached, and false if otherwise.

However, the *eof* function is not as reliable with text files as it is with binary files in detecting the end of the file. The *eof* function's return value may not accurately reflect if the end of the file was reached if the last item in the file is followed by one or more whitespace characters. This is not an issue with binary files since they do not contain whitespace characters.

A better choice is the *fail* member function, discussed in the earlier section "Checking if the File Was Opened." The following code fragment shows how to use the *fail* member function in reading a file until the end of the file is reached:

```
ifstream infile;
infile.open("students.dat");
infile >> data;
while(!infile.fail())
{
    infile >> data;
    cout << data;
}
infile.close();
```

The preceding code fragment has two *infile >> data* statements, one before the loop begins, the other inside the loop. The reason is that the end of file is not detected until *after* a read attempt is made. Thus, if the *infile >> data* statement before the loop was omitted and the file was empty, the *cout << data* statement would execute before an attempt was made to detect if the end of file had been reached.

NOTE: *A do while loop could be used instead of a while loop. This would dispense with the need to check for end of file before entering the loop, but add the requirement to check inside the loop if (using an if statement) end of file had been reached. This is the usual tradeoff between while and do while loops.*

Modifying the previous program, the code now would read

```
#include <fstream>
#include <iostream>
#include <string>
using namespace std;

int main ()
{
    string data;
    ofstream outfile;
    outfile.open("students.dat");
    cout << "Writing to the file" << endl;
    cout << "====================" << endl;
    cout << "Enter class name: ";
    getline(cin, data);
```

```
    outfile << data<< endl;
    cout << "Enter number of students: ";
    cin >> data;
    cin.ignore();
    outfile << data<< endl;
    outfile.close();
    ifstream infile;
    cout << "Reading from the file" << endl;
    cout << "====================" << endl;
    infile.open("students.dat");
    getline(infile, data);
    while(!infile.fail())
    {
        cout << data << endl;
        getline(infile, data);
    }
    infile.close();
    return 0;
}
```

File Stream Objects as Function Arguments

Chapter 9 explained how you can use functions to make your code more modular. In that spirit, let's rewrite the previous program to add two functions, each to be called from *main: writeFile* to open a file for writing using an *ofstream* object, and *readFile* to open a file for reading using an *ifstream* object. Each function includes code to check if the file was opened successfully and returns a Boolean value indicating whether the file was opened successfully:

```
#include <fstream>
#include <iostream>
#include <string>
using namespace std;
bool writeFile (ofstream&, char*);
bool readFile (ifstream&, char*);

int main ()
{
    string data;
    bool status;
    ofstream outfile;
```

```cpp
      status = writeFile(outfile, "students.dat");
      if (!status)
      {
         cout << "File could not be opened for writing\n";
         cout << "Program terminating\n";
         return 0;
      }
      else
      {
         cout << "Writing to the file" << endl;
         cout << "===================" << endl;
         cout << "Enter class name: ";
         getline(cin, data);
         outfile << data<< endl;
         cout << "Enter number of students: ";
         cin >> data;
         cin.ignore();
         outfile << data<< endl;
         outfile.close();
      }
      ifstream infile;
      status = readFile(infile, "students.dat");
      if (!status)
      {
         cout << "File could not be opened for reading\n";
         cout << "Program terminating\n";
         return 0;
      }
      else
      {
         cout << "Reading from the file" << endl;
         cout << "=====================" << endl;
         getline(infile, data);
         while(!infile.fail())
         {
            cout << data << endl;
            getline(infile, data);
         }
         infile.close();
      }
      return 0;
}

bool writeFile (ofstream& file, char* strFile)
```

```
{
    file.open(strFile);
    if (file.fail())
        return false;
    else
        return true;
}

bool readFile (ifstream& ifile, char* strFile)
{
    ifile.open(strFile);
    if (ifile.fail())
        return false;
    else
        return true;
}
```

For each function, the file stream object is passed by reference instead of by value even though neither function changes the contents of the file. The reason is that the internal state of a file stream object may change with an open operation even if the contents of the file may not change.

Summary

Data is persistent when it survives after the program is finished or even after the computer is turned off. Data stored in variables does not persist because RAM, where the variables are stored, is cleared when the program (or the computer) stops running. It is necessary to save data to a file on the computer's hard drive or other storage medium so that data later can be retrieved when needed.

This chapter showed you how to make your data persistent by saving it to a file. Since saving the data accomplishes little unless you can later retrieve it, this chapter also showed you how to retrieve data from a file.

A file is a collection of data. It is located on persistent storage, such as a hard drive, CD-ROM, or other storage device.

Files store data in one of two formats, text and binary. Text files store data that has been converted into strings of ASCII characters. By contrast, binary files store data in the same format in which data is stored in RAM, fundamentally ones and zeroes. Notepad and other plain-text editors use text files. Binary files may store more complex data, and therefore are used in more complex programs, such as word processing, spreadsheet, or database programs.

You should include the *fstream* standard library when your program reads from, or writes to, files. This standard library defines three data types. The *ofstream* data type represents the output file stream, the direction of output being from your program out to a file. The *ifstream* data type represents the input file stream, the direction of input being from a file into your program. Finally, the *fstream* data type represents the file stream generally, and has the capabilities of both *ofstream* and *ifstream* in that it may both write information to files and read information from files.

The process of accessing a file, whether to read it, write to it, or both, goes through the following steps. First, the file first must be opened to establish a path of communication between the file and a stream object in your program—*fstream, ofstream,* or *ifstream*—used to access the file. Second, your program then reads from, or writes to, the file. Third, and finally, your program closes the file, using the *close* member function, to free system resources that are required to maintain the path of communication between the file and the stream object in your program, and also to avoid a "sharing" problem caused by trying in one part of your program to open a file that in another part of the program previously was opened but not closed.

You use either the *open* member function or a constructor to open a file. A constructor is a function that is automatically called when you attempt to create an *instance* of an object, such as an *fstream, ofstream,* or *ifstream* object. Either the *open* member function or a constructor may use two arguments. The first argument is the relative or absolute path to the file. The second argument, which may be optional, is one or more file mode flags, which define how the file should be opened, whether for input, output, appending, or something else.

You cannot assume that a file was successfully opened for reading or writing. You can use the *fail* member function to check if a file was successfully opened. You also can check to see if the file stream object used to open the file is NULL.

You write information to a file from your program using the *stream insertion* operator (<<) just as you use that operator to output information to the screen, except that you use an *ofstream* or *fstream* object instead of the *cout* object. Similarly, you read information from a file into your program using the *stream extraction* operator (>>) just as you use that operator to input information from the keyboard, except that you use an *ifstream* (or *fstream*) object instead of the *cin* object.

You read a line of a file using either the *getline* member function if you are working with C-strings or the *getline* function if you are working with the C++ string class. You use the *fail* member function to test for the end of the file as you read line by line through a file.

File stream objects may be passed as function arguments. They should be passed by reference rather than by value since the internal state of a file stream object may change with an open operation even if the contents of the file have not changed.

Quiz

1. What does it mean for data to be persistent?

2. What is a file?

3. What are the two formats in which files store data?

4. What standard library should you include when your program reads from, or writes to, files?

5. Which of the three objects, *fstream, ifstream,* or *ofstream,* may be used both for file input and file output?

6. What are the two functions you can use to open a file?

7. What is the purpose of opening a file?

8. What is the purpose of closing a file?

9. What is a constructor?

10. Which is a better choice for detecting end of file in a text file, the *eof* member function or the *fail* member function?

11. Should file stream objects be passed as function arguments by value or by reference?

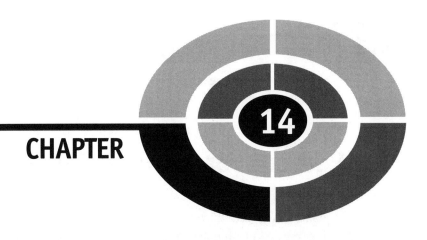

CHAPTER

14

The Road Ahead: Structures and Classes

Late one evening, at the end of the final session of a computer programming class I taught that left off where the last several chapters do, one of my students asked me: "Where do I go from here?" My suggestion was: "Home."

My answer, while technically accurate, was not very helpful, so my student attempted to follow up: "No, I mean, what can I expect from the next class?" My prediction was, quoting from Mr. T when asked his prediction for the outcome of his upcoming rematch with Rocky Balboa in *Rocky III:* "Pain."

That answer too might have been accurate (depending on which teacher he took next) but it also was not very helpful, so I then spared my student further stale humor and described to him what I am about to tell you in this chapter. Of course, the student received a much more condensed explanation since it was late in the evening. Before getting to that though, I have a question for you: "Why are you reading this book?"

Your Reasons for Reading This Book?

I knew the student well from other classes he had taken with me, so I knew his future plans, which were relevant to the answer I gave him. However, I don't know yours. Therefore, I need to ask you, or perhaps you need to ask yourself, which of the following best describes why you are reading this book:

- I am reading this book to help me with a course I am taking as part of my plan to obtain a degree.
- I am reading this book to help me upgrade my skills for my current job or to retrain for a new job.
- I am reading this book because programming is my hobby.
- I am reading this book because I have nothing better to do.

If you chose the last statement, then you may need to get out more often. Otherwise, whether your primary reason for reading this book is higher education, a job, or a hobby will, of course, influence your next steps in programming. For example, if you are retraining for a particular programming position, your focus will be much more specific than a student who is planning to obtain a higher degree in computer science.

Nevertheless, regardless of whether your focus is specific or general, the major area that follows the subjects covered in this book is Object-Oriented Programming, often known by its acronym OOP. OOP (described in the following section) heavily uses two programming concepts: structures and classes. Therefore, this chapter, and book, concludes by covering these two concepts.

Object-Oriented Programming

Object-Oriented Programming, often known by its acronym, OOP, is a term used more than it is understood. However, understanding OOP principles is important, since OOP really is the next step. Indeed, the previous chapters have given you the foundation to learn OOP.

I am not going to attempt to cover the entire subject of OOP in this chapter; entire books are written about OOP. Indeed, one of the companion books in the Demystified series to which this book belongs is *Object-Oriented Programming Demystified.* Nevertheless, let me try to briefly describe OOP.

While game programs are fun, the usual purpose of a program is to provide a solution to real-world tasks, which involve persons, places, things, or concepts. Programs use objects to represent a real-world person, place, thing, or concept.

Objects generally are *abstractions,* simplifying the real-world person, place, thing, or concept they represent. Just as you don't need to know how an internal combustion engine works to drive a car, you don't need to understand the inner workings of the object to know how to use it.

For example, as recently as the last chapter, we used objects, specifically the file stream objects, *fstream, ofstream,* and *ifstream.* We did not need to understand the inner workings of these objects, as detailed in the *fstream* standard library, to use them to open, read from, write to, and close files.

Objects are not limited to something as abstract as a file stream object, however. You are a person object. This book is a book object. The car you drive is a car object. A character in a game also is an object. The number and variety of possible objects is limited only by the programmer's imagination and creativity.

Real-world objects also have relationships with other real-world objects. These relationships are either an "is a" relationship or a "has a" relationship.

An example of an "is a" relationship is that a teacher *is a* person. Some of my students have questioned this in respect to certain teachers, but then we call a truce after I remind them that a student also "is a" person, even though there are a few whom I've had my doubts about.

An "is a" relationship is important because if you already have created a person class, when you write the teacher class you don't need to write code for those attributes that a teacher has in common with all persons, such as a name, birthday, height, weight and so forth. Rather, the teacher class can "inherit" those attributes from the person class, so you only need to write code for those attributes that a teacher has in addition to, or different than, all persons generally, such as tenure status, a higher education level, and so on.

This ability of one class to inherit from another is called, naturally enough, inheritance. Inheritance enables you to reuse existing code, such as the person class, when creating classes that represent more specialized objects, like teachers.

An example of a "has a" relationship is that a car *has an* engine. This type of relationship also is referred to as composition or, the term I will use, containership. Containership also enables you to reuse existing code, such as the engine class, when creating classes that represent the containing object, like cars.

Code reusability makes application development faster since you don't have to "reinvent the wheel." Additionally, the applications you develop are less buggy since the code you are reusing already has been tested (hopefully).

Since structures and classes are heavily used in OOP, let's discuss them now.

Structures

Objects generally are too complex to be described by a single variable. An array can store multiple values, but all the values in that array must be of the same data type.

The restriction that all values must be of the same data type usually is not workable for objects. For example, each of us as human beings shares common characteristics such as a name and height. The value of each may be stored in a variable. However, these variables have different data types. Height may be stored in an integer or other numeric variable, but a name would be stored in a C-string or a C++ string class variable.

The name and height variables are related in the sense that they both describe different characteristics of the same person. However, if you declare them as follows, they do not belong together, but instead simply are two separate, independent variables:

```
string name;
int height;
```

C++ enables you to package related variables together into a structure. A structure may contain multiple variables of different data types, permitting the program to more faithfully emulate the complexity of a real-world object.

A structure, in reality, is a data type. However, it is not a data type built into C++, such as an int or a C-string. Instead, it is a programmer-defined data type.

Declaring a Structure

Since a structure is a programmer-defined data type, you must declare it so the compiler will understand what it is. The following code fragment declares a structure representing a person with two characteristics, name and height:

```
struct Person {
    string name;
    int height;
};
```

The declaration commences with *struct,* which is a keyword indicating that a structure is being declared. "Person" is the name I gave for this structure. I could have used another name. As with naming variables, you should give the structure a name which indicates what it represents.

The open and close curly braces define the body of the structure. Structures, like functions, have a body, enclosed in open and close curly braces. However, unlike functions, the close curly brace must be followed by a semicolon.

NOTE: *Forgetting the semicolon after the close curly brace is a common rookie mistake. You may not experience a compiler error, but instead a run-time error, particularly on multiple file projects, with the error message providing little or no clue that the real reason for the error is that you forgot the semicolon.*

The variables that are related to each other are declared in the body of the structure. Each such variable is referred to as a *member variable*. A structure may have many member variables. Indeed, as discussed in a later section in this chapter, "Nesting Structures," a variable of one structure may be a member variable of another structure.

A structure may be declared pretty much anywhere in your code. However, by convention, a structure usually is declared just below the preprocessor directives and above *main,* as in the following code fragment:

```
#include <iostream>
#include <string>
using namespace std;
struct Person {
    string name;
    int height;
};
int main ()
{
    // code
    return 0;
}
```

You may be wondering: "Wait a minute! He is declaring a structure the same place a global variable would be declared and he taught us not to use global variables unless absolutely necessary."

Don't worry, this is not a case of "Do what I say, not what I do." When we declare a structure, we are not declaring a variable. Instead, we are declaring a data type. By declaring the data type globally, we will be able to use that data type throughout the program. The reasons for not making variables global don't apply to declaring a data type. For example, you can't assign a value to a Person structure any more than you can assign a value to an int. Instead, you need to declare variables of the structure. That issue is discussed next.

Declaring a Structure Variable

Late on a Saturday evening, I drove to a party to pick up my teenage daughter. The party was noisy, packed with perhaps one hundred teenagers, each in programming parlance an instance of a Person structure, with their own name and height. Some also had nose rings, but I won't talk about that variable. Anyway, I was looking for just one particular person, my daughter. When I went up to the parent hosting the party, I did not ask if they knew where a generic Person was. Instead, I asked if they knew where I could find a particular person, identifying her specifically.

A generic person is the Person structure that in the previous section I showed you how to declare. However, each particular person is an instance of the Person structure, and each such instance needs to be declared as a Person structure variable.

You declare a structure variable essentially the same as you declare a variable of a built-in data type. The following code declares a Person variable:

```
Person p1;
```

As with the declaration of a variable of a built-in data type, the declaration of a structure variable starts with the data type, then a variable name, and closes with a semicolon to indicate to the compiler the end of the statement.

You also can declare multiple Person variables, such as:

```
Person p1, p2, p3;
```

Indeed, for the mob scene at the party where I went to pick up my daughter, you might want to declare an array of Person variables:

```
Person p[100];
```

You may declare a structure variable essentially anywhere in your program; the same scope and lifetime rules apply just the way they do for integer, float, and other types of variables.

Accessing Structure Member Variables

Declaring a structure variable does not assign values to its member variables. You can access a member variable by the name of a structure variable, a dot operator, which looks like a period, and the name of the member variable. The following code assigns the value "Emily Kent" to the *name* member variable of the Person variable *p1*:

```
p1.name = "Emily Kent";
```

Similarly, you could output the value of the member variable using the same syntax:

```
cout << "The name of p1 is " << p1.name;
```

Don't make the beginner's mistake of using the name of the structure, rather than the name of the structure variable, as in the following example:

```
Person.name = "Emily Kent";    // won't work!
```

The following program declares a three-element Person array, assigns values to the member variables of each element, and then outputs their values:

```cpp
#include <iostream>
#include <string>
using namespace std;
const int MAX = 3;
struct Person {
    string name;
    int height;
};
int main ()
{
    Person p[MAX];
    for (int x = 0; x < MAX; x++)
    {
        cout << "Enter person's name: ";
        getline(cin, p[x].name);
        cout << "Enter height in inches: ";
        cin >> p[x].height;
        cin.ignore();
    }
    cout << "Outputting person data\n";
    cout << "=====================\n";
    for (x = 0; x < MAX; x++)
        cout << "Person #" << x + 1 << "'s name is "
            << p[x].name << " and height is "
            << p[x].height << endl;
    return 0;
}
```

Some sample input and output could be

```
Enter person's name: Genghis Khent
Enter height in inches: 78
Enter person's name: Jeff Kent
Enter height in inches: 72
Enter person's name: Dante Kent
Enter height in inches: 10
Outputting person data
=====================
Person #1's name is Genghis Khent and height is 78
Person #2's name is Jeff Kent and height is 72
Person #3's name is Dante Kent and height is 10
```

Initializing a Structure

There are two ways you may initialize a structure. The first way is to use an initialization list. The second way is to use a constructor.

Initialization Lists

The following code fragment demonstrates how you can initialize a structure with an initialization list:

```
Person p1 = {"Jeff Kent", 72};
```

This may seem like déjà vu, since an array is similarly initialized with an initialization list. However, there is an important difference. While all of the elements of an array share the same data type, the member variables of a structure may have different data types. This makes the order of the values in the initialization list particularly important. For example, the following code will result in a compiler error because the first member variable of the structure is a C-string and you cannot assign an integer to a C-string:

```
Person p1 = {72, "Jeff Kent"};   // won't work
```

Constructors

The constructor was discussed in Chapter 13 in connection with file stream objects. The constructor is a function that is automatically called when you attempt to create an instance of an object.

Default Constructors

You do not need to write a constructor. Indeed, we did not write a constructor in the previous program that declared a three-element Person array, assigned values to the member variables of each element, and then outputted their values.

If you do not write a constructor, then a default constructor is called. The term default means the constructor is supplied by default since you did not write one.

The following program demonstrates the use of the default constructor:

```
#include <iostream>
#include <string>
using namespace std;
const int MAX = 3;
struct Person {
   string name;
   int height;
```

```
};

int main ()
{
   Person p1;
   cout << "The person's name is "
        << p1.name << " and height is "
        << p1.height << endl;
   return 0;
}
```

The output is

```
The person's name is  and height is -858993460
```

The default constructor was called by the following statement, which created a Person instance:

```
   Person p1;
```

The result was that a Person instance was created by the default constructor. However, the member variables were not assigned values. Consequently, the value of the *name* member variable is an empty string and the value of the *height* member variable is a "garbage" value.

No-Argument Constructors

You can write a no-argument constructor that, unlike the default constructor, assigns default values to the member variables. The following code shows the addition of a no-argument constructor inside the body of the declaration of the Person structure:

```
struct Person {
   string name;
   int height;
   Person()
   {
      name = "No name assigned";
      height = -1;
   }
};
```

The constructor itself reads

```
   Person()
   {
      name = "No name assigned";
      height = -1;
   }
```

The name of the constructor is always the same as the name of the structure itself; no exceptions. Additionally, the constructor has no return value; again, no exceptions. Indeed, some compilers will object if you put a void return value in the function header.

Modify the program by adding the no-argument constructor to the declaration of the Person structure. The program now reads

```cpp
#include <iostream>
#include <string>
using namespace std;
const int MAX = 3;
struct Person {
    string name;
    int height;
    Person()
    {
        name = "No name assigned";
        height = -1;
    }
};

int main ()
{
    Person p1;
    cout << "The person's name is "
        << p1.name << " and height is "
        << p1.height << endl;
    return 0;
}
```

The output now reflects the default values:

```
The person's name is No name assigned and height is -1
```

NOTE: *This no-argument constructor, like the default constructor, is called by the statement* Person p1. *Though a no argument constructor is called, there are no empty parentheses following* p1 *since it is not a function call but instead a variable declaration.*

Constructors with Arguments

Declaring a no-argument constructor is an improvement over the default constructor since now the member variables have default values. However, it would be even better if we could truly initialize the member variables with values supplied by the user when the program is running. This is possible if we add arguments to the constructor, each argument being the value used to initialize a member variable. Accordingly, add the following two-argument constructor to the definition of the Person structure:

```
Person(string s, int h)
  {
     name = s;
     height = h;
  }
```

The program now reads

```
#include <iostream>
#include <string>
using namespace std;
const int MAX = 3;
struct Person {
   string name;
   int height;
   Person()
   {
      name = "No name assigned";
      height = -1;
   }
   Person(string s, int h)
   {
      name = s;
      height = h;
   }
};

int main ()
{
   int inches;
   string strName;
   cout << "Enter person's name: ";
   getline(cin, strName);
   cout << "Enter height in inches: ";
   cin >> inches;
   cin.ignore();
   Person p1(strName, inches);
   cout << "The person's name is "
      << p1.name << " and height is "
      << p1.height << endl;
   return 0;
}
```

The sample input and output could be

```
Enter person's name: Jeff Kent
Enter height in inches: 72
The person's name is Jeff Kent and height is 72
```

The two-argument constructor is called by the following declaration of a Person instance:

```
Person p1(strName, inches);
```

The parentheses are necessary because there are arguments. The arguments must be in the order the constructor is expecting. If the constructor expects the first argument to be a string and the second to be an integer, a compiler error will result if you declare the Person instance with the first argument being an integer and the second a string.

Separating the Constructor Prototype and Implementation

The following code modifies the previous program by separating the prototype of the constructors from the implementation of the constructors. The prototypes are inside the declaration of the structure. However, the implementations are outside the declaration of the structure:

```
#include <iostream>
#include <string>
using namespace std;
const int MAX = 3;
struct Person {
    string name;
    int height;
    Person();
    Person(string, int);
};

    Person::Person()
    {
        name = "No name assigned";
        height = -1;
    }
    Person::Person(string s, int h)
    {
        name = s;
        height = h;
    }
```

```
int main ()
{
    int inches;
    string strName;
    cout << "Enter person's name: ";
    getline(cin, strName);
    cout << "Enter height in inches: ";
    cin >> inches;
    cin.ignore();
    Person p1(strName, inches);
    cout << "The person's name is "
        << p1.name << " and height is "
        << p1.height << endl;
    return 0;
}
```

In the function header of each of the constructors, the function name is preceded by the class name and the scope resolution operator (::):

```
Person::Person()
Person::Person(string s, int h)
```

The reason is that since the function implementation is outside of the class, preceding the function name with the structure name and the scope resolution operator (::) is necessary to tell the compiler that the function belongs to the structure rather than being just another standalone function like the ones you created in Chapter 9.

While the preceding discussion should explain how you can separate the prototype and implementation of the constructors, the question thus far unanswered is why. The reason is in OOP—one principle is to separate what a function does from how it does it. This enables programmers to later improve how a function does its job without affecting the function's signature (arguments and return value) on which existing programs using the function depend.

Passing Structures as Function Arguments

The following program passes a Person structure instance as an argument to two functions. The *setValues* function assigns values to the member variables of the structure instance, whereas the *getValues* function outputs the values of the member variables of the structure instance:

```
#include <iostream>
#include <string>
using namespace std;
struct Person {
```

```
      string name;
      int height;
};
void setValues(Person&);
void getValues(const Person&);

int main ()
{
      Person p1;
      setValues(p1);
      cout << "Outputting person data\n";
      cout << "=====================\n";
      getValues(p1);
      return 0;
}

void setValues(Person& pers)
{
      cout << "Enter person's name: ";
      getline(cin, pers.name);
      cout << "Enter height in inches: ";
      cin >> pers.height;
      cin.ignore();
}

void getValues(const Person& pers)
{
      cout << "Person's name is " << pers.name
            << " and height is " << pers.height << endl;
}
```

The following is some sample input and output:

```
Enter person's name: Genghis Khent
Enter height in inches: 78
Outputting person data
=====================
Person's name: Genghis Khent
Person's height in inches is: 78
```

Unlike an array name, a structure's value is not an address. Therefore, to change the values of its member variables when passing a structure as a function argument, the structure needs to be passed by reference or by address. Therefore, in the *setValues* function, which changes the member variables of the structure passed to it, the structure is passed by reference.

However, the structure also is passed by reference to the *getValues* function even though that function does not change the value of its member variables. The reason is that less memory is required to pass the address of an object than the object itself, which may take up a lot of bytes. However, here the structure instance in the *getValues* function's argument list is preceded with the *const* keyword to prevent the function from inadvertently changing the values inside the structure instance.

Nesting Structures

In previous chapters, we have nested if statements within if statements, and loops within loops. You also may nest a structure within another structure.

Of course, your mother may have told you (or at least mine told me) "Just because you can do something doesn't mean you *should* do it." Here, however, nesting structures is a good idea.

Using our Person structure example, every person has a birthday. A birthday is a date. A date, in turn, may be defined by a structure that contains three member variables, all integers, which represent the month, day, and year of the particular date. The Date structure could be declared as follows:

```
struct Date
{
    int month;
    int day;
    int year;
};
```

The Person structure declaration then would be modified to add a member variable, of the structure Date, named *bDay,* to represent the person's birthday:

```
struct Person {
    string name;
    int height;
    Date bDay;
};
```

The following code modifies the previous one by adding the Date structure and the *bDay* Date member variable to the Person structure, as well as modifying the *setValues* function to also assign a value to the *bDay* Date member variable and the *getValues* function to output the value of that member variable:

```
#include <iostream>
#include <string>
using namespace std;
struct Date
```

```
{
    int month;
    int day;
    int year;
};
struct Person {
    string name;
    int height;
    Date bDay;
};
void setValues(Person&);
void getValues(const Person&);

int main ()
{
    Person p1;
    setValues(p1);
    cout << "Outputting person data\n";
    cout << "======================\n";
    getValues(p1);
    return 0;
}

void setValues(Person& pers)
{
    cout << "Enter person's name: ";
    getline(cin, pers.name);
    cout << "Enter height in inches: ";
    cin >> pers.height;
    cin.ignore();
    cout << "Enter month, day and year of birthday separated by spaces: "
    cin >> pers.bDay.month >> pers.bDay.day >> pers.bDay.year;
    cin.ignore();
}

void getValues(const Person& pers)
{
    cout << "Person's name: " << pers.name << endl;
    cout << "Person's height in inches is: " << pers.height << endl;
    cout << "Person's birthday in mm/dd/yyyy format is: "
        << pers.bDay.month << "/" << pers.bDay.day
        << "/" << pers.bDay.year << endl;
}
```

The following is some sample input and output:

```
Enter person's name: Genghis Khent
Enter height in inches: 78
Enter month, day and year of birthday separated by spaces: 3 4 1211
```

```
Outputting person data
======================
Person's name: Genghis Khent
Person's height in inches is: 78
Person's birthday in mm/dd/yyyy format is: 3/4/1211
```

The Date structure must be declared before the Person structure. Otherwise, the compiler would not know what Date was in the declaration of the *bDay* member variable of the Person structure.

The *setValues* function sets the value of the person's birthday. It cannot do so by:

```
cin >> pers.bDay
```

The reason is that *bDay* is not an integer that can be assigned user input of an integer. Instead, it itself is also a structure. Therefore, it is necessary to drill down further into the member variables of *bDay*, *month*, *day,* and *year*, as in the following statement:

```
cin >> pers.bDay.month >> pers.bDay.day >> pers.bDay.year;
```

Similarly, the *getValues* function cannot output the person's birthday with the statement:

```
cout << pers.bDay;
```

Instead, it must also drill down further into the member variables of *bDay*, *month, day,* and *year*, as in the following statement:

```
cout << "Person's birthday in mm/dd/yyyy format is: "
    << pers.bDay.month << "/" << pers.bDay.day
    << "/" << pers.bDay.year << endl;
```

The nesting of a Date structure variable in a Person structure is an example of containership (discussed previously in this chapter in the section "Object-Oriented Programming") in that a person "has a" birthday.

Classes

Most of the previous discussion on structures applies also to classes. Indeed, for the most part you can simply substitute the *class* keyword for the *struct* keyword when declaring the class.

However, there is an important difference between structures and classes. To illustrate that difference, let's run the following program which is identical to the one in the earlier section, "Passing Structures as Function Arguments," with one exception: the *class* keyword has been substituted for the *struct* keyword when declaring the Person class:

```cpp
#include <iostream>
#include <string>
using namespace std;
class Person {
    string name;
    int height;
};
void setValues(Person&);
void getValues(const Person&);

int main ()
{
    Person p1;
    setValues(p1);
    cout << "Outputting person data\n";
    cout << "======================\n";
    getValues(p1);
    return 0;
}

void setValues(Person& pers)
{
    cout << "Enter person's name: ";
    getline(cin, pers.name);
    cout << "Enter height in inches: ";
    cin >> pers.height;
    cin.ignore();
}

void getValues(const Person& pers)
{
    cout << "Person's name: " << pers.name << endl;
    cout << "Person's height in inches is: " << pers.height << endl;
}
```

The unfortunate result is a number of compiler errors in *getValues* and *setValues*. Each reference to *pers.name* and *pers.height* is flagged by an error message that you are unable to access a private member declared in class Person. What happened?

The reason why we experienced compiler errors when Person is a class but not when it is a structure is that, by default, member variables of a class are *private,* whereas member variables of a structure are *public.*

A public member variable may be accessed anywhere in the program. Therefore, when Person was a structure instead of a class, the compiler did not object when we attempted to access *pers.name* and *pers.height* in *getValues* and *setValues* because *name* and *height* are public variables.

By contrast, a private member variable may be accessed only by a member function of the same class. The *getValues* and *setValues* functions are not member functions of the Person class, as a Person constructor would be, for example. Since the *getValues* and *setValues* functions are outside the class, they are not permitted to access the Person private member variables *name* and *height.* The result of this impermissible attempt is a compiler error.

The solution is to create public member functions to read from, and write to, the private member variables. These member functions are public so they can be accessed outside the class.

In the following program, the *getName* member function reads from the *name* member variable and the *setName* member function writes to it. Similarly, the *getHeight* member function reads from the *height* member variable, and the *setHeight* member function writes to it.

```cpp
#include <iostream>
#include <string>
using namespace std;

class Person {
   private:
      string name;
      int height;
   public:
      string getName() const;
      void setName(string);
      int getHeight() const;
      void setHeight(int);
};

   string Person::getName() const
   { return name; }

   void Person::setName(string s)
   {
      if (s.length() == 0)
         name = "No name assigned";
      else
         name = s;
   }

   int Person::getHeight() const
   { return height; }
```

```
        void Person::setHeight(int h)
        {
           if (h < 0)
              height = 0;
           else
              height = h;
        }

void setValues(Person&);
void getValues(const Person&);

int main()
{
   Person p1;
   setValues(p1);
   cout << "Outputting person data\n";
   cout << "=====================\n";
   getValues(p1);
   return 0;
}

void setValues(Person& pers)
{
   string str;
   int h;
   cout << "Enter person's name: ";
   getline(cin,str);
   pers.setName(str);
   cout << "Enter height in inches: ";
   cin >> h;
   cin.ignore();
   pers.setHeight(h);
}

void getValues(const Person& pers)
{
   cout << "Person's name: " << pers.getName() << endl;
   cout << "Person's height in inches is: " <<
        pers.getHeight() << endl;
}
```

Note: *The earlier section on "Passing Structures as Function Arguments"*
explains why the getValues function passes its argument by reference and why that

argument is preceded by the const keyword. Similarly, the getName and getHeight member functions are followed by the const keyword to indicate they will not change the values of the Person object that calls them.

Now the program compiles and runs and provides the expected output:

```
Enter person's name: Jeff Kent
Enter height in inches: 72
Outputting person data
======================
Person's name: Jeff Kent
Person's height in inches is: 72
```

While this program works fine, you legitimately may wonder why we went to the trouble of using public member functions to read from, and write to, private member variables, rather than just make the member variables public.

When Person was a structure instead of a class, there was nothing in the structure to prevent invalid values from being assigned to its member variables since the structure permitted direct access to these variables from outside the structure. Therefore, the assigned input could be a blank name and negative height:

```
Enter person's name:
Enter height in inches: -5
Outputting person data
======================
Person's name:
Person's height in inches is: -5
```

However, when Person is a class, the member functions could perform input validation before assigning the input value to the member variable. In this regard, the *setName* member function checks if the input string is blank, and if it is, assigns "No name assigned" rather than a blank string to the *name* member variable. Similarly, the *setHeight* member function checks if the input number is negative, and if it is, assigns zero instead of the negative number to the *height* member variable. The following sample input and output demonstrates this:

```
Enter person's name:
Enter height in inches: -5
Outputting person data
======================
Person's name: No name assigned
Person's height in inches is: 0
```

This demonstrates another aspect of OOP, encapsulation or information-hiding. The applicability of information hiding is that the class' data or information, contained

in its member variables, is hidden from the "outside world" and access to them is restricted to member functions. Encapsulation applies because a member variable is packaged together with the member functions that read or write to it.

One benefit, as this example demonstrated, is for the member functions that write to member variables to perform input validation. Another benefit could be for the member functions that read from member variables and return their values to restrict read access to only those users who in the particular system have the right to access that information.

Summary

Object-Oriented Programming (often known by its acronym, OOP) concerns, as its name indicates, objects. A common purpose of a program is to provide a solution to real-world tasks, which involve persons, places, things, or concepts. Programs use objects to represent real-world persons, places, things, or concepts.

Real-world objects also have relationships with other real-world objects. These relationships are either an "is a" relationship or a "has a" relationship.

An example of an "is a" relationship is that a teacher *is a* person. This type of relationship is referred to as inheritance. Inheritance enables you to reuse existing code, such as the person class, when creating classes that represent more specialized objects, like teachers.

An example of a "has a" relationship is that a car *has an* engine. This type of relationship also is referred to as containership. In addition, containership enables you to reuse existing code, such as the engine class, when creating classes that represent the containing object, like cars.

Code reusability makes application development faster since you don't have to "reinvent the wheel." Additionally, the applications you develop are less buggy since the code you are reusing already has been tested. Accordingly, OOP enables programmers to model programming objects after complex real-world objects, and reuse existing, tested code.

Objects generally are too complex to be described by a single variable. Additionally, the several variables necessary to describe an object may have different data types, so an array is not an option.

A solution is to use a structure to describe complex objects. A structure is a programmer-defined data type that enables you to package related variables together, even if the variables are of different data types. The variables that belong to a structure are called member variables.

This chapter showed you how to declare a structure. The declaration commences with *struct,* which is a keyword indicating that a structure is being declared. The *struct* keyword is followed by a name that indicates what the structure represents.

Structures, like functions, have a body, enclosed in open and close curly braces. However, unlike functions, the close curly brace must be followed by a semicolon. The body of the structure contains the member variables of the structure.

The effect of declaring a structure is similar to declaring your own data type. Accordingly, you need to declare a structure variable to create an instance of a structure. If you have many structure instances, you may declare a separate variable for each instance, or instead declare an array of structure instances.

You use the dot operator (.) with the structure instance name to access the member variables, whether the access is to obtain the value of the variable or to assign a value to it.

There are two ways you may initialize a structure. The first way is to use an initialization list. The second way is to use a constructor. As you learned in Chapter 13, a constructor is a function that is automatically called when you attempt to create an instance of an object. You may create more than one constructor, such as one with no arguments and one with several arguments.

In OOP, one principle is to separate what a function does from how it does it. In this spirit, programmers often separate a constructor's prototype from its implementation, implementing the constructor outside of the body of the structure. If you do this, then in the function header of the constructor's implementation, you need to precede the constructor name with the structure name and the scope resolution operator (::) to tell the compiler that the implementation is of a structure member function.

A structure may be passed as a function argument. Unlike an array name, a structure's value is not an address. So, to change the values of its member variables, a structure needs to be passed by reference or address. However, a structure often is passed by reference even if the function will not change the value of its member variables because less memory is required to pass the address of an object than the object itself, which may take up a lot of bytes. You precede the structure instance in the function argument list with the *const* keyword to prevent the function from inadvertently changing the values inside the structure instance.

You may nest a structure within another structure. Using the Person structure example, every person has a birthday. A birthday is a date, and a date, in turn, may be defined by a Date structure that contains three member variables which represent the month, day, and year of the particular date. You then could add to the Person structure declaration a member variable of the structure Date to represent the person's birthday. This is an example of the OOP concept of containership in that a person "has a" birthday.

Classes are quite similar to structures. You declare a class similarly to how you declare a structure, just substituting the *class* keyword for the *struct* keyword.

An important difference between a structure and a class is that member variables are, by default, public in a structure but private in a class. A public member variable may be accessed anywhere in the program. By contrast, a private member variable may be accessed only by a member function of the same class.

In classes, typically member functions are used to read from, and write to, the private member variables. These member functions are public so they can be accessed outside the class. One benefit of keeping the member variables private and using public member functions for read and write access is input validation. Keeping the member variables private is an example of the OOP concepts of encapsulation and information-hiding.

I hope you enjoyed this book as much as I enjoyed writing it, and I wish you the best of luck in your future programming endeavors.

Quiz

1. What are some major benefits of OOP?

2. What is an example of information hiding or encapsulation?

3. What type of relationship is involved in inheritance?

4. What type of relationship is involved in containership?

5. What is a structure?

6. When you declare a structure, are you declaring an instance or a data type?

7. What are the two ways to initialize a structure?

8. Can you nest one structure within another structure?

9. Why may a structure be passed by reference even if the function will not change the value of its member variables?

10. What is an important difference between a structure and a class?

Final Exam

1. What is a computer program?

2. What is a programming language?

3. What is a function?

4. How many main functions should a C++ program have?

5. What is a standard library file?

6. What is the purpose of an include directive?

7. What does a preprocessor do?

8. What does a compiler do?

9. What does a linker do?

10. Which of the following types of memory is not temporary: cache memory, RAM, or persistent storage?

11. What is the amount of information that may be stored at a particular memory address?

12. Is the size of a data type always the same no matter which computer you may be working on?

13. What is the difference between an unsigned and a signed data type?

14. What is an ASCII value?

15. What is a literal string?

16. What is an expression?

17. What is the effect of declaring a variable?

18. Can you refer to a variable before declaring it as long as you declare it later?

19. What is the difference between the *address* and *sizeof* operators?

20. What is the difference between initialization and assignment?

21. What is overflow?

22. Do you use the cin object for compile-time or run-time assignment of values to variables?

23. Which of the four arithmetic operations has more than one operator?

24. Which of the arithmetic operators cannot have a floating-point operand?

25. Which of the arithmetic operators cannot have a zero as a second operand?

26. Assuming *total* is an integer variable, how else could you express in code *total = total + 5?*

27. What is the result of 4 + 3 * 2?

28. What is the result of the expression 8 / 2 * 4?

29. What is the result of the expression 15 / 4?

30. What operator or function do you use to raise a number to a certain power?

31. What is an algorithm?

32. How many operands are in a relational expression?

33. What is the data type of the expression following the *if* keyword?

34. In an if / else if / else statement, which part must you have one, but only one, of?

35. In an if / else if / else statement, which part may you have more than one of?

36. In an if / else if / else statement, which part may you omit?

37. In a switch statement, what is the required data type of expression following the switch keyword?

38. In a switch statement, may the expression following a case keyword be a variable?

39. Which keyword in a switch statement corresponds to the *else* keyword in an if / else if / else statement?

40. Can you use nested if statements as an alternative to the logical And and Or operators?

41. For which of the logical operators do both Boolean expressions have to be true for the overall Boolean expression to be true?

42. For which of the logical operators do both Boolean expressions have to be false for the overall Boolean expression to be false?

43. Which of the logical operators reverses the "truth" of a Boolean expression, making a true expression false and a false expression true?

44. What does the increment operator do?

45. What does the decrement operator do?

46. In the statement *cout << --num,* which occurs first, decrementing *num* or the outputting of the value of *num?*

47. What is an iteration?

48. What is the usual purpose of the first expression in the parentheses following the *for* keyword?

49. What is the purpose of the second expression in the parentheses following the *for* keyword?

50. What is the usual purpose of the third expression in the parentheses following the *for* keyword?

51. Can one or more of the expressions in the parentheses following the *for* keyword be empty?

52. What is the purpose of the *break* keyword in a for loop?

53. What is the purpose of the *continue* keyword in a for loop?

54. If you were going to use nested for loops to print rows and columns, which for loop would print the columns—inner or outer?

55. Which of the three loops—for, while, or do while—executes at least once?

56. Which of the three loops—for, while, or do while—is the best choice when the number of iterations is predictable?

57. Is the parenthetical expression following the while keyword for initialization, condition, or update?

58. What is a flag?

59. What is the difference between variable scope and lifetime?

60. Must a function other than main be prototyped?

61. Is a function required to have at least one argument?

62. May a function have more than one argument?

63. What is the effect on a variable in *main* if it is passed by value to another function that changes the argument corresponding to that variable?

64. What is the effect on a variable in *main* if it is passed by reference to another function that changes the argument corresponding to that variable?

65. Must a function have a return value?

66. May a function have more than one return value?

67. May a function have neither a return value nor any arguments?

68. May a function have both a return value and arguments?

69. Can a particular array contain integers, floats, and characters?

70. What is the number of the starting index of an array?

71. What is the number of the ending index of an array?

72. What are the two alternative methods of initializing an array?

73. What is the purpose of the null character in a character array?

74. What is the value of the name of an array?

75. When you pass an array name as a function argument, are you passing it by value, reference, or address?

76. What is a pointer?

77. What is the difference between declaring an integer variable and declaring an integer pointer variable?

78. What is the meaning of the data type in the declaration of a pointer?

79. What is the meaning and purpose of NULL when being assigned to a pointer?

80. What operator do you use to assign a pointer the address of another variable or constant?

81. What is the purpose of the indirection operator?

82. What is the effect of incrementing a pointer variable?

83. What are the purposes of the *new* and *delete* operators?

84. Can you use an assignment operator to assign the value of one C-string to another?

85. What does it mean for data to be persistent?

86. What is a file?

87. What standard library should you include when your program reads from, or writes to, files?

88. Which of the three objects, *fstream, ifstream,* or *ofstream,* may be used both for file input and file output?

89. What are the two functions you can use to open a file?

90. What is the purpose of opening a file?

91. What is the purpose of closing a file?

92. What is a constructor?

93. Should file stream objects be passed as function arguments by value or by reference?

94. What type of relationship is involved in inheritance?

95. What type of relationship is involved in containership?

96. What is a structure?

97. What are the two ways to initialize a structure?

98. Can you nest one structure within another structure?

99. Why may a structure be passed by reference even if the function will not change the value of its member variables?

100. What is an important difference between a structure and a class?

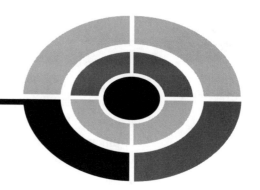

Answers to Quizzes and Final Exam

Chapter 1

1. A computer program consists of step-by-step instructions to the computer from a computer programmer.

2. Computers can store greater amounts of information, can recall that information more quickly and accurately, and can perform calculations faster and more accurately.

3. A programming language is a language that resembles the structure and syntax of human language, and that is used by computer programmers to write instructions for computers.

4. C++ is a good programming language to learn because it is very widely used in industry and in education, and also because many other programming languages, including Java and C#, are based on C++.

5. A function is a group of related instructions, also called statements, which together perform a particular task.

6. A C++ program must have one main function, no more, no less.

7. A standard library file is a file that defines commonly used objects, such as cout.

8. The purpose of an include directive is to tell the program to include a particular standard library file in your application.

9. A preprocessor is a program that scans the source code for include directives, and then inserts them into the source code of all files included by the include directives.

10. The compiler is a program that translates the preprocessed source code (the source code after the insertions made by the preprocessor) into corresponding machine language instructions that are stored in an object file.

11. The linker is a program that combines the object file with the necessary parts of the run-time library and creates an executable file.

Chapter 2

1. The CPU can most quickly access instructions or data from cache memory because that memory is on the CPU itself.

2. Persistent storage is not temporary like the other two: cache memory and RAM.

3. One byte of information may be stored at a particular memory address.

4. No. The size of a data type may vary depending on the compiler and operating system.

5. The range of a data type is the highest and lowest value that that data type may represent.

6. The value of an unsigned data type is either zero or positive, never negative, whereas the value of a signed data type may be negative also.

7. .0051 is represented by 5.1E-3 in E notation.

8. An ASCII value is a number between 0 and 255 that corresponds to a particular character.

9. The sizeof operator returns the size in bytes of a data type on the compiler and operating system on which the program is running.

10. A literal string is a string, generally encased in double quotes, that is outputted literally, without evaluation.

11. An expression is a code statement with a value that has to be evaluated when the program runs.

Chapter 3

1. Declaring a variable reserves memory for the storage of information and provides a name by which that information later can be referred to in code.

2. No. An "undeclared identifier" compiler error will occur even though the variable is declared after it is referred to because the compiler reads the code from top to bottom, so when it reaches the first reference to the variable, it has not seen the variable declaration.

3. Yes, as long as the variables are of the same data type.

4. A naming convention is a consistent method of naming variables.

5. The address operator is used to obtain the hexadecimal value of a variable's memory address, whereas the size of operator is used to determine the number of bytes in memory required to store the variable.

6. Initialization is when you assign a value to a variable as part of the same statement that declares that variable.

7. Overflow occurs when a variable is assigned a value too large for its range.

8. A compiler error is the consequence of using an assignment operator to assign a string value to an integer variable.

9. You use the cin object for run-time assignment of values to variables.

10. Yes. You can use one cin statement to assign values to several variables of different data types.

Chapter 4

1. Division has more than one operator, / and %.

2. The addition operator can operate on string as well as numeric operands.

3. The modulus operator cannot have a floating point operand.

4. The two division operators, / and %, cannot have zero as a second operand.

5. total + = 2

6. The result of 2 + 3 * 4 is 14, not 20, because multiplication has precedence over addition.

7. The result of the expression 8 / 2 * 4 is 16, not 1, because of associativity. Multiplication and division have equal precedence, so the operations are performed from left to right.

8. The result of the expression 10 / 4 is 2, not 2.5, because of integer division.

9. C++, unlike some other programming languages, does not have an exponent operator. Instead, you use the *pow* function, defined in the *cmath* standard library, to raise a number to a certain power.

10. An algorithm is a step-by-step logical procedure for solving a problem.

Chapter 5

1. There are two operands in a relational expression.

2. The purpose of a flowchart is to visually depict the flow of a program.

3. The data type of the expression following the if keyword is Boolean.

4. In an if /else if / else statement, you must have one, but only one, if part.

5. In an if /else if / else statement, you may have more than one else if part.

6. In an if /else if / else statement, you may omit the else part, in which case the statement becomes an if/else if statement.

7. In a switch statement, the required data type of expression following the switch keyword is integer.

8. In a switch statement, an expression of the character data type may follow the switch keyword because the ANSI or ASCII value of a character is an integer.

9. In a switch statement, the expression following a case keyword must be a constant and therefore cannot be a variable.

10. The default keyword in a switch statement corresponds to the else keyword in an if /else if / else statement.

Chapter 6

1. You can use nested if statements as an alternative to the logical And and Or operators.

2. An if statement can be nested in the else if or else part of an if / else if / else statement, as well as the if part.

3. With the logical And operator, both Boolean expressions have to be true for the overall Boolean expression to be true.

4. With the logical Or operator, both Boolean expressions have to be false for the overall Boolean expression to be false.

5. The logical Not operator reverses the "truth" of a Boolean expression, making a true expression false and a false expression true.

6. Assuming *resident* is a Boolean variable, *if(resident)* is the same as *if(resident == true)*.

7. The logical Not operator is a unary rather than binary operator.

8. The logical Not operator has a higher precedence than the relational operators.

9. The logical And operator has a higher precedence than the logical Or operator.

10. A Boolean value of either true or false can be used following the case keyword in a switch statement since both true and false have corresponding integer values.

Chapter 7

1. The increment operator increases a value by one.

2. The decrement operator decreases a value by one.

3. In the statement *cout << --num,* decrementing occurs before the outputting of the value of num because the decrementing is prefix.

4. An iteration is each time a loop repeats.

5. The usual purpose of the first expression in the parentheses following the for keyword is to initialize a variable which usually serves as the counter.

6. The purpose of the second expression in the parentheses following the for keyword is to set the condition which must be true for the loop to continue to execute.

7. The usual purpose of the third expression in the parentheses following the for keyword is to update a value, usually a counter.

8. One or more of the expressions in the parentheses following the for keyword may be empty if handled elsewhere in the code.

9. The purpose of the break keyword in a for loop is to prematurely terminate the loop.

10. The purpose of the continue keyword in a for loop is to prematurely terminate the iteration of a loop.

11. If you were going to use nested for loops to print rows and columns, you would use the inner for loop to print the columns.

Chapter 8

1. The do while loop executes at least once.

2. The for loop is the best choice when the number of iterations is predictable.

3. The parenthetical expression following the while keyword is for the condition.

4. The parenthetical condition following the while keyword may always be true, such as *while (true)*. However, to avoid an infinite loop, the break keyword would need to be used in the body of the loop.

5. The parenthetical condition following the while keyword may combine two expressions using a logical && or || operator.

6. The purpose of the break keyword in a while loop is the same as it is in a for loop—to prematurely terminate the loop.

7. The purpose of the continue keyword in a while loop is the same as it is in a for loop, to prematurely terminate the iteration of a loop.

8. A flag is a Boolean variable whose value indicates whether a condition exists.

9. If you were going to use nested while loops to print rows and columns, you would use the outer for loop to print the rows.

10. A variable declared inside the body of a do while loop does not have scope in the parenthetical expression following the while keyword.

Chapter 9

1. A variable's scope determines where it can be referred to in the code. A variable's lifetime determines when it is destroyed.

2. No. A function other than *main* does not have to be prototyped if it is defined above where it is called. However, it is a good idea to prototype each function other than *main*.

3. No. A function need not have any arguments. If it has none, then the *void* keyword may be used in the parentheses following the function name.

4. Yes. A function may have more than one argument. If so, the arguments are separated by commas.

5. If a variable in *main* is passed by value to another function which changes the argument corresponding to that variable, the variable in *main* is not changed.

6. If a variable in *main* is passed by reference to another function which changes the argument corresponding to that variable, the variable in *main* is changed.

7. No. A function does not have to have a return value. If it doesn't have a return value, the keyword *void* is used in its place.

8. No. A function may not have more than one return value.

9. Yes. A function does not have to have a return value nor any arguments.

10. Yes. A function may have both a return value and arguments.

Chapter 10

1. While the data type of an array may be integer, float, or character, a particular array cannot contain integers, floats, and characters. All the elements of an array must be of the same data type.

2. The number of the starting index of an array is zero.

3. The number of the ending index of an array is one less than the number of elements in the array.

4. Initialization is when you assign a value to a variable in the same statement in which you declare that variable. By contrast, assignment is when you assign a value to a variable in a statement after the one in which you declare that variable.

5. The two alternative methods of initializing an array are explicit initialization, in which the square brackets contain a numerical constant indicating the size of the array, or implicit initialization, in which the square brackets are empty and the size of the array is indicated by the number of elements on the right side of the assignment operator.

6. The purpose of the null character is to signal cout when to end the output of a character array.

7. The value of the name of an array is the base address of the array.

8. The last element of a character array need not always be a null character. When each element of a character array is separate from the other, such as a separate grade for each test, there is no need to use a null character.

However, if the character array elements are related, such as a character array representing a person's name, then usually the last element should be a null character.

9. The *get* function reads the user's input up to, but not including, the newline character, whereas the *getline* function reads the user's input up to and including the newline character.

10. When you pass an array name as a function argument, you are passing it by address.

Chapter 11

1. A pointer is a variable or constant whose value is the address of another variable or constant.

2. Dynamic memory allocation requires a pointer to be performed.

3. The only difference between declaring an integer variable and an integer pointer variable is that the pointer variable declaration includes an asterisk, which either follows the data type or precedes the variable name.

4. The data type in the declaration of a pointer refers to the data type of another variable (or constant) whose memory address is the value of the pointer.

5. NULL is a constant defined in several standard libraries, including *iostream*. You assign a pointer NULL if it is too early in your code to know which address to assign to the pointer. The value of NULL, the memory address 0, signals that the pointer is not intended to point to an accessible memory location.

6. You use the address operator to assign a pointer the address of another variable or constant.

7. The purpose of the indirection operator is to obtain the value of the variable or constant to which the pointer points. This operation is said to dereference the pointer.

8. A pointer may point to different memory addresses at different times in the program if the pointer is declared as a variable instead of as a constant.

9. Yes. More than one pointer may point to the same memory address.

10. Incrementing a pointer variable increases its value by the number of bytes of its data type.

11. The purpose of the new operator is to dynamically allocate memory. The purpose of the delete operator is to deallocate dynamically created memory.

Chapter 12

1. The cin object with the stream extraction operator (>>) will ignore a leading newline character in the input buffer.

2. The *getline* member function will not leave a newline character in the input buffer.

3. You should always follow the cin object with the stream extraction operator (>>) with the no-argument *ignore* member function because the cin object with the stream extraction operator (>>) always leaves a newline character in the input buffer.

4. You should never follow the *getline* member function with the no-argument *ignore* member function because the *getline* member function always removes the newline character that terminated input from the input buffer.

5. The argument of the *isdigit* function is a character.

6. The argument of the *atoi* function is a C-string.

7. A C++ string class variable cannot directly use the *atoi* function to convert the string representation of a number to a number. However, it can copy its contents to a C-string using either the *c_str* or *data* member functions, after which the C-string can use the *atoi* function.

8. The functions in the C++ standard library *cctype*, such as *toupper* and *isdigit*, are used with characters.

9. The functions in the C++ standard library *cstdlib*, such as *atoi* and *itoa*, are used with C-strings.

10. You cannot use an assignment operator to assign the value of one C-string to another. You will be assigning an address instead of a value.

Chapter 13

1. Data is persistent when it survives after the program is finished.

2. A file is a collection of data that is located on persistent storage, such as a hard drive, a CD-ROM, or other storage device.

3. Files store data in either text or binary format.

4. You should include the *fstream* standard library when your program reads from, or writes to, files.

5. The *fstream* object may be used both for file input and file output.

6. You can open a file with either the open member function or a constructor.

7. The purpose of opening a file is to establish a path of communication between the file and a file stream object in your program.

8. The purpose of closing a file is to free system resources that are required to maintain the path of communication between the file and the file stream object in your program.

9. A constructor is a function that is automatically called when you attempt to create an instance of an object.

10. The *fail* member function is a better choice than the *eof* member function for detecting end of file in a text file.

11. File stream objects should be passed as function arguments by reference rather than by value.

Chapter 14

1. OOP enables programmers to model programming objects after complex real-world objects, and to reuse existing, tested code.

2. An example in this chapter of information hiding or encapsulation is the use of public member functions to govern read and write access to private member variables.

3. Inheritance involves an "is a" relationship. An example is a student *is a* person.

4. Containership involves a "has a" relationship. Examples include that a car *has an* engine and a person *has a* birthday.

5. A structure is a programmer-defined data type that enables you to package related variables that may be of different data types.

6. When you declare a structure, you are declaring a data type. You need to declare a variable of that structure to create an instance of it.

7. You may initialize a structure using either an initialization list or a constructor.

8. You can nest one structure within another structure, such as a birthday member variable of a Person structure being a Date structure itself.

9. A structure may be passed by reference even if the function will not change the value of its member variables because less memory is required to pass the address of an object than the object itself, which may take up a lot of bytes. In this situation, you may precede the structure instance in the function

argument list with the *const* keyword to prevent the function from inadvertently changing the values inside the structure instance.

10. Member variables are, by default, public in a structure but private in a class.

Final Exam

1. A computer program consists of step-by-step instructions to the computer from a computer programmer.

2. A programming language is a language that resembles the structure and syntax of human language, and that is used by computer programmers to write instructions for computers.

3. A function is a group of related instructions, also called statements, which together perform a particular task.

4. A C++ program must have one main function, no more, no less.

5. A standard library file is a file that defines commonly used objects, such as cout.

6. The purpose of an include directive is to tell the program to include a particular standard library file in your application.

7. A preprocessor is a program that scans the source code for include directives, and then inserts them into the source code of all files included by the include directives.

8. The compiler is a program that translates the preprocessed source code (the source code after the insertions made by the preprocessor) into corresponding machine language instructions that are stored in an object file.

9. The linker is a program that combines the object file with the necessary parts of the run-time library and creates an executable file.

10. Persistent storage is not temporary like the other two: cache memory and RAM.

11. One byte of information may be stored at a particular memory address.

12. No. The size of a data type may vary depending on the compiler and operating system.

13. The value of an unsigned data type is either zero or positive, never negative, while the value of a signed data type may be negative also.

14. An ASCII value is a number between 0 and 255 that corresponds to a particular character.

15. A literal string is a string, generally encased in double quotes, that is outputted literally, without evaluation.

16. An expression is a code statement with a value that has to be evaluated when the program runs.

17. Declaring a variable reserves memory for the storage of information and provides a name by which that information later can be referred to in code.

18. No. An "undeclared identifier" compiler error will occur even though the variable is declared after it is referred to because the compiler reads the code from top to bottom, so when it reaches the first reference to the variable, it has not yet seen the variable declaration.

19. The *address* operator is used to obtain the hexadecimal value of a variable's memory address, whereas the *sizeof* operator is used to determine the number of bytes in memory required to store the variable on the compiler and operating system where the program is running.

20. Initialization is when you assign a value to a variable in the same statement in which you declare that variable. By contrast, assignment is when you assign a value to a variable in a statement after the one in which you declare that variable.

21. Overflow occurs when a variable is assigned a value too large for its range.

22. You use the cin object for run-time assignment of values to variables.

23. Division has more than one operator, / and %.

24. The modulus operator cannot have a floating-point operand.

25. The two division operators, / and %, cannot have zero as a second operand.

26. total + = 5

27. The result of 4 + 3 * 2 is 10, not 14, because multiplication has precedence over addition.

28. The result of the expression 8 / 2 * 4 is 16, not 1, because of associativity. Multiplication and division have equal precedence, so the operations are performed from left to right.

29. The result of the expression 15 / 4 is 3, not 3.75, because of integer division.

30. C++, unlike some other programming languages, does not have an exponent operator. Instead, you use the *pow* function, defined in the *cmath* standard library, to raise a number to a certain power.

31. An algorithm is a step-by-step logical procedure for solving a problem.

32. There are two operands in a relational expression.

33. The data type of the expression following the *if* keyword is Boolean.

34. In an if / else if / else statement, you must have one, but only one, if part.

35. In an if / else if / else statement, you may have more than one else if part.

36. In an if / else if / else statement, you may omit the else part, in which case the statement becomes an if / else if statement.

37. In a switch statement, the required data type of expression following the switch keyword is integer.

38. In a switch statement, the expression following a case keyword must be a constant or a literal and therefore cannot be a variable.

39. The default keyword in a switch statement corresponds to the *else* keyword in an if / else if / else statement.

40. You can use nested if statements as an alternative to the logical And and Or operators.

41. With the logical And operator, both Boolean expressions have to be true for the overall Boolean expression to be true.

42. With the logical Or operator, both Boolean expressions have to be false for the overall Boolean expression to be false.

43. The logical Not operator reverses the "truth" of a Boolean expression, making a true expression false and a false expression true.

44. The increment operator increases a value by one.

45. The decrement operator decreases a value by one.

46. In the statement *cout << --num,* decrementing *num* occurs before the outputting of the value of *num* because the decrementing is a prefix.

47. An iteration is each time a loop repeats.

48. The usual purpose of the first expression in the parentheses following the *for* keyword is to initialize a variable which usually serves as the counter.

49. The purpose of the second expression in the parentheses following the *for* keyword is to set the condition which must be true for the loop to continue to execute.

50. The usual purpose of the third expression in the parentheses following the *for* keyword is to update a value, usually a counter.

51. One or more of the expressions in the parentheses following the *for* keyword may be empty if handled elsewhere in the code.

52. The purpose of the *break* keyword in a for loop is to prematurely terminate the loop.

53. The purpose of the *continue* keyword in a for loop is to prematurely terminate the iteration of a loop.

54. If you were going to use nested for loops to print rows and columns, you would use the inner for loop to print the columns.

55. The do while loop executes at least once.

56. The for loop is the best choice when the number of iterations is predictable.

57. The parenthetical expression following the *while* keyword is for the condition.

58. A flag is a Boolean variable whose value indicates whether a condition exists.

59. A variable's scope determines where it can be referred to in the code. A variable's lifetime determines when it is destroyed.

60. No. A function other than *main* does not have to be prototyped if it is defined above where it is called. However, it is a good idea to prototype each function other than *main.*

61. No. A function need not have any arguments. If it has none, then the *void* keyword may be used in the parentheses following the function name.

62. Yes. A function may have more than one argument. If so, the arguments are separated by commas.

63. If a variable in *main* is passed by value to another function that changes the argument corresponding to that variable, the variable in *main* is not changed.

64. If a variable in *main* is passed by reference to another function that changes the argument corresponding to that variable, the variable in *main* is changed.

65. No. A function does not have to have a return value. If it doesn't have a return value, the keyword *void* is used in its place.

66. No. A function may not have more than one return value.

67. Yes. A function does not have to have a return value nor any arguments.

68. Yes. A function may have both a return value and arguments.

69. While the data type of an array may be integer, float, or character, a particular array cannot contain integers, floats, and characters. All the elements of an array must be of the same data type.

70. The number of the starting index of an array is zero.

71. The number of the ending index of an array is one less than the number of elements in the array.

72. The two alternative methods of initializing an array are explicit initialization, in which the square brackets contain a numerical constant indicating the size

of the array, or implicit initialization, in which the square brackets are empty and the size of the array is indicated by the number of elements on the right side of the assignment operator.

73. The purpose of the null character is to signal cout when to end the output of a character array.

74. The value of the name of an array is the base address of the array.

75. When you pass an array name as a function argument, you are passing it by address.

76. A pointer is a variable or constant whose value is the address of another variable or constant.

77. The only difference between declaring an integer variable and an integer pointer variable is that the pointer variable declaration includes an asterisk, which either follows the data type or precedes the variable name.

78. The data type in the declaration of a pointer refers to the data type of another variable (or constant) whose memory address is the value of the pointer.

79. NULL is a constant defined in several standard libraries, including *iostream.* You assign a pointer NULL if it is too early in your code to know which address to assign to the pointer. The value of NULL, the memory address 0, signals that the pointer is not intended to point to an accessible memory location.

80. You use the *address* operator to assign a pointer the address of another variable or constant.

81. The purpose of the indirection operator is to obtain the value of the variable or constant to which the pointer points. This operation is said to dereference the pointer.

82. Incrementing a pointer variable increases its value by the number of bytes of its data type.

83. The purpose of the *new* operator is to dynamically allocate memory at run-time. The purpose of the *delete* operator is to deallocate dynamically created memory.

84. You cannot use an assignment operator to assign the value of one C-string to another. You will be assigning an address instead of a value.

85. Data is persistent when it survives after the program is finished.

86. A file is a collection of data that is located on persistent storage, such as a hard drive, a CD-ROM, or other storage device.

87. You should include the *fstream* standard library when your program reads from, or writes to, files.

88. The *fstream* object may be used both for file input and file output.

89. You can open a file with either the *open* member function or a constructor.

90. The purpose of opening a file is to establish a path of communication between the file and a file stream object in your program.

91. The purpose of closing a file is to free system resources that are required to maintain the path of communication between the file and the file stream object in your program.

92. A constructor is a function that is automatically called when you attempt to create an instance of an object.

93. File stream objects should be passed as function arguments by reference rather than by value.

94. An "is a" relationship is involved in inheritance. An example is a student *is a* person.

95. A "has a" relationship is involved in containership. Examples include that a car *has an* engine and a person *has a* birthday.

96. A structure is a programmer-defined data type that enables you to package related variables that may be of different data types.

97. You may initialize a structure using either an initialization list or a constructor.

98. You can nest one structure within another structure, such as a birthday member variable of a Person structure being a Date structure itself.

99. A structure may be passed by reference even if the function will not change the value of its member variables because less memory is required to pass the address of an object than the object itself, which may take up a lot of bytes. In this situation, you may precede the structure instance in the function argument list with the *const* keyword to prevent the function from inadvertently changing the values inside the structure instance.

100. Member variables are, by default, public in a structure but private in a class.

INDEX

INTERNATIONAL CONTACT INFORMATION

AUSTRALIA
McGraw-Hill Book Company
Australia Pty. Ltd.
TEL +61-2-9900-1800
FAX +61-2-9878-8881
http://www.mcgraw-hill.com.au
books-it_sydney@mcgraw-hill.com

CANADA
McGraw-Hill Ryerson Ltd.
TEL +905-430-5000
FAX +905-430-5020
http://www.mcgraw-hill.ca

GREECE, MIDDLE EAST, & AFRICA
(Excluding South Africa)
McGraw-Hill Hellas
TEL +30-210-6560-990
TEL +30-210-6560-993
TEL +30-210-6560-994
FAX +30-210-6545-525

MEXICO (Also serving Latin America)
McGraw-Hill Interamericana Editores
S.A. de C.V.
TEL +525-1500-5108
FAX +525-117-1589
http://www.mcgraw-hill.com.mx
carlos_ruiz@mcgraw-hill.com

SINGAPORE (Serving Asia)
McGraw-Hill Book Company
TEL +65-6863-1580
FAX +65-6862-3354
http://www.mcgraw-hill.com.sg
mghasia@mcgraw-hill.com

SOUTH AFRICA
McGraw-Hill South Africa
TEL +27-11-622-7512
FAX +27-11-622-9045
robyn_swanepoel@mcgraw-hill.com

SPAIN
McGraw-Hill/
Interamericana de España, S.A.U.
TEL +34-91-180-3000
FAX +34-91-372-8513
http://www.mcgraw-hill.es
professional@mcgraw-hill.es

UNITED KINGDOM, NORTHERN,
EASTERN, & CENTRAL EUROPE
McGraw-Hill Education Europe
TEL +44-1-628-502500
FAX +44-1-628-770224
http://www.mcgraw-hill.co.uk
emea_queries@mcgraw-hill.com

ALL OTHER INQUIRIES Contact:
McGraw-Hill/Osborne
TEL +1-510-420-7700
FAX +1-510-420-7703
http://www.osborne.com
omg_international@mcgraw-hill.com

The fast and easy way to understanding computing fundamentals

- *No formal training needed*
- *Self-paced, easy-to-follow, and user-friendly*
- *Amazing low price*

0-07-225454-8
Available May 2004

0-07-225363-0
Available April 2004

0-07-225514-5
Available July 2004

0-07-225359-2
Available March 2004

0-07-225370-3
Available May 2004

0-07-225364-9
Available March 2004

For more information on these and other McGraw-Hill/Osborne titles, visit www.osborne.com.